Praise for *High-Impact ePortfolio Practice*

"Eynon and Gambino have written the book I've been waiting for. It demonstrates the power of ePortfolios to transform college learning and offers practical strategies for realizing this potential. As an extraordinarily insightful, comprehensive guide to designing an effective ePortfolio initiative, *High-Impact ePortfolio Practice* will take its place as the reference of choice for campus and program ePortfolio leaders."

—*Susan Kahn, Director, ePortfolio Initiative, Indiana University-Purdue University Indianapolis*

"The Eynon and Gambino book will become an instant classic; readable, authoritative, reflecting the experience of many diverse institutions and finally settling the question "What is an ePortfolio?" I recommend this book to anyone in higher education."

—*Trent Batson, Founder of the Association for Authentic, Experiential and Evidence-Based Learning (AAEEBL, the international ePortfolio organization)*

"Challenging the noisy legion of digital gurus who see job-specific training as the best choice for first-generation learners, Eynon and Gambino provide compelling evidence that ePortfolios can help underserved students achieve those distinctively twenty-first century liberal arts: agency as motivated learners, creativity in connecting myriad kinds of formal and informal learning, and reflective judgment about their own roles in building solutions for the future. An invaluable resource for all."

—*Carol Geary-Schneider, Fellow, Lumina Foundation; President Emerita, Association of American Colleges and Universities*

"This timely volume shows that ePortfolio is a powerful pedagogical framework at any type of institution, benefitting all participating students in desirable ways, as with other High-Impact Practices. Happily, Eynon and Gambino explain how and why by illustrating the requisite steps and conditions to do ePortfolio well, in the classroom and beyond."

—*George D. Kuh, Chancellor's Professor of Higher Education Emeritus at Indiana University; Founder and Senior Scholar, National Institute for Learning Outcomes Assessment; and author of* Using Evidence of Student Learning to Improve Higher Education

"I have witnessed on three continents the beneficial impact ePortfolio practice has on learning—when done well. Employability, study abroad, collaborative projects—the growing number of educational challenges for which ePortfolios are the solution makes this book timely; the complexity of successful campus implementation makes

it indispensable. Eynon and Gambino's wisdom, collaborative learnings, and vast experience leap from the pages of this excellent book."

—**Shane Sutherland**, *Founder, PebblePad*

"A handbook of everything educators need to know about the current state of the art, capped off with a provocative look at the synergy of ePortfolios with other student success interventions."

—**John N. Gardner**, *President, Gardner Institute for Excellence in Undergraduate Education; and* **Betsy O. Barefoot**, *Senior Scholar, Gardner Institute for Excellence in Undergraduate Education*

"Many years ago I had students in my poetry course develop portfolios, and I sure wish this volume, with its much larger vision of purpose, had been available then. This book is the perfect mix of practical examples and research pointing to the many ways that ePortfolio can transform student learning, how we work as teachers, and the character of our institutions."

—**Pat Hutchings**, *National Institute for Learning Outcomes Assessment*

"Drawing on years of work with campuses nationwide, the authors provide excellent analyses of best practices in ePortfolio use, and they situate their examples in critical contexts that demonstrate the role ePortfolios play in facilitating reflection and integration, essential elements of impactful education. This book will be an indispensable resource for colleges and universities."

—**Natalie McKnight**, *Dean, College of General Studies, Boston University*

"A call to arms for thoughtful and effective educational reform and renewal. Eynon and Gambino show us how student ePortfolios have effectively reshaped teaching and learning in a range of undergraduate classrooms. They describe the successes and setbacks of the Connect to Learn national network to design and scale up effective ePortfolio programs on their 24 campuses. With honesty and insight this book reminds us that digital technologies are only as effective as the pedagogical principles and practices that undergird them."

—**Steve Brier**, *Founder, Interactive Technology & Pedagogy program, CUNY Graduate Center; Co-Author,* Austerity Blues: Fighting for the Soul of Public Higher Education

"The *Catalyst Framework* constitutes a watershed contribution in our understanding of ePortfolios 'done well.' Each chapter includes engaging vignettes and practical exercises that will be both enlightening and immediately accessible to readers."

—**Gail Matthews-DeNatale**, *Associate Director, Center for Advancing Teaching and Learning through Research, Northeastern University*

"I enjoyed this book enormously and was delighted to discover that many of my 'dreams' regarding ePortfolio practice, like 'social learning' and 'community portfolios' are gaining ground. *High-Impact ePortfolio Practice* eloquently demonstrates how *informed practice* can contribute to transforming individual and organizational learning. Gives me hope!"

—**Serge Ravet**, *Co-Director of Europortfolio (the European network of ePortfolio practitioners)*

"Rich with theoretical grounding and examples of actual practice at a wide variety of colleges and universities, *High-Impact ePortfolio Practice* reveals the power of combining reflective pedagogy with a technology that showcases signature work. It is an essential contribution to the field. Eynon and Gambino lay out a comprehensive framework that guides the effective design and implementation of ePortfolio initiatives at both departmental and institutional scales."

—**David Hubert**, *Assistant Provost for Learning Advancement, Salt Lake Community College*

"Over the last decade, higher education has learned that the hard part about ePortfolios isn't finding a vendor, but fully realizing ePortfolio's potential to make learning purposeful, integrative, and visible. It's a daunting task, but we procrastinate at our peril; employers, students, and their supporters all want real evidence of our value, and they deserve no less. In *High-Impact ePortfolio Practice* we get crucial help, from leading practitioners in the field."

—**Ken O'Donnell**, *Associate Vice President, California State University, Dominguez Hills*

"Electronic portfolios have held promise for enhancing student learning and success for two decades. But on many campuses that promise has not been realized. Thanks to the work of 24 Connect to Learning institutions, we now have principles and examples of good practice that will enable more institutions to use ePortfolio effectively. I salute Eynon and Gambino for synthesizing research on authentic assessment and productively connecting pedagogy that works, professional development, and outcomes assessment.

—**Trudy W. Banta**, *Professor, Vice Chancellor Emerita, Indiana University-Purdue University Indianapolis*

"At a time when preparing students to address complex, real-world problems is more critical than ever, Eynon and Gambino offer a compelling case for ePortfolios as essential to student success. Positioning ePortfolios as High-Impact Practices and detailing the unique role ePortfolios can play in twenty-first-century learning, this work is an exceptional resource for faculty and staff committed to helping students connect deep learning across academic and co-curricular experiences as a catalyst for intellectual growth and development."

—*Lynn Pasquerella*, *President, Association of American Colleges & Universities*

"Eynon and Gambino put inquiry at the center of ePortfolio practice, where it belongs. Students do not simply document their achievements in ePortfolios. Rather, they compose themselves as new members of academic and professional communities. . . . The Connect to Learning campuses undertook ePortfolio initiatives linked in *collective* inquiry into student learning and institutional change. With this book, we can all share in the benefits."

—*Darren Cambridge, Barbara Cambridge, and Kathy Yancey*, *Co-Directors of the Inter/National Coalition for Electronic Portfolios Research*

"Spotlighting Inquiry, Reflection, and Integration, Eynon and Gambino provide a comprehensive resource for faculty, staff and administrators for all things ePortfolio. From investigation to implementation to transformation, they outline principles and practices for ePortfolio success. This book will clearly become the definitive guide on ePortfolio done well!"

—*Alison Carson*, *Professor of Psychology, Manhattanville College*

"This is an essential book for anyone working with faculty and staff colleagues to improve student learning. Eynon and Gambino provide a practical framework, concrete examples, and evidence-based guidance to support individual and institutional improvement. Their recommendations for professional development are particularly insightful. This book is not just a blueprint for excellent ePortfolios; it offers an inspiring vision for learning and change in higher education."

—*Peter Felten,* *Assistant Provost, Elon University; and former President, Professional and Organizational Developers Network*

HIGH-IMPACT ePORTFOLIO PRACTICE

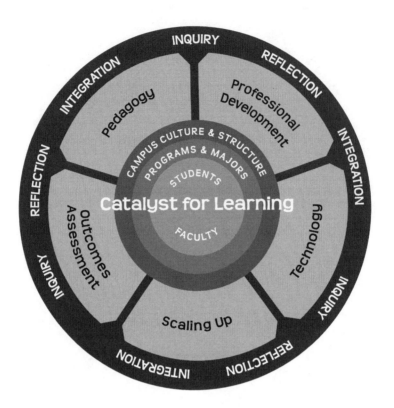

HIGH-IMPACT ePORTFOLIO PRACTICE

A Catalyst for Student, Faculty, and Institutional Learning

Bret Eynon and Laura M. Gambino

Foreword by George D. Kuh

Published in association with AAC&U

Association of American Colleges and Universities

STERLING, VIRGINIA

COPYRIGHT © 2017 BY
STYLUS PUBLISHING, LLC.

Published by Stylus Publishing, LLC.
22883 Quicksilver Drive
Sterling, Virginia 20166-2102

All rights reserved. No part of this book may be reprinted or reproduced in any form or by any electronic, mechanical, or other means, now known or hereafter invented, including photocopying, recording, and information storage and retrieval, without permission in writing from the publisher.

Library of Congress Cataloging-in-Publication Data

Names: Eynon, Bret, author. | Gambino, Laura M., 1968- author.
Title: High impact ePortfolio practice:
a catalyst for student, faculty, and institutional learning/Bret Eynon and
Laura M. Gambino.
Description: Sterling, Virginia: Stylus Publishing, LLC, 2017. |
Includes bibliographical references and index.
Identifiers: LCCN 2016029514 (print) |
LCCN 2016049167 (ebook) |
ISBN 9781620365045 (casebound : alk. paper) |
ISBN 9781620365052 (pbk. : alk. paper) |
ISBN 9781620365069 (library networkable e-edition) |
ISBN 9781620365076 (consumer e-edition) |
Subjects: LCSH: Electronic portfolios in education. |
Education, Higher--Effect of technological innovations on. |
Education, Higher--Aims and objectives |
Universities and colleges--Planning--Technological innovations.
Classification: LCC LB1029.P67 E97 2017 (print) |
LCC LB1029.P67 (ebook) | DDC 371.39--dc23
LC record available at https://lccn.loc.gov/2016029514

13-digit ISBN: 978-1-62036-504-5 (cloth)
13-digit ISBN: 978-1-62036-505-2 (paperback)
13-digit ISBN: 978-1-62036-506-9 (library networkable e-edition)
13-digit ISBN: 978-1-62036-507-6 (consumer e-edition)

Printed in the United States of America

All first editions printed on acid-free paper
that meets the American National Standards Institute
Z39-48 Standard.

Bulk Purchases

Quantity discounts are available for use in workshops
and for staff development.
Call 1-800-232-0223

First Edition, 2017

10   9   8   7   6   5

CONTENTS

And Now There Are 11

Initially, I was taken aback by the title of this volume, which declares that ePortfolios are a High-Impact Practice (HIP). Since the introduction of the term *HIP* along with data supporting the benefits to students who do one or more, HIPs have become something of a juggernaut in the United States. The 64-campus State University of New York (SUNY) system now requires every student to have at least one "applied learning experience," its language for a HIP. The 23-campus California State University (CSU) system in partnership with the National Association of System Heads is working to make more high-quality HIPs available to more CSU students. Many private institutions including Cornell University, Elon University, and Hendrix College are also promoting their distinctive versions of such activities.

It is not unusual in my experience to visit a campus and discover that many faculty and staff are eager to point to something they do with their students to be a high-impact activity. Most of those who say so, however, are not talking about one of the 10 practices on the "officially approved" list that appeared in the first HIP publication[1] since promulgated by the Association of American Colleges and Universities (AAC&U).

I understand the motivation for joining the effort to improve undergraduate education; surely more than a few of the activities colleagues claim to be "high-impact" are thoughtfully designed and well implemented and may well have effects similar to those on the AAC&U list. At the same time, I and others worry that appropriating the HIP label in the absence of compelling evidence could dilute and draw attention away from the important, challenging work institutions are trying to do to scale what appears to be a most promising set of approaches to enhancing student learning and success.

Against this backdrop, and with a raised eyebrow, I agreed to pen this foreword, secretly hoping that the text and supporting documents demonstrated that students who created an ePortfolio benefitted in ways comparable to the activities on the AAC&U HIP list. Indeed, it was clear to me that if the ePortfolio did not exist, the field would have to invent something akin to what it promises to adequately address current and emerging circumstances to ensure that all students attain a high-quality credential. I'll return to this important point later. But first, on what basis can the authors—Bret Eynon and Laura M. Gambino, who are national leaders of the ePortfolio movement—claim the ePortfolio qualifies as a HIP?

Show Me the Data

The ePortfolio process is conceptually and theoretically sound, drawing on complementary strands of research from the learning sciences and allied areas. Equally impressive and persuasive is the empirical case the authors make for declaring the ePortfolio to be a HIP.

Working over several years with colleagues and students at the two dozen colleges and universities participating in the Connect to Learning (C2L) network, the authors systematically documented the implementation procedures that ensure high-quality implementation of the ePortfolio process, what they call the *Catalyst for Learning Framework*. In doing so, they empirically demonstrated that, when done well, students who create and continue to add to their ePortfolio as intended benefit in ways similar to students who participate in one or more of the 10 HIPs on the AAC&U list.[2] That is, compared with their counterparts who did not use ePortfolios, students taking courses requiring ePortfolios were generally more engaged in educationally purposeful activities, earned higher grades, and were more likely to complete courses and persist. This pattern of outcomes is widely accepted as key to student success.

And there's more. C2L and the nature of interpersonal connections required to do ePortfolio work well as described in this book are levers for student-centered culture bending.[3] That is, the educationally purposeful focused nature of interactions students have with their teachers, advisors, and other students and those interactions between instructors and other personnel fuel the development of a supportive, learning-intensive, positively restless ethos mindful of the high-performing institutions featured in *Student Success in College*.[4]

To their credit, the authors appropriately note the limitations of their inquiry, citing the somewhat mixed findings across the wide variety of types of schools in the C2L consortium. Still, the scope and complexity of the effort are impressive and the pattern of positive findings are consistent enough to substantiate the claim that the ePortfolio—when done well—warrants joining the AAC&U HIPs list.

The timing could not be better for extolling the virtues of ePortfolios. Here is why.

The ePortfolio as a Meta HIP

Several years ago, the National Institute for Learning Outcomes Assessment (NILOA) titled one of its publications *Knowing What Students Know and Can Do*.[5] This is the classic student learning outcomes (SLO) assessment challenge, which continues to bedevil many colleges and universities and animate accreditation processes. Doing assessment well enough to adequately respond to accountability expectations and guide institutional improvement has always been a critical but difficult task. Now dynamic student enrollment patterns—sometimes referred to as *swirl*—make ensuring collegiate quality and SLO assessment work even more complicated.

One aspect of swirl is the nontrivial proportions of students—in recent years more than 60%—who attend two or more institutions on the way to earning a baccalaureate degree. Another aspect of swirl is taking courses from two or more different colleges or universities during the same academic term; about one-quarter of students do so, which is likely a conservative estimate. As the availability of online learning in various forms increases, this fraction of undergraduates will only grow.

Two more contemporary enrollment features further complicate the challenge of ensuring that students earn a high-quality credential: (a) the reverse transfer phenomenon and (b) the emergence of an expanded credentialing system.

Reverse transfer has multiple manifestations. One version is those students who start at a four-year college and transfer to a two-year institution; some later may return to a four-year degree-granting school (but not necessarily the one where they started). Other students pursue an even more complicated pattern of course-taking from multiple degree-granting institutions.

The appearance of a broader, more inclusive credentialing system is prompted by the need to recognize and record the short-term learning that may result in a badge, certification, or some other nondegree postsecondary credential that represents a specific set of competencies, especially those sought by employers.[6] These learning opportunities may be independent of or pursued simultaneously with enrollment in a degree-granting institution.

Taken together, these patterns and trends have made the traditional academic transcript increasingly less relevant. Moreover, when presented with multiple transcripts, employers cannot easily or adequately discern the proficiencies of a prospective employee. Graduate school admissions committees face similar challenges. In addition, these circumstances muddle responding to the larger accountability agenda. Which institutions are responsible for what aspects of what students know and can do when they complete their degree?

Bringing coherence to, synthesizing, and integrating one's learning inside and outside the classroom are considered markers of a high-quality undergraduate education.[7] Making connections and creating coherence is difficult enough for those students who attend only one institution. With an increasing majority of undergraduates aggregating credits from multiple providers, what kind of record-keeping and quality assurance mechanisms can validate the learning that occurs in these various venues? Equally important, how can postsecondary institutions help students make meaningful connections across their many courses and out-of-class activities, including employment, to bring some sense of coherence and deeper meaning to their various learning experiences?

Herein lies the powerful potential of the ePortfolio when done well: It serves as a portable, expandable, and updatable vehicle for accumulating and presenting evidence of authentic student accomplishment including the curation of specific proficiencies and dispositions at given points in time.

But as the authors of this book emphasize, the ePortfolio is much more than a just-in-time twenty-first-century electronic record keeping system. It is an intentionally designed instructional approach that, among other advantages, prompts students to periodically reflect on and deepen what they are learning and helps them connect and make sense of their various experiences inside and outside the classroom that—taken together—add up to more than the sum of their parts.

In addition, the ePortfolio is especially well suited to document, integrate, and enhance the positive effects of other HIPs. That is, research shows the unusually powerful cumulative additive effects of participating in multiple HIPs over the course of the undergraduate experience.[8] In addition, ePortfolios will make the extended educational transcript (something like a co-curricular transcript on steroids) initiative now being tested even more attractive to employers, institutions, and students themselves.[9]

So, count me among those bullish on the potential and promise of ePortfolios. Indeed, as the field gains more experience with ePortfolios, it is possible that the data will show that students who begin building their ePortfolio at the start of their postsecondary education evidence outcomes that warrant the claim that this instructional vehicle is a "meta HIP."

So Now We Have 11

In recent years I have encouraged colleagues to identify and document the impact of additional activities and experiences that qualify as HIPs. Among the activities found on many campuses that have many or even most of the conditions common to those on the AAC&U HIP list are writing for school publications and participating in touring choirs, bands, or other performing groups (theater and dance) that require major investments of time and energy. I am convinced that even intercollegiate athletic coaches who ascribe to a developmentally powerful philosophy in sync with the institution's mission can have nontrivial salutary effects on how athletes connect and make meaning of their experiences in the classroom and the playing fields. What we lack are the kinds of quality data the C2L ePortfolio project has produced.

There is much to be gained from scaling ePortfolio work, and this book offers many important principles for doing so. And there is much to cheer and for which to thank the authors and their colleagues and students at the diverse set of C2L campuses. One of the main takeaways for me is that good ePortfolio work can be done effectively at any type of institution. Happily, Eynon and Gambino explain how, by illustrating the requisite steps and conditions to do ePortfolio well in the classroom and beyond.

Moreover, all students benefit, especially those who are less well prepared for college, which is one of the most important and necessary features of a HIP.

The other noteworthy lesson for me personally is that the field now has another HIP to add to the officially approved list.

My sincere thanks and congratulations to all those involved for producing this important work and providing the guidance the enterprise needs to strengthen undergraduate education and enrich and deepen student learning. Bravo.

George D. Kuh
Senior Scholar, National Institute for Learning Outcomes Assessment
Chancellor's Professor of Higher Education Emeritus, Indiana University

Notes

1. George Kuh, *High-Impact Educational Practices: What They Are, Who Has Access to Them, and Why They Matter* (Washington, DC: Association of American Colleges and Universities, 2008).

2. Ibid; George Kuh, Ken O'Donnell, and Sally Reed, *Ensuring Quality & Taking High-Impact Practices to Scale* (Washington, DC: Association of American Colleges and Universities, 2013).

3. George Kuh, "Culture Bending to Foster Student Success" in *Building Bridges for Student Success: A Sourcebook for Colleges and Universities,* ed. Gerry McLaughlin, Richard Howard, Josetta McLaughlin, and William E. Knight (University of Oklahoma: Consortium for Student Retention Data Exchange, 2013), 1–15.

4. George D. Kuh, Jillian Kinzie, John H. Schuh, Elizabeth J. Whitt, and Associates, *Student Success in College: Creating Conditions That Matter* (San Francisco, CA: Jossey-Bass, 2005/2010).

5. George D. Kuh, Natasha Jankowski, Stanley O. Ikenberry, and Jillian Kinzie, *Knowing What Students Know and Can Do: The Current State of Learning Outcomes Assessment at U.S. Colleges and Universities* (Urbana, IL: University of Illinois and Indiana University, National Institute for Learning Outcomes Assessment, 2014).

6. Dewayne Matthews, Holly Zanville, and Amber Garrison Duncan, *The Emerging Learning System: Report on the Recent Convening and New Directions for Action*, (Indianapolis: Lumina Foundation, 2016). Retrieved from https://www.luminafoundation.org/resources/the-emerging-learning-system

7. Association of American Colleges and Universities (AAC&U), *Greater Expectations: A New Vision for Learning as a Nation Goes to College* (a national panel report) (Washington, DC: Author, 2002); Association of American Colleges and Universities (AAC&U), *Our Students' Best Work: A Framework for Accountability Worthy of Our Mission* (2nd ed., a Statement from the Board of Directors) (Washington, DC: Author, 2008).

8. Ashley Finley and Tia McNair, *Assessing Underserved Students' Engagement in High-Impact Practices* (Washington, DC: Association of American Colleges and Universities, 2013).

9. Matthews et al., 2016.

ACKNOWLEDGMENTS

*H*igh-Impact ePortfolio Practice: A Catalyst for Student, Faculty, and Institutional Learning* emerged from the collaborative work and efforts of the Connect to Learning (C2L) Project, a community of practice of 24 campus teams that worked together for four years, from 2011 to 2015.

Our most important acknowledgment is to the students, faculty, and staff who took part in and supported this effort. The Connect to Learning project involved hundreds of faculty and staff and tens of thousands of students working on the C2L campuses. Information technology staff, institutional research offices, and campus executive leadership supported campus innovation and change. Each campus was represented by a multiperson leadership team of faculty and staff that spent hours and days and weeks and months in designing, testing, documenting, sharing, and refining new practices. Participation in the collaborative community of practice added burdens to already overloaded schedules. This book would not have been possible without the collective energy and expertise, creativity and commitment of this community. Thank you for sharing your time, your practices, and your wisdom.

Campus teams worked together with the C2L leadership team in an ongoing process of collaboration and co-invention. Together we learned and developed and refined our thinking about transformative ePortfolio practice. The *Catalyst for Learning Framework* emerged from our collective work, and for that we are so proud and thankful.

On the C2L leadership team, we are most pleased to thank our two C2L Senior Scholars, Stanford University's Helen L. Chen and Georgetown University's Randy Bass. Helen's expertise as a researcher and her ability to design and guide statistical analysis added rigor to our research. Randy's visionary insights into learning, teaching, and change in higher education inspired some of our most productive community conversations and profoundly shaped our understanding of the implications of our findings.

We also wish to acknowledge other members of the leadership team who provided project management and website development, including Judit Torok, Mikhail Valentin, Jiyeon Lee, and Niranjan Khadka. At its best, this team carried the project forward through an arduous but exciting educational journey.

C2L would not have been possible without external funding, supplementing the internal support provided by campuses. We are deeply grateful to the Fund for the Improvement of Post-Secondary Education for its sustained support for this grant project. We also thank the Association for Authentic, Experiential and Evidence-Based Learning (AAEEBL) and, in particular, Trent Batson and Judy Williamson-Batson for their support of this project and for their ongoing efforts to advance the ePortfolio field.

In this vein, we also express our appreciation to Jeff Yan, CEO of Digication, for donating the use of the Digication platform for our use in the C2L project and to Alex McCormick at the National Survey of Student Engagement (NSSE) for giving us permission to adapt a set of NSSE questions for use in the C2L Core Survey.

We recognize that our work builds on the intellectual foundation developed by many across higher education. Most notably, we have learned deeply from the work of George D. Kuh and others who have advanced higher education with scholarship and advocacy related to High-Impact Practices, including Carol Geary Schneider, Ken O'Donnell, Tia McNair, and Ashley Finley. We are particularly indebted to George Kuh for asking tough questions and pushing us to deepen our work—and now generously agreeing to review our manuscript and preparing a powerful and significant foreword.

We are proud and delighted to acknowledge the Association of American Colleges & Universities (AAC&U) for their sustained and essential leadership work related to High-Impact Practices, ePortfolio, and integrative learning. Guided by Carol Geary Schneider, Terrel Rhodes and others, AAC&U has made a crucial difference in American higher education, and our work has benefited significantly from our long collaboration. As AAC&U enters a new era, we look forward to exciting future collaborations with its new president, Lynn Pasquerella.

Our debts to other scholars are too many to detail. But we wish to particularly highlight the work of Dewey scholar Carol Rodgers, who shaped our thinking about reflection, and Marcia Baxter Magolda, whose work on purposeful authorship we found deeply insightful. We are in debt to Pat Hutchings, not only for her leadership of the Integrative Learning Project, sponsored by AAC&U and the Carnegie Foundation for the Advancement of Teaching, but also for her provision of sustained support and inspiration, modeling what it means to be a thoughtful and generous educational collaborator. We also thank Eddie Watson, editor of the *International Journal of ePortfolio* for his contributions to the field, helping to build and strengthen research on the impact of ePortfolio on student learning and success.

This project would not have been possible without sustained support from our home institutions. Bret is pleased to thank President Gail O. Mellow and Provost Paul Arcario for inspiring and supporting this particular effort and the broader work of LaGuardia's Making Connections National Resource Center. The LaGuardia Center for Teaching and Learning was an invaluable resource; Roslyn Orgel, Priscilla Stadler, and Dean Howard Wach stepped forward at key moments and made essential contributions. Pioneers in ePortfolio innovation, LaGuardia faculty, staff, peer mentors and students are the source of new ideas and ongoing inspiration.

Similarly, Laura thanks Tunxis Community College President Cathryn Addy. Laura began her C2L journey at Tunxis while working as a faculty and ePortfolio coordinator. She is grateful to Cathryn for encouraging her to pursue this work, even though it meant leaving Tunxis. And, she thanks her current president at Guttman,

Scott Evenbeck, for always pushing her thinking and for his continual support and encouragement of this work and her other projects.

Special thanks go to the trusted readers who gave us invaluable feedback as we developed this manuscript: Peter Felten, Gail Matthews-DeNatale, Trent Batson, Susan Kahn, and Susan Scott. We thank Priscilla Stadler for the design of the *Catalyst Framework* graphic. Our thanks also go to Pablo C. Avila for shooting the cover photo for this volume. We thank our vignette authors, Helen L. Chen, Terry Rhodes, Gail Matthews-DeNatale, Susan Kahn, Susan Scott, Kati Lewis, and G. Alex Ambrose. Special thanks, again, to Randy Bass for preparing two significant essays for inclusion in this volume.

The work of the Connect to Learning project, as represented in this book, is complete. But the larger work of inventing high-impact ePortfolio practice is ongoing. In this regard we are pleased to thank all of our readers and all of our collaborators: past, present, and future. Higher education is in the midst of turbulent change, with broad and far-reaching implications. But the history of the future is still being written. Our collective work together can make a difference.

INTRODUCTION

Electronic student portfolios, or ePortfolios, are an intriguing element of the emerging digital learning ecosystem. According to an Educause report,[1] 57% of U.S. colleges now offer ePortfolios to their students, reflecting dramatic growth over the past decade. Furthermore, more than half of college students nationwide report they have used ePortfolio at some point in their time at college. And yet systematic knowledge about how to make ePortfolio practice most effective has been slow to emerge, as has concrete evidence of its impact. This book addresses the need for deeper understanding of effective ePortfolio practice and its potential benefits for students, faculty, and their colleges. Based primarily on research undertaken by 24 campus teams in the Connect to Learning project (C2L),[2] a national community of practice, this book outlines the strategies needed to ensure that ePortfolio fulfills its promise.

Student ePortfolios are Web-based, student-generated collections of learning artifacts (papers, multimedia projects, speeches, images, etc.) and related reflections, focused on learning and growth. ePortfolio practice builds over time and across boundaries, linking courses and disciplines, co-curricular and life experiences. ePortfolio's digital qualities—the ePortfolio platform and its features—can facilitate the linking process and help make learning visible to students themselves, to their peers and faculty, and to external audiences. But meaningful student ePortfolio practice requires much more than an effective platform. The process of curating the connected collection—making meaning through reflection and thereby developing deeper, more intentional identities as learners—requires thoughtful student action guided by well-informed faculty and staff and supported by a broad coalition of college stakeholders. We hope this book will serve as a resource for faculty, staff, and campus leaders as they work to make ePortfolio practice meaningful and effective.

> ePortfolios make student learning visible to students themselves, to their peers and faculty, and to external audiences.

In this book, we argue that ePortfolio practice can play a unique role in twenty-first-century higher learning. We present evidence from C2L campuses demonstrating that ePortfolio offers powerful avenues for enhanced student, faculty, and institutional learning. In a landscape of proliferating educational services and increasingly fragmented learning experiences, we suggest that ePortfolio has demonstrated the capacity to support coherence and integration. We offer a set of comprehensive, field-tested strategies for strengthening ePortfolio's value as a High-Impact Practice (HIP). Based on the practices of the C2L network, the *Catalyst Framework* can guide the work of faculty, staff, and campus leaders who want to mobilize ePortfolio practice to enhance learning and teaching.

The Connect to Learning network brought together ePortfolio innovators from a diverse set of campuses, including Boston University, Virginia Tech, and San Francisco State University as well as LaGuardia, Guttman, Three Rivers, and Salt Lake Community Colleges. Collaborating over the course of four years, campus-based teams gathered evidence, shared ePortfolio practices, and discussed what made ePortfolio practice effective. Together we created the *Catalyst for Learning: ePortfolio Resources and Research* website (see Figure I.1) to share our work with the field.

Reviewing C2L's broad collection of evidence, our findings suggest that, done well, ePortfolio practice can help institutions balance aspirations for deep learning and student success and translate pressures for accountability into meaningful institutional learning. We propose that effective ePortfolio practice can help students engage more deeply and take ownership of their learning, leading to greater student success,

Figure I.1. The *Catalyst for Learning: ePortfolio Resources and Research* Website

Note. Working together in a community of practice from 2011 to 2015, the 24 campuses in the C2L project created the *Catalyst for Learning: ePortfolio Resources and Research* website (c2l.mcnrc.org) to share their work with the broader ePortfolio field.

Catalyst for Learning Value Propositions

Proposition 1: ePortfolio practice done well advances student success. At a growing number of campuses with sustained ePortfolio initiatives, student ePortfolio usage correlates with higher levels of student success as measured by pass rates, grade point average (GPA), and retention.

Proposition 2: ePortfolio practice done well makes student learning visible and supports reflection, integration, and deep learning. Helping students reflect on and connect their learning across academic and co-curricular experiences, sophisticated ePortfolio practices transform the learning experience. Advancing higher order thinking and integrative learning, the connective ePortfolio helps students construct purposeful identities as learners.

Proposition 3: ePortfolio practice done well catalyzes learning-centered institutional change. Focusing attention on student learning and prompting connection and cooperation across departments and divisions, ePortfolio initiatives can catalyze campus cultural and structural change, helping colleges and universities develop as learning organizations.

including measurable improvements in retention and graduation. We find that ePortfolio practice can help link a set of fragmented experiences—for example, a set of High-Impact Practices based in different parts of campus—bringing greater coherence and meaning. Our findings can be summarized in three related value propositions.

Summarized in Chapter 1 and detailed in Chapter 8, these findings represent a step forward for the ePortfolio field. Evidence linked to Proposition 1 shows how ePortfolio practice can advance student success, helping students progress toward graduation. Evidence related to Proposition 2 suggests that ePortfolio practice helps educators balance a focus on completion with an emphasis on quality, the deep learning that makes education meaningful. Proposition 3 outlines the ways that ePortfolio initiatives have a broader impact, helping colleges become more cohesive and agile learning organizations. These three propositions organize important evidence for strategic planning and institutional decision-making related to ePortfolio practice. They also provide a coherent set of propositions to be tested through further research.

Together, these value propositions undergird our argument that ePortfolio should be recognized as a High-Impact Practice. Spearheaded by George D. Kuh; the American Association of Colleges & Universities (AAC&U); and other scholars, including Ken O'Donnell, Tia McNair, and Ashley Finley, the body of research on HIPs has highlighted the broadly demonstrated power of 10 widely used higher education innovations, such as first-year seminars and undergraduate research.[3] As we shall see, C2L data suggest that ePortfolio practice shows a pattern of benefit comparable to other HIPs.

The benefit of all HIPs depends on being done well. First-year seminars can help new college students persist and thrive, for example, but only if they are instituted

Figure I.2. The *Catalyst Framework.*

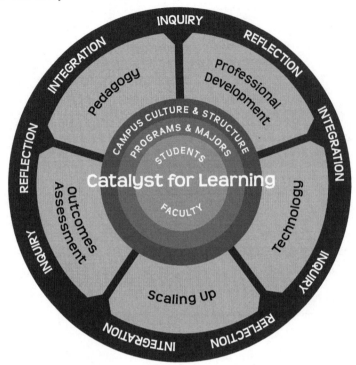

with a high degree of attention to quality and depth. Our study of ePortfolio practice reveals a similar pattern. Done poorly, without insight or careful attention to the qualities that make ePortfolio practice powerful, ePortfolios will have few benefits for students or their institutions. Done well, ePortfolio practice can powerfully advance student, faculty, and institutional learning.

In this book we propose a detailed guide or set of precepts for doing ePortfolio well: The *Catalyst Framework for Effective ePortfolio Practice* (see Figure I.2). We highlight integrative social pedagogy as a key factor for success and provide examples of such pedagogy in practices designed by faculty nationwide. Drawing on the experiences of C2L teams, we also discuss the kinds of support that faculty and students need, addressing professional development, outcomes assessment, and ePortfolio technology as well as the institutional strategies that advance the power of ePortfolio practice.

Using This Book

This book is designed as a resource for faculty, staff, and administrators who want to employ ePortfolio practice to deepen and transform student learning. It is not a teacher's handbook, but it can provide invaluable guidance to educators seeking to advance educational improvement at multiple levels, from classroom practice to institutional outcomes assessment and campus planning and change.

Chapter 1 introduces the ePortfolio field and its development. It outlines the work of the C2L project, summarizing what we and the C2L teams learned from each other and spotlighting the website we jointly created, *Catalyst for Learning: ePortfolio Resources and Research* (c2l.mcnrc.org). Readers interested in a quick overview can find in this chapter the highlights of our collective findings.

Chapters 2 through 7 illuminate the conceptual and practical qualities of ePortfolio practice done well. Chapter 2 provides an overview of the *Catalyst Framework* and highlights the Catalyst design principles: Inquiry, Reflection, and Integration (I-R-I). Subsequent chapters focus on specific *Framework* sectors, from Pedagogy (Chapter 3) to Professional Development (Chapter 4) and Outcomes Assessment (Chapter 5). Chapter 6 examines the role of ePortfolio Technology in effective ePortfolio practice. Chapter 7 considers the institutional strategies C2L campuses used to build and deepen their ePortfolio work. These chapters offer examples of the work needed in each sector, drawn from C2L campus practices.

Each of Chapters 3 through 7 includes a boxed set of tips titled "Getting Started," which list the first steps and issues to keep in mind in launching an ePortfolio project. Multiple chapters include short vignettes written by colleagues in C2L and the broader field, highlighting particular issues and practices. In Chapters 3 and 7, we are pleased to include two short essays by C2L Senior Scholar Randy Bass, exploring particular issues related to the *Catalyst Framework*.

Chapter 8 addresses the following questions: Why ePortfolio? How can ePortfolio practice help students and faculty? What does it offer program directors, deans, provosts, and other institutional stakeholders? It details our three propositions, discussing the quantitative and qualitative evidence supplied by C2L teams.

Chapter 9 discusses the ways ePortfolio is used in conjunction with other High-Impact Practices such as first-year experiences, capstone courses, and service- and community-based learning. C2L research suggests that effective ePortfolio practice can deepen the impact of other HIPs and that the longitudinal and connective quality of ePortfolio facilitates integration of multiple HIPs, helping students understand and articulate them as a cohesive signature learning experience.

Chapter 10, the book's final chapter, goes beyond current practice to consider the future of ePortfolio practice and the ePortfolio field. We argue that connecting ePortfolio with emergent practices such as e-advising, digital badging, and learning analytics can advance critical strategies to address the whole student. In a higher education landscape marked by disruption and change, next-generation ePortfolio practice can help colleges and universities become more integrated, agile, and adaptive learning organizations.

The development of effective ePortfolio practice is an evolving process. We do not see our work as conclusive; rather, we hope that it contributes to an ongoing dialogue. More research will be needed and new approaches must be tried if ePortfolio practice is to serve the needs of twenty-first-century students and faculty. We invite all readers to join us on the *Catalyst for Learning* resource site to discuss new questions and insights, to share best practices, and to build a living resource for this growing and exciting field.

Notes

1. Eden Dahlstrom, with D. Christopher Brooks, Susan Grajek, and Jamie Reeves. *ECAR Study of Students and Information Technology, 2015* (research report) (Louisville, CO: ECAR, December 2015).

2. Bret Eynon and Laura M. Gambino, *Catalyst for Learning: ePortfolio Resources and Research Website,* January 2014, http://c2l.mcnrc.org

3. George Kuh, *High-Impact Educational Practices: What They Are, Who Has Access to Them, and Why They Matter* (Washington, DC: Association of American Colleges and Universities, 2008); George Kuh and Ken O'Donnell, *Ensuring Quality & Taking High Impact Practices to Scale* (Washington, DC: Association of American Colleges and Universities, 2013); Jayne E. Brownell and Lynn E. Swaner, *Five High-Impact Practices: Research on Learning Outcomes, Completion, and Quality* (Washington, DC: Association of American Colleges and Universities, 2010); Ashley Finley and Tia McNair, *Assessing Underserved Students' Engagement in High-Impact Practices* (Washington, DC: Association of American Colleges and Universities: 2013).

PART ONE

HIGH-IMPACT ePORTFOLIO
PRACTICE AND THE
CONNECT TO LEARNING PROJECT

I

ePORTFOLIO

A High-Impact Practice

ePortfolios are increasingly common in higher education, and are now used on more than half of U.S. college campuses.[1] As higher education adapts to the pressures of the twenty-first century, the capacity of ePortfolio practice to enhance integration and make learning visible can further elevate its value. Yet key elements of effective ePortfolio practice are often overlooked; as a result, many campus ePortfolio initiatives struggle. To realize its potential, the field must gather and examine evidence of ePortfolio's impact on student learning and generate clear frameworks for effective practice.

This book directly speaks to these needs. It draws on the work of the Connect to Learning (C2L) network, 24 teams from campuses with sustained ePortfolio projects engaged in a national community of practice. It analyzes C2L campus data on the benefits of ePortfolio practice for students, faculty, and institutions, generating three evidence-based value propositions. It also offers the *Catalyst Framework*, a linked set of campus-tested strategies for building an effective ePortfolio initiative, connecting effective pedagogy to professional development and outcomes assessment. In doing so, it aligns effective ePortfolio practice with the framework George D. Kuh, the Association of American Colleges & Universities (AAC&U), and others have developed for educationally effective High-Impact Practices.[2]

This chapter begins by briefly reviewing the history of ePortfolio practice. It summarizes the evidence gathered by the C2L project, introduces the *Catalyst Framework*, and positions

> ### Connect to Learning: ePortfolio Value Propositions
>
> Findings from C2L revealed three mutually reinforcing value propositions of the benefits of ePortfolio practice done well.
>
> 1. ePortfolio practice done well advances student success.
> 2. Making learning visible, ePortfolio practice done well supports reflection, integration, and deep learning.
> 3. ePortfolio practice done well catalyzes learning-centered institutional change.

ePortfolio in the growing literature related to educationally effective High-Impact Practices.

A History of Growth

The spread of ePortfolio practice in twenty-first-century higher education has been rapid but uneven. Growing numbers of colleges and universities offer ePortfolio services. Hundreds of thousands of students use ePortfolio each year. The proliferation of ePortfolio vendors, journals, networks, and conferences is striking. Yet in educational technology circles, ePortfolios are often seen as passé, and many campus ePortfolio projects struggle to grow beyond the pilot stage. While the field has progressed in significant ways, broad understanding of ePortfolio practice is still limited.

ePortfolios have deep historical roots. Disciplines such as writing and architecture have long used portfolios to collect student work and present a curated demonstration of skill and accomplishment. Sophisticated practitioners understood that this process created opportunities for self-critique and the development of reflective practice.[3]

In the 1990s three developments energized the transformation of portfolio practice. First, new research in learning science spurred the growth of learner-centered and constructivist pedagogies, demonstrating that students learned best by doing and creating, connecting new knowledge with preexisting frameworks of understanding. Bransford, Brown, and Cocking's magisterial synthesis of this research highlighted the crucial learning role of reflection or metacognitive thinking.[4] This research literature has only continued to grow in size and sophistication, offering important insights into cognition as well as the noncognitive or affective elements of student learning and growth, such as grit and resilience.[5]

Second, the digital revolution empowered students to create and share collections of text, images, and multimedia artifacts. Although ePortfolios emerged as part of what was later called Web 1.0, they in some ways anticipated Web 2.0 by focusing on user-generated content.

Third, federal agencies and accreditation bodies spurred new attention on assessment and accountability, the measurement of student learning. The movement to advance authentic assessment took an important turn, and colleges and universities nationwide began to look for ways to satisfy assessment pressures.

These developments fueled the emergence of ePortfolios as a multifaceted practice that links digital technology with reflective learning, integrative pedagogy, and authentic assessment. A handful of educators saw the broad potential of ePortfolio as a student-curated collection of learning artifacts and reflections, which together made a student's learning visible to the student and to others. In 2002 Trent Batson noted with some surprise,

> The term "electronic portfolio" or "ePortfolio" is on everyone's lips. We often hear it associated with assessment, but also with accreditation, reflection, student resumes, and career tracking. It's as if this new tool is the answer to all of the questions we didn't realize we were asking.[6]

Batson and others believed ePortfolio practice could address multiple needs. It could help students deepen their learning by reflecting on their own growth. By making artifacts of student learning more visible, it could make assessment more meaningful than standardized tests, and it had potential as a vehicle students could use to present accomplishments to external audiences, including employers. Alverno College, Kalamazoo College, Wesleyan University, and Portland State University were among the early ePortfolio pioneers, but others soon followed, including LaGuardia Community College and Indiana University–Purdue University Indianapolis (IUPUI). The broad possibilities envisioned for ePortfolio practice led a small but growing number of colleges to launch ePortfolio initiatives, with growth accelerating after 2009. In 2010 Terrel Rhodes, vice president of the Association of American Colleges & Universities wrote,

> Electronic portfolios are emerging on campuses across the country as a means for students to reflect systematically on their own learning; for faculty to represent and evaluate multimodal ways for students to demonstrate their learning through text, performance and visual or audio media; and for institutions to assess, document and share student learning through the curriculum and co-curriculum. The growth in student and faculty interest in electronic portfolios is evidenced by the growth in the varieties of portfolio software available in the marketplace.[8]

> **What Is ePortfolio for Students?**
>
> Campuses define *ePortfolio* in different ways. LaGuardia Community College defines *ePortfolio* for its students as the following:
>
> For students, ePortfolio practice asks questions, such as,
>
> - Who am I?
> - Who am I becoming?
> - Who do I dare to be?
>
> Asking these questions, ePortfolio practice helps students connect their past and their future, their challenges and their growth, their learning and their lives.
>
> More than a technology, ePortfolio is a guided process that helps students tell their stories. Documenting and reflecting on their learning in the classroom and beyond, returning to the process semester after semester, students transform experience into meaning.
>
> A space for planning, collaborating, and sharing, ePortfolio not only builds success but also helps students develop more purposeful identities as learners and emerging professionals.[7]

In the years since Rhodes wrote, new developments have unsettled higher education. Pressure over costs and accountability have risen at the same time that growing numbers of minority and first-generation college students have transformed student demographics. Massive open online courses (MOOCs), digital badging, online advisement tools, and other elements of a new digital learning environment exploded onto the scene, creating opportunities for "unbundling"[9] the traditional campus; in the future, some observers have predicted, students will use digital tools and systems to "learn everywhere," not from a single university but from a variety of education providers, scattered across the country and around the globe.

The future of this upheaval is not yet clear, but change is inevitable. To the extent that higher education becomes in some way "unbundled," that learning occurs in and beyond the walls of the classroom, ePortfolio practice can help students connect and synthesize those learning experiences. Linking learning in diverse settings, ePortfolio can support more integrative processes of reflection and assessment. In the emerging educational ecosystem, effective ePortfolio practice can link digital badges and learning analytics to broader structures for student, faculty, and institutional learning. At a time when many forces are fragmenting the educational experience, what we discuss as next-generation ePortfolio practice has the potential to create opportunities for strengthening connection and meaning.

What Is ePortfolio for Faculty and Staff?

LaGuardia Community College defines *ePortfolio* for its faculty and staff as the following:

For faculty, staff, advisors, and the institution, ePortfolio practice asks questions such as the following:

- Who are our students?
- What experiences do they bring to the college?
- How can I see and better understand their patterns of learning and growth?

Done well, ePortfolio practice makes learning visible across boundaries and over time. As students tell their stories, they help faculty understand who sits in their classes, and how their classes connect with each other.

As students craft plans for education and careers, they create opportunities for faculty and staff advisors to offer deeper, more informed guidance.

Moving past standardized tests, students' ePortfolio work helps degree programs assess their own impact and helps an institution become a more integrated and adaptive learning organization.[10]

A Promise Not Yet Realized

Despite growing use of ePortfolio and its emerging role in the new learning ecosystem, the full promise of ePortfolio has yet to be realized. Campus ePortfolio projects confront multiple challenges, from choosing the right platform to providing technical support, building faculty engagement, developing effective pedagogy, and balancing conflicting goals. There is a deeper issue as well: ePortfolio initiatives require coordinated efforts on multiple fronts, cross-institutional collaborations that can challenge long-standing assumptions. As a result, many campus ePortfolio projects have been short lived; others have survived but never thrived or gone to scale.

Part of the problem is that many campuses have launched ePortfolio initiatives with limited understanding of effective ePortfolio practice. Many colleges approach ePortfolios as a technology and fail to grasp that their value depends on sophisticated pedagogy and institutional practice. Campuses lack access to comprehensive discussions of implementation issues and well-organized collections of campus-tested practices. They have no guide to help them plan the complex effort needed to achieve success.

This is a significant gap in the field. Although the ePortfolio field has matured, no comprehensive framework has yet emerged to guide the design of ePortfolio initiatives. There is a need for an overarching conceptual structure that embraces the complexity of ePortfolio initiatives, the strategic potential of their integrative nature, and the rich and evolving nature of ePortfolio itself as an emerging set of practices.

Another gap has also hobbled ePortfolio development. ePortfolio practitioners have produced surprisingly little evidence regarding ePortfolio's role in student learning. Bryant and Chittum reviewed the research literature and found a striking paucity of hard research; of 118 articles on ePortfolio published in peer-reviewed journals between 1996 and 2012, they found that most were descriptive or self-reporting in nature. Only 15% of the articles they reviewed provided empirical evidence related to student outcomes, and less than 2% used measures Bryant and Chittum considered reliable and valid.[11]

Although legitimate questions could be raised about Bryant and Chittum's categories and methodologies, the broader point is indisputable. Up until now, relatively little data have been published on the role of ePortfolio experience in shaping student outcomes such as learning, retention, and completion. In an era of tight higher education budgets and increased attention to student completion and accountability, the need for evidence of impact is only growing.

Fortunately, new evidence is now emerging. The C2L network gathered evaluation evidence from multiple campuses, showing strong correlations between ePortfolio experience and improved student learning and success. C2L campuses also worked together to generate a comprehensive framework for effective ePortfolio practice. C2L findings can support educators nationwide, and those findings are the basis for our claim that ePortfolio is a High-Impact Practice for twenty-first-century learning.

The Connect to Learning Project: A Community of Inquiry

Active from 2011 to 2015, the C2L project brought together teams from 24 campuses nationwide to respond to questions confronting the field: What difference can ePortfolio make? Can an ePortfolio initiative improve student learning? Does ePortfolio-based outcomes assessment really work? Is ePortfolio worth an investment of institutional resources? What evidence demonstrates the broader value of an ePortfolio initiative? What strategies have produced success for students and institutions?

Supported by a grant from the Fund for the Improvement of Post-Secondary Education (FIPSE), C2L assembled 24 institutions with established ePortfolio projects into a national community of practice. Engaged in a recursive knowledge-generation process, partner campuses represented a cross-section of higher education, from community colleges to Research I universities, ranging from Boston University

C2L Partner Institutions

Boston University
City University of New York
(CUNY) School of Professional
Studies
Empire State College (State Uni-
versity of New York [SUNY])
Georgetown University
Stella and Charles Guttman
Community College (CUNY)
Hunter College (CUNY)
Indiana University-Purdue Uni-
versity Indianapolis
LaGuardia Community College
(CUNY)
Lehman College (CUNY)
Manhattanville College
Northeastern University
Northwestern Connecticut Com-
munity College
Norwalk Community College
Pace University
Queensborough Community
College (CUNY)
Rutgers University
St. John's University
Salt Lake Community College
San Francisco State University
Stony Brook University (SUNY)
Three Rivers Community College
Tunxis Community College
University of Delaware
Virginia Polytechnic Institute
and State University

to San Francisco State, IUPUI, and Three Rivers Community College. C2L was coordinated by the Making Connections National Resource Center of LaGuardia Community College, in partnership with the Association for Authentic, Experiential, and Evidence-Based Learning. LaGuardia's associate provost for academic affairs, Bret Eynon, was the project's principal investigator; Laura M. Gambino, associate dean for assessment and technology at Guttman Community College, was the C2L research director. Judit Torok helped manage C2L. Georgetown's Randy Bass and Stanford's Helen L. Chen served as C2L's senior scholars.

C2L used a hybrid community-building model that integrated online conversations and face-to-face meetings to link teams as they explored the literature, exchanged practices, and expanded their campus ePortfolio projects.[12] Campus projects reflected local needs. Some teams focused on a few disciplines, such as education, nursing, or art history; others used ePortfolio campus-wide, sometimes tied to general education. Many C2L teams linked their ePortfolio work with first-year seminars and capstone courses.

Each campus team built a portfolio to represent its ePortfolio story. These portfolios and a set of cross-cutting analytical essays form a jointly created website titled *Catalyst for Learning: ePortfolio Resources and Research* (c2l.mcnrc.org). This book draws on that site to make a narrative argument and provide a book-format resource to the field (see Figure 1.1).

The Difference ePortfolio Makes

Each C2L campus team was asked to gather local evidence about the effectiveness of ePortfolio practice. Teams focused on student learning and success, but made choices about how to measure it, using indicators appropriate to their campus and students.

Figure 1.1. The *Catalyst for Learning: ePortfolio Resources and Research* Website.

Note. Each campus team created an ePortfolio on the *Catalyst for Learning* site, such as this one from San Francisco State University, with practices, stories, links to student ePortfolios, and other multimedia resources.

They all used a common survey instrument, the C2L Core Survey, that included questions used with permission from the National Survey of Student Engagement (NSSE). They shared annual reports analyzing the local impact of ePortfolio on teaching, learning, and assessment.

The groundbreaking research conducted by C2L campuses represents a systematic, multicampus effort to examine the impact ePortfolio practice can have on student learning and success, and it generated important evidence suggesting that sophisticated ePortfolio practice, or ePortfolio done well, makes a difference for students, faculty, and institutions. On multiple campuses, ePortfolio-enhanced courses demonstrated higher student success outcomes than comparison courses. Data on GPA, retention, and graduation showed similar patterns. Meanwhile, data from the C2L Core Survey suggested that ePortfolio practice engaged students in deep and integrative learning. Moreover, the impact documented by C2L campuses was not limited to students; it indicated that sophisticated campus ePortfolio practice can also advance faculty learning and institutional change.[13]

The C2L findings can be summarized in three mutually reinforcing value propositions, previewed here and discussed fully in Chapter 8.

Proposition 1: ePortfolio Practice Done Well Advances Student Success

At a growing number of campuses with sustained ePortfolio initiatives, student ePortfolio usage correlates with higher levels of student success as measured by pass rates, GPA, and retention.

C2L campuses studied the role of ePortfolio in student success. A constellation of campuses, from Manhattanville College to IUPUI to San Francisco State University, presented evidence of ePortfolio-related student success such as retention rates and GPA data.

In the Douglass Women's College of Rutgers University, ePortfolio was introduced into a required first semester mission course in the 2008–2009 school year; student performance improved significantly. The students' average grade point average (GPA) in the course improved and, perhaps more important, so did their cumulative GPA across all courses.

At LaGuardia Community College, data from multiple years show that across disciplines, the one-semester retention rate for students in ePortfolio courses is an average of 9 to 11 percentage points higher than the rate for students in comparison courses. Students enrolled in ePortfolio courses also had higher course completion and course pass rates than students in comparison courses.

At Tunxis Community College, a year-long comparison between ePortfolio and non-ePortfolio sections of developmental English courses showed that ePortfolio sections had 3.5 percentage points higher pass rates and an almost 6 percentage points higher retention rate.

San Francisco State University integrated ePortfolio into the Metro Health Academy, a learning community for high-risk students. Data show that improved success rates at every stage, including a graduation rate 10 percentage points higher than university-wide averages.

Detailed in Chapter 8, these studies and others represent an emergent pattern and provide a suggestive body of evidence for the proposition that sophisticated ePortfolio initiatives can help campuses improve student success and meet the challenge of improved rates of graduation and completion.

We must note an important caveat: We recognize that the data from C2L campuses have limitations. Proving causal connections related to learning is always challenging. C2L teams did not have the capacity to conduct randomized control group studies. The network spanned diverse campus contexts, marked by differences in focus, purpose, and level of student preparation. Not all teams succeeded in mobilizing their campus institutional research team to conduct the study. While the C2L data are limited in rigor and consistency, they are nonetheless suggestive and intriguing.

Proposition 2: Making Learning Visible, ePortfolio Practice Done Well Supports Reflection, Integration, and Deep Learning

Helping students reflect on and connect their learning across academic and co-curricular learning experiences, sophisticated ePortfolio practices transform the student learning experience. Advancing higher order thinking and integrative learning, the connective nature of ePortfolio helps students construct purposeful identities as learners.

To go beyond completion and begin to address issues of quality learning, C2L teams and project leaders worked with Stanford University researcher Helen L. Chen to develop a survey tool that would help illuminate the effect of sophisticated ePortfolio practice on the nature of the student learning experience. We incorporated (with permission) and adapted a set of questions from the widely respected National Survey on Student Engagement, along with more specific questions about ePortfolio experience. Used on campuses across the network with a wide range of students (n = 10,170), the C2L Core Survey sheds important light on the ways ePortfolio practice can shape student experiences.

On questions about ePortfolio, wide majorities of students reported that building their ePortfolios helped them "think more deeply" about course content, "make connections between ideas," and become "more aware" of their growth and development as learners. They also demonstrated high degrees of engagement in what Laird, Shoup, and Kuh have identified as a deep learning scale—synthesizing and organizing ideas, engaging in critical thinking, and applying theoretical concepts in unfamiliar situations.[14]

Analysis of these data, detailed in Chapter 8, suggests that ePortfolio processes shaped by integrative social pedagogies help students make connections and deepen their learning. The data also suggest that ePortfolio practice done well helps students take ownership of their learning, building not only academic skills but also the affective understandings of self critical to student success. In this way, a sophisticated ePortfolio initiative can help educators address issues of learning quality without sacrificing success outcomes.

Proposition 3: ePortfolio Practice Done Well Catalyzes Learning-Centered Institutional Change

Focusing attention on student learning and prompting connection and cooperation across departments and divisions, ePortfolio initiatives can catalyze campus cultural and structural change, helping colleges and universities develop as learning organizations.

Although the first two value propositions focus on students, we found that effective ePortfolio practice had a broader impact as well, linked to faculty, staff, and institutional learning. The winds of change now swirling across higher education give particular importance to our third proposition. How can colleges and universities build their capacity to respond and adapt to changing conditions and new possibilities? How can administrators thoughtfully engage faculty and staff expertise to advance campus innovation focused on student learning? At a time when some argue that higher education should be "unbundled," how can campuses develop a shared purpose, a more concerted effort to advance student learning and development? How can colleges build learning cultures and become more integrated and adaptive learning organizations?

Addressing this challenging agenda, our third value proposition is based on stories and practices shared by the C2L teams that described their multifaceted work and how it reshaped campus culture. We found that the most effective C2L teams undertook a broad range of activities, connecting with faculty and staff in diverse sectors of the campus, from departments and programs to student life, institutional research and assessment, information technology (IT) and Centers for Teaching and Learning (CTLs). Bringing together diverse campus groups for collaboration focused on student learning, we found, helped campuses illuminate the holistic nature of student learning, spark integrative structural change, and build campus-wide commitment to organizational learning.

All three value propositions are explored in Chapter 8, on the *Catalyst for Learning* website, and in peer-reviewed articles.[15] While still emergent, they represent an important first step in documenting the difference that ePortfolio can make in higher education. We encourage others to gather evidence that can confirm, extend, and refine these findings. As we move forward, such research will advance our understanding of ePortfolio's multifaceted benefits.

What It Takes to Make a Difference: The *Catalyst Framework*

The C2L campuses also worked together to document and analyze the strategies needed to do ePortfolio effectively. While reading literature in the field, including the research on High-Impact Practices, they also reviewed and discussed each other's practices. Out of this conversation emerged the *Catalyst Framework* (see Figure 1.2). By the project's end, campuses were explicitly using the *Framework* to strengthen their own campus efforts.

The *Catalyst Framework* starts with classroom pedagogy, but it extends further. Because ePortfolio is most effective when it is implemented longitudinally and horizontally across disciplines and semesters, and because effective ePortfolio practice involves faculty and institutional learning as well as student learning, the *Framework* goes beyond the boundaries of the classroom. It speaks to not only the work of students and faculty but also that of departments and programs as well as broader institutional structures. Across these different levels of institutional life, we found that effective ePortfolio initiatives intentionally structure work in five interlocking sectors:

- **Integrative Social Pedagogy**: The theory and practice that guide the use of ePortfolio to support and deepen student learning, including practices related to ePortfolio for career and advisement. C2L focused particularly on practices that involve integrative learning and social pedagogy and centered on reflection as a key to deep learning.
- **Professional Development**: The active processes (workshops, seminars, online tutorials, and institutes) designed to help faculty and staff learn about ePortfolio technology and pedagogy and more effectively advance student learning and growth.

Figure 1.2. The *Catalyst Framework*

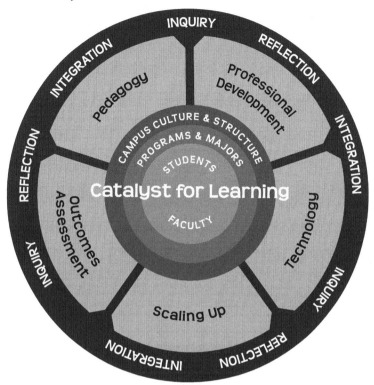

- **Outcomes Assessment**: The ways campuses use ePortfolio and authentic classroom work to support holistic assessment of programs and general education outcomes.
- **Technology**: The choices campuses make about ePortfolio platforms and related support mechanisms can have a profound impact on the shape and the success of a campus ePortfolio initiative.
- **Scaling Up**: The planning, building, and evaluating of an ePortfolio initiative—the active role of campus ePortfolio leaders, and the way they work with students, faculty, administrators, and other stakeholders to build ePortfolio culture, allocate resources, and make the connections that can catalyze institutional change.

The Pedagogy sector of the *Catalyst Framework* is critical, and it is the area that has the most in common with the literature on High-Impact Practices. But C2L campus teams concluded that other sectors were also essential. No matter how effective their pedagogy, faculty acting alone in their individual classrooms cannot realize the full potential of ePortfolio practice. Broader institutional effort is required. The sectors of the *Catalyst Framework* suggest a way to conceptualize and organize that effort.

We found that work done in these interlocking sectors can be enhanced by attention to the three Catalyst design principles: Inquiry, Reflection, and Integration (I-R-I). C2L research suggests that effective ePortfolio initiatives use these principles in their pedagogy as well as other sectors, guiding the planning and implementation of activities campus-wide.

- **Inquiry**, or inquiry learning, is a well-developed pedagogy involving generating questions, examining evidence, and solving authentic problems. For students, ePortfolios can be understood as an inquiry into their own learning. In sophisticated ePortfolio-related professional development programs, faculty too are engaged in collective inquiry into practice. Programs and institutions use ePortfolio-based outcomes assessment as part of their inquiry into learning and teaching.
- **Reflection**, as understood by Dewey and others, stands at the core of deep learning and is key to processing experience and the generation of meaning.[16] Guided reflective learning is widely understood as essential to powerful ePortfolio practice, and becoming a reflective practitioner is key to the success of ePortfolio-related professional development and outcomes assessment efforts.
- **Integration**, or integrative learning, engages students in connecting learning across time, space, and discipline, and developing the capacity to transfer knowledge and skill from one setting to another. Faculty and institutions as well as students must work to advance integration, thereby overcoming fragmentation and more intentionally applying insights and innovations to the broader process of building more cohesive and effective educational institutions. ePortfolios and outcomes assessment practices can be powerful processes in this regard.

To be used effectively as design principles, the overarching concept of Inquiry, Reflection, and Integration must be understood as connected, not discrete. Together they form a dynamic cycle, most powerful when recursive and ongoing. As design principles, they can inform the planning and execution of action across sectors, deepening cohesive strategies on diverse fronts of a campus-wide ePortfolio initiative.

The *Catalyst Framework* can help campuses understand what it takes to do ePortfolio well. Building an effective ePortfolio initiative is a developmental process that must unfold over time. Because ePortfolio practice is most meaningful as a process of connection and integration, ePortfolio "done well" requires cohesive vision and design. The diversity of the *Framework* sectors suggests the necessary breadth of the effort, and the Catalyst design principles help ensure cohesion and quality.

ePortfolio as a High-Impact Practice

The concept of High-Impact Practices is well established in higher education. Under the direction of the AAC&U, George Kuh and others have conducted, reviewed, and drawn on a wide range of educational research to identify a set of practices that when done well, "engage participants at levels that elevate their performance across multiple engagement and desired-outcome measures such as persistence."[17] The AAC&U and Kuh codified a list of 10 practices that qualify.

These teaching and learning practices "have been widely tested and shown to be beneficial for college students from many backgrounds."[18] Evidence from multiple institutions shows these practices "have special benefit" on student outcomes such as engagement, persistence, retention, higher GPA,

> **High-Impact Practices**
>
> First-Year Seminars
> Common Intellectual
>   Experiences
> Learning Communities
> Writing-Intensive Courses
> Collaborative Assignments and
>   Projects
> Undergraduate Research
> Diversity and Global Learning
> Service-Learning, Community-
>   Based Learning
> Internships
> Capstone Courses and Projects

and graduation from college. Moreover, research shows they are particularly valuable for first-generation and minority students, helping them even more than they help traditional college students. "While participation in effective educational activities generally benefits all students," Kuh writes, "the salutary effects are even greater for students who begin college at lower achievement levels, as well as students of color, compared with white students."[19]

In this book, we argue that ePortfolio should be recognized as a High-Impact Practice (sometimes abbreviated in the field and this book as HIP), along with first-year seminars, undergraduate research, and capstone courses. We believe that ePortfolio practice meets the criteria laid out in various HIP-related publications. The C2L data reviewed in Chapter 8 suggest that ePortfolio practice has been widely tested, shows a recurring pattern of benefit comparable to other HIPs, and meets other HIP criteria as well.

Key to the discussion of HIPs is the issue of implementation quality. As Kuh has written, "to engage students at high levels, these practices *must be done well*" (emphasis in the original).[20] Research has identified a framework for quality implementation of each HIP, identifying the essential elements, for example, of a first-year seminar done well.[21] These frameworks are crucial to helping institutions plan, launch, and sustain any given HIP. The *Catalyst Framework* establishes a done-well structure for ePortfolio practice comparable to the equivalent structure for other HIPs. Extending from the classroom to broader institutional practice, the *Catalyst Framework* identifies a developmental process that can help educators develop and scale high-impact ePortfolio practice.

Finally, Kuh, O'Donnell, and others have argued that there is a set of key operational characteristics common to varying degrees across HIPs. No one HIP encompasses all characteristics, but all encompass some. As Kuh has written, "High-Impact Practices are developmentally powerful because they combine and concentrate other empirically validated pedagogical approaches into a single multi-dimensional activity that unfolds over an extended period of time."[22] Sometimes termed *behaviors* or *educationally effective practices*, these traits can be understood as key dimensions of high-impact student learning experiences, the qualities that make HIPs high-impact. These include the following:

- performance expectations set at appropriately high levels
- significant investment of time and effort by students over an extended period of time
- interactions with faculty and peers about substantive matters
- experiences with diversity
- frequent, timely, and constructive feedback
- periodic, structured opportunities to reflect and integrate learning
- opportunities to discover relevance of learning through real-world applications
- public demonstration of competence[23]

Throughout this book, we will demonstrate that high-impact ePortfolio practice embodies many of these characteristics. The core of ePortfolio practice is the act of making student learning more visible and connected, using the combination of guided reflection and networked digital technology. This core behavior aligns directly with two of Kuh and O'Donnell's dimensions noted previously: periodic, structured opportunities to reflect and integrate learning; and public demonstration of competence. As we shall see, it also facilitates learning experiences along many of the other dimensions, including significant investment of time and effort by students over an extended period of time; experiences with diversity; frequent, timely, and constructive feedback; and opportunities to discover relevance of learning through real-world applications.

Throughout this book, we consider the behaviors facilitated by ePortfolio practice and do so in the context of the *Catalyst Framework*, looking not only at integrative ePortfolio pedagogy but also the key factors that support such pedagogy and the improved learning associated with it.

Done well, ePortfolio practice supports measurably improved student learning and success as well as the key behaviors common among HIPs. But doing ePortfolio well is more challenging than many educators realize. Planning, piloting, leading, and sustaining an effective ePortfolio project takes a careful understanding of what ePortfolio pedagogy looks like. It also requires attention to professional development, assessment, technology, and institutional support. The chapters that follow provide a sector-by-sector review of the *Catalyst Framework*, illuminated by an array of thoughtful practices developed, tested, and shared by C2L campuses.

Notes

1. Eden Dahlstrom, with D. Christopher Brooks, Susan Grajek, and Jamie Reeves, *ECAR Study of Undergraduate Students and Information Technology, 2015* (research report) (Louisville, CO: ECAR, December 2015).

2. George Kuh, *High-Impact Educational Practices: What They Are, Who Has Access to Them, and Why They Matter* (Washington, DC: Association of American Colleges & Universities, 2008); George Kuh and Ken O'Donnell, *Ensuring Quality & Taking High-Impact Practices to Scale* (Washington, DC: Association of American Colleges & Universities, 2013); Jayne E. Brownell and Lynn E. Swaner, *Five High-Impact Practices: Research on Learning Outcomes, Completion, and Quality* (Washington, DC: Association of American Colleges & Universities, 2010); Ashley Finley and Tia McNair, *Assessing Underserved Students' Engagement in High-Impact Practices* (Washington, DC: Association of American Colleges & Universities: 2013).

3. Darren Cambridge, *e-Portfolios for Lifelong Learning and Assessment* (Chichester, UK: Wiley, 2010).

4. John D. Bransford, Ann L. Brown, and Rodney R. Cocking, eds., *How People Learn: Brain, Mind, Experience, and School* (Washington, DC: National Academies Press, 2000).

5. Peter C. Brown, Henry L. Roediger III, and Mark A. McDaniel, *Make It Stick: The Science of Successful Learning* (Cambridge, MA: Belknap Press, 2014); Richard E. Mayer, *Applying the Science of Learning* (Upper Saddle River, NJ: Pearson, 2010); Susan A. Ambrose, Michael W. Bridges, Michele DiPietro, Marsha C. Lovett, and Marie K. Norman, *How Learning Works: Seven Research-Based Principles for Smart Teaching* (San Francisco: Jossey-Bass, 2010); Ken Bain, *What the Best College Teachers Do* (Cambridge, MA: Harvard University Press, 2004); Richard Keeling, ed., *Learning Reconsidered: A Campus-Wide Focus on the Student Experience* (Washington DC: National Association of Student Personnel Administrators and American College Personnel Association, 2004); David C. Hodge, Marcia Baxter Magolda, and Carolyn A. B. Haynes, "Engaged Learning: Enabling Self-Authorship and Effective Practice," *Liberal Education*, 95, no. 4 (Fall 2009); Carol S. Dweck, *Mindset: The New Psychology of Success* (New York, NY: Random House, 2006).

6. Trent Batson, "The Electronic Portfolio Boom: What's It All About?" *Campus Technology*, accessed November 15, 2015, https://campustechnology.com/articles/2002/11/the-electronic-portfolio-boom-whats-it-all-about.aspx

7. "What is ePortfolio?," LaGuardia Community College, 2016.

8. Terrel Rhodes, foreword to *Electronic Portfolios and Student Success: Effectiveness, Efficiency, and Learning*, by Helen L. Chen and Tracy Penny Light (Washington, DC: Association of American Colleges & Universities, 2010), vi.

9. Randy Bass and Bret Eynon, *Open and Integrative: Designing Liberal Education for the New Digital Ecosystem* (Washington, DC: Association of American Colleges & Universities, 2016), 4.

10. "What Is ePortfolio?," LaGuardia Community College, 2016.

11. Lauren H. Bryant and Jessica R. Chittum, "ePortfolio Effectiveness: A(n Ill-Fated) Search for Empirical Support," *International Journal of ePortfolio* 3, no. 2 (2014): 189–198.

12. Bret Eynon, Laura M. Gambino, and Judit Torok, "Connect to Learning: Using e-Portfolios in Hybrid Professional Development," *To Improve the Academy* 32 (2013): 109–126.

13. Bret Eynon, Laura M. Gambino, and Judit Torok, "What Difference Can ePortfolio Make? A Field Report from the Connect to Learning Project," *International Journal of ePortfolio* 4, no. 1 (2014), 95–114.

14. Thomas F. Laird, Rick Shoup, and George D. Kuh, "Measuring Deep Approaches to Learning Using the National Survey of Student Engagement" (paper, Annual Meeting of the Association for Institutional Research, Chicago, IL, May 2005).

15. Bret Eynon, Laura M. Gambino, and Judit Torok, "What Difference Can ePortfolio Make? A Field Report from the Connect to Learning Project," *International Journal of ePortfolio* 4, no. 1 (2014), 95–114; Bret Eynon, Laura M. Gambino, and Judit Torok, "Completion, Quality, and Change: The Difference E-Portfolios Make," *Peer Review* 16, no. 1 (2014), 8–14.

16. John Dewey, *Experience and Education* (New York, NY: Touchstone, 1997); Jack Mezirow, ed., *Learning as Transformation: Critical Perspectives on a Theory in Progress* (San Francisco, CA: Jossey-Bass, 2000); Bransford et al., *How People Learn.*

17. George Kuh, *High-Impact Educational Practices: What They Are, Who Has Access to Them, and Why They Matter* (Washington, DC: American Association of Colleges and Universities, 2008), 14.

18. Kuh, *High-Impact Educational Practices,* 9.

19. Ibid., 19.

20. Ibid., 20.

21. Jayne E. Brownell and Lynn E. Swaner, "High Impact Practices: Applying the Learning Outcomes Literature to the Development of Successful Campus Programs," *Peer Review,* 11, no. 2 (Washington, DC: AAC&U, 2009), 28–29.

22. George Kuh, foreword to *Five High-Impact Practices: Research on Learning Outcomes, Completion, and Quality,* by Jayne E. Brownell and Lynn E. Swaner (Washington, DC: Association of American Colleges & Universities, 2010), xi.

23. George Kuh and Ken O'Donnell, *Ensuring Quality & Taking High-Impact Practices to Scale* (Washington, DC: Association of American Colleges & Universities, 2013), 8.

PART TWO

ePORTFOLIO DONE WELL

The *Catalyst Framework*

2

THE *CATALYST FRAMEWORK*

An Evidence-Based Approach to ePortfolio Practice

How can educators best employ ePortfolio practice to improve learning and teaching? What strategies, both in and out of the classroom, have proven effective? How can pedagogy, technology, and assessment be synergized? What issues and questions need to be addressed? Which stakeholders and what resources need to be mobilized? What does it take to make a difference? This chapter launches us into a broad examination of what it takes to "do ePortfolio well."

As discussed in Chapter 1, the work of the Connect to ·Learning (C2L) network shows that ePortfolio practice can help colleges meet the pressing challenges of contemporary higher education. Done well, ePortfolio practice plays a valuable role in improving student success and encouraging deep learning. Through outcomes assessment and professional development, it spurs faculty learning and institutional change. C2L senior scholar Randy Bass has argued that although other digital technologies may be more glamorous, ePortfolio practice has an unmatched capacity to connect learning across boundaries:

> In a landscape of unbundled educational services and increasingly granular learning experiences, ePortfolios are agents of integration. They are demonstrating the capacity to create an integrative and coherent context for students to make sense of their learning and for institutions to get an unmatched, holistic view into the impact of their curricular and institutional designs.[1]

"Done well," ePortfolio can serve as a powerful agent of integration, unfolding over time, linking disciplines and dimensions of learning. But what does ePortfolio practice "done well" look like? What different facets of ePortfolio practice need to be addressed? What does it take to make productive links between pedagogy and platforms, outcomes assessment and campus-wide change? To realize ePortfolio's full potential, campus leaders need a comprehensive, evidence-based framework for addressing the multifaceted tasks of building a successful, high-impact ePortfolio initiative. There is a broad need for an overarching conceptual structure that explains the complexity of ePortfolio initiatives; the strategic potential of their integrative nature; and the rich, evolving nature of ePortfolio itself as an emerging set of practices.

The *Catalyst Framework* addresses this need. It can help campus communities think through not only their goals but also the collaborative strategies ePortfolio initiatives require to enhance student, faculty, and institutional learning. It is designed to further the capacity of campuses to use ePortfolio to address pressing needs and make a meaningful difference. This chapter provides an overview of the *Framework*, outlining its key sectors and discussing the cross-cutting Catalyst design principles: Inquiry, Reflection, and Integration (I-R-I). And in so doing, it sets the stage for Chapters 3 through 7, which explore specific *Framework* sectors in greater detail.

The *Catalyst Framework*

In C2L, ePortfolio leaders from our partner campuses worked together to document and share their practices, exploring the following question: What strategies and approaches do successful ePortfolio campuses employ to launch, build, and sustain their ePortfolio initiatives?

The answer that emerged had multiple layers, linking pedagogy with broader institutional practices. Any definition of powerful ePortfolio practice must, of course, be rooted in the design of rich student learning experiences. However, in part because of the longitudinal and integrative nature of ePortfolio, meaningful initiatives must encompass not only the practice of individual faculty but also programs, departments, and other institutional groupings. This brings ePortfolio initiatives into challenging territory. As Michigan's Melissa Peet has suggested, much of the conversation about ePortfolio is "really about organizational change."[2] Successful ePortfolio initiatives must be active across many dimensions of campus structure and culture.

The *Catalyst Framework* addresses the multiple facets of ePortfolio practice and the ways they connect to build a high-impact ePortfolio initiative. The *Framework* consists of a learning core, five interlocking sectors, and three design principles, each of which is described in the following sections.

Learning Core

The hypothesis emerging from our research states that effective integrative ePortfolio initiatives address at least three levels of campus life and learning (see Figure 2.1):

- **Students and Faculty:** the active engagement of students, faculty, and other front-line staff (advisors, student affairs staff, etc.) who shape core student learning experiences;
- **Programs and Majors:** the crucial organizational units campus life and learning (academic and co-curricular) are most often organized around; and
- **Campus Culture and Structure:** the broad campus-wide mission, policy, stakeholders, and culture that conditions educational practice and shapes the learning experience for all—students, faculty, staff and institutional leaders.

Figure 2.1. The *Catalyst Framework*: The Learning Core

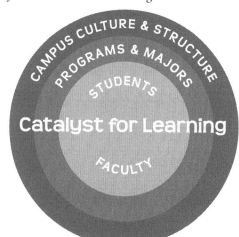

Interlocking Sectors

Our research further suggests that high-impact integrative ePortfolio initiatives address these core-learning levels with work that takes place in five interlocking sectors (see Figure 2.2).

Figure 2.2. The *Catalyst Framework*: Five Interlocking Sectors

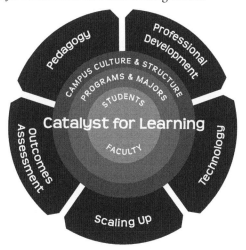

Pedagogy

Successful campus ePortfolio initiatives employ ePortfolio as an integrative social pedagogy that enhances student learning and success. When learning is connected, or integrated, it is more meaningful and enduring. We argue that such integration is promoted through systematic and disciplined reflection that helps students make the cognitive and affective connections that intensify their learning; and that reflection is more meaningful when it includes social elements, making learning more visible to others.

Reflective pedagogy encourages students to connect and make meaning from diverse learning experiences. Helping students deepen and integrate their learning, reflection is central to powerful ePortfolio practice. Meanwhile, what we call social pedagogy engages students in communication-intensive tasks where the representation of knowledge for an authentic audience is central to the construction of knowledge. Social pedagogy transforms ePortfolio learning from a solitary experience to one in which students engage with and construct knowledge through a community of learners.

Integrative learning helps students develop their ability to connect and apply their learning across disciplines and semesters, linking academic and lived curricula. When it incorporates reflective, social and integrative pedagogy, ePortfolio practice encourages the types of deep learning and high-impact behaviors that enable students to be successful and provides opportunities to build the twenty-first-century skills employers value. Chapter 3 draws on the practices shared by C2L faculty and staff to analyze and illustrate this pedagogy.

Professional Development

Professional development refers to the active processes (workshops, seminars, online tutorials, and institutes) that help faculty and staff learn about ePortfolio pedagogy and technology and the ways they can together encourage behaviors that advance student learning and growth. Professional development and Centers for Teaching and Learning play pivotal roles in advancing effective ePortfolio initiatives and developing an institutional learning culture.

Integrating ePortfolio pedagogy into a course or program can be challenging; in fact, many consider it a disruptive force. Effective ePortfolio pedagogy requires faculty and staff to rethink many assumptions about teaching and learning. ePortfolio is not a plug-and-play technology but one that requires guidance and skill to use its features effectively.

By engaging participants in planning, testing, and reflecting on ways to integrate ePortfolio into their work, professional development helps shift ePortfolio from a disruptive to a transformative practice that enhances student, faculty, and staff learning. Detailed in Chapter 4, professional development is a central component of high-impact ePortfolio projects and perhaps the most important of the five Catalyst sectors in terms of advancing effective classroom use, student learning, and broader scaling processes.

Outcomes Assessment

During the past decade, discussion of assessment and accountability in higher education has grown increasingly charged. Legislators, federal agencies, and accreditation bodies have pushed colleges to report on the quality of the education they provide.

For many faculty and staff, assessment is associated with standardized testing, something done for others that has (at best) no value for their own practice.

But assessment can be entirely different, a meaningful way for educators to deepen our understanding of our craft. ePortfolio practice can help campuses ground outcomes assessment in the authentic work of students and faculty. In addition, the design principles of Inquiry, Reflection, and Integration (discussed further in this chapter) help campuses make ePortfolio-based assessment more meaningful, spurring improvement at every level of the learning experience, from students and faculty to programs, departments, and entire institutions. Framing assessment as an inquiry into student learning highlights its scholarly nature, making it more engaging. Incorporating reflection helps transform assessment into a collective learning opportunity and moves the focus from findings to recommendations for change. And in an assessment context, integration involves "closing the loop," moving from recommendations to the active process of changing pedagogy and practice, curricula, and even institutional structure. Chapter 5 draws on the outcomes assessment stories of C2L teams to suggest strategies that campuses can use to make student learning visible for collegewide inquiry and reflection and become more adaptive learning colleges.

Technology

Experienced ePortfolio practitioners know that "pedagogy should drive technology" and that meaningful ePortfolio practices involve a complex interplay among teaching, learning, and technology. Effective ePortfolio platforms can, nevertheless, play a critical role in supporting campus efforts to realize ePortfolio's transformative potential.

The *e* in ePortfolio can make a difference for students, faculty, staff, and administrators. ePortfolios are distinct from traditional learning management systems because they extend beyond traditional course structures, providing a way for students to make connections between and among their courses and co-curricular experiences at an institution. Effective ePortfolio technology helps make student learning visible to students themselves, to their peers, and to faculty and others across the campus. High-functioning ePortfolio platforms facilitate students' interaction with faculty and peers about substantive matters, which Kuh identified as a high-impact educational activity.[3]

An effective ePortfolio platform also supports professional development, where it can be used as an integral part of workshops and seminars, mirroring and modeling the types of pedagogy that enhance student learning. And many ePortfolio platforms provide technical structures to facilitate the outcomes assessment process for faculty, staff, and assessment leaders.

If an effective ePortfolio platform can facilitate high-impact ePortfolio practice, a clumsy or poorly functioning platform can, conversely, cause problems, frustrating users and diminishing the effectiveness of ePortfolio engagement. Campus leaders need to select platforms carefully and plan for sustained technical support. Distilling lessons from C2L technology stories, Chapter 6 provides insights about ePortfolio technology from the C2L network.

Scaling Up

Scaling an ePortfolio project is a developmental process. Projects often emerge in one part of an institution and then grow as more faculty, courses, and programs start to work with ePortfolio. As they scale, ePortfolio projects increasingly serve as networks of connections, linking students and faculty, programs and majors, as well as high-impact practices and campus initiatives such as general education, outcomes assessment, co-curricular learning, and advisement. Scaling these connections provides opportunities for greater numbers of students to have access to ePortfolio and its effective activities and practices. And through such connections, ePortfolio projects introduce rich views of student learning into the everyday flows of teaching, assessment, and curriculum design.

Scaling doesn't happen by itself. Effective campus ePortfolio leaders must be active on multiple fronts, connecting with faculty and departments, collaborating with those responsible for professional development, assessment, and instructional technology. At the same time, ePortfolio leaders must take on a range of additional scaling tasks, such as gathering evidence of impact, organizing campus outreach, and building administrative support, all of which nurture the growth of an ePortfolio-based learning culture. When done well, the scaling process of an ePortfolio initiative stimulates a network of connections, leading to broader institutional learning and change. Chapter 7 examines the developmental histories of selected C2L campuses and distills a set of key strategies for effectively scaling a campus ePortfolio project.

The five sectors of the *Catalyst Framework* are highly interconnected. ePortfolio-related professional development can focus on pedagogy, technology, or outcomes assessment or combinations of the three. The choices made by campuses about ePortfolio technology can facilitate (or hinder) the growth of integrative ePortfolio pedagogy and shape the student learning experience. The ability of campus ePortfolio proponents to effectively involve departments and college leaders shapes the curricular and cultural context for learning at all levels. The relationships among these elements are complex and profoundly significant for implementing a high-impact institutional ePortfolio practice.

We found that the most successful campus ePortfolio initiatives worked at multiple levels of the institution, from classroom and co-curricular learning to programmatic and institutional change. Across these levels, their work addressed interlocking issues in the five Catalyst sectors: Pedagogy, Professional Development, Technology, Outcomes Assessment, and Scaling Up. And when the work in the various sectors was guided by the design principles of Inquiry, Reflection, and Integration, institutions were well positioned to attain ePortfolio's full potential.

Design Principles

Three overarching design principles embrace and help unify sectors of the *Catalyst Framework*: Inquiry, Reflection, and Integration. C2L research suggests that the practices of effective ePortfolio initiatives demonstrate a more or less explicit use of these design principles in not only Pedagogy, but also other sectors (see Figure 2.3).

Figure 2.3. The *Catalyst Framework*: Design Principles

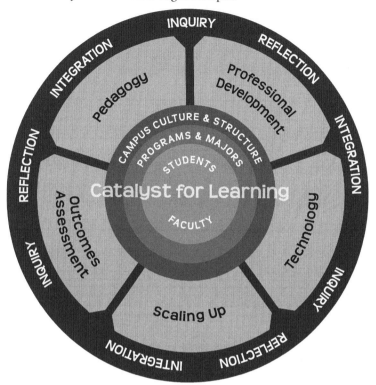

Inquiry

By inquiry, we mean the investigative, problem-based learning described by David Kolb and others, a cyclical process that involves asking questions about authentic problems, analyzing relevant evidence, creating and presenting evidence-based solutions, reflecting on the learning process, and developing new questions and plans for further inquiry.[4] In contrast to lecture models, where students passively absorb the authoritative viewpoint of a single professor or textbook, inquiry approaches push students to grapple with conflicting points of view and confront ambiguity and uncertainty. Encouraging students to take responsibility for their learning and giving them freedom to pursue questions that arouse their curiosity, inquiry practices foster intellectual maturity and self-authorship. At its best, ePortfolio pedagogy provides students with a way to showcase the products of their inquiries; at a deeper level, it also engages students in a recursive inquiry into their own learning and their evolving identities as learners.

Inquiry has a rich history in professional development and outcomes assessment. Professional development programs with an emphasis on collective inquiry ask faculty and staff to raise questions, explore issues, and use their classrooms as laboratories for scholarly experiments with new pedagogies. Taken to a deeper level, such inquiries can become the basis for the scholarship of teaching and learning. Meanwhile, the National Institute for Learning Outcomes Assessment has argued that meaning-ful outcomes assessment engages faculty and staff in a process of structured inquiry into programmatic and institutional teaching and learning effectiveness.[5] Through sustained collective inquiry in ePortfolio-related professional development and out-comes assessment, faculty, staff, and the broader institution construct new knowledge and understandings about the teaching and learning process.

Reflection

Reflection can build on inquiry but can also stand alone. From a Deweyan perspective, reflection complements experience. The purpose of reflection is to make connections among experiences, deepening continuities and empowering the meaning-making process.

> We learn by doing, constructing, building, talking and writing [and] we also learn by thinking about events, activities, and experiences. This confluence of experiences (action) and thought (reflection) combines to create new knowledge. Reflection is then the vehicle for critical analysis, problem-solving, synthesis of opposing ideas, evaluation, identifying patterns and creating meaning—in short, many of the higher order thinking skills we strive to foster in our students.[6]

Reflection is pivotal to meaningful student ePortfolio practice. Guided by faculty, staff, and peer mentors, as well as carefully crafted questions embedded in ePortfolio templates, ePortfolio practice can prompt, intensify, and share students' reflection on their learning. Students can reflect on specific artifacts and experiences or on broader processes. Their reflections can be written, oral, artistic, or multimedia in form, and take place individually or in community. Kathleen Blake Yancey described reflection as the centerpiece of powerful ePortfolio learning.[7] Reflective pedagogy transforms ePortfolio from a push-button technology into an engaging process of connection, linking students' academic learning and life experience to the most profound pro-cesses of personal growth.

Reflection also deepens professional development and outcomes assessment processes. In professional development settings, reflective activities help participants learn from their experiences and develop as reflective practitioners. And reflection can help move outcomes assessment beyond accountability as individuals and programs reflect on assessment findings and their implications for curricular and pedagogical change. In professional development and outcomes assessment, reflection takes place in the community as well as on an individual level. The combination of inquiry and reflection in ePortfolio-related professional development and outcomes assessment helps colleges transform into learning organizations.

Integration

Integration, or integrative learning, has gained new visibility in higher education. For students, integrative learning involves making connections and transferring knowledge across courses, disciplines, and semesters, linking academic learning with co-curricular and lived experience into a more intentional whole. The AAC&U suggests giving greater attention to integrative learning as a key priority for American higher education.[8] In 2004, the AAC&U and the Carnegie Foundation for the Advancement of Teaching issued the following statement:

> Many colleges and universities are creating opportunities for more integrative, connected learning through first-year seminars, learning communities, interdisciplinary studies programs, capstone experiences, individual portfolios, advising, student self-assessment, and other initiatives. . . . A variety of opportunities to develop the capacity for integrative learning should be available to all students throughout their college years, and should be a cornerstone of a twenty-first century education.[9]

In an ePortfolio context, integration has multiple layers of meaning. Guided by integrative pedagogy, students use ePortfolios to bring together work from multiple contexts, consider the relationship between their classrooms and their lives outside of class, and construct new identities as learners. In ePortfolio-related professional development, an integrative approach prompts faculty to develop and test strategies that help students integrate their learning and also help faculty and staff to transfer knowledge and insight from specific instances to broader contexts and applications. We see integration in ePortfolio-focused professional development practices that move from "my course" to "our program" and "our students," turning creative, one-shot experiments into broadly adopted and linked changes in practice.

In outcomes assessment, integration can be associated with closing the loop, taking action based on evidence-based recommendations. In professional development and outcomes assessment, integration ultimately means addressing campus curricula, structure, and culture, steps that involve campus leaders, budgets, and governance. As Randy Bass writes,

> We must fully grasp that students will learn to integrate deeply and meaningfully only insofar as we design a curriculum that cultivates that; and designing such a curriculum requires that we similarly plan, strategize and execute integratively across the boundaries within our institutions.[10]

As design principles, we see a role for Inquiry, Reflection, and Integration in every sector of the *Catalyst Framework*. Some principles have particular resonance in specific sectors. In ePortfolio Pedagogy, for example, reflection and integration are particularly critical. Integration is central to Scaling Up efforts. All three principles combine to deepen the work of Professional Development and Outcomes Assessment. Technology may be a special case. In some sense, the role of technology in terms of the I-R-I design principles is one of enabler or obstacle. Does the campus ePortfolio platform facilitate or frustrate individual reflection? Does it support reflection in community as a social pedagogy? Does it support or hinder integrative learning by students? By faculty and staff? Technology that facilitates the deployment of I-R-I-shaped practices can enhance the transformative potential of an ePortfolio project and vice versa.

I-R-I is not a magic formula that solves all problems or makes all the challenges of building an ePortfolio initiative suddenly disappear. But our findings suggest that if thoughtfully and persistently employed as design principles, Inquiry, Reflection, and Integration can guide intentional planning and development at all levels, deepen the power and meaning of ePortfolio practice, and help ePortfolio projects become catalysts for the transformative changes needed to help colleges and universities move toward becoming learning organizations.

Conclusion

The *Catalyst Framework* helps us understand that building and sustaining a successful and high-impact ePortfolio initiative is in many ways an institutional change effort. As Bass powerfully argued, "For any large-scale version of ePortfolios to be successful, they will require at the program and institutional level . . . a goals-driven, systems-thinking approach that requires multiple players to execute successfully."[11] Building an integrative ePortfolio initiative involves intentional and far-reaching institutional change.

Emerging from the examination of campus practices, the *Catalyst Framework* helps ePortfolio leaders "plan, strategize, and execute integratively"[12] across an institution as they develop effective ePortfolio initiatives. Analyzing the developmental stories and practices of C2L campuses, it illuminates specific strategies and the overarching, coordinated attention to diverse sectors of campus life needed to build effective ePortfolio implementations. Requiring careful design and cross-campus collaboration, such initiatives can play a powerful role in advancing the learning of students, faculty, and higher education institutions.

The *Catalyst Framework* offers a comprehensive campus-tested conceptual structure for understanding the developmental work of ePortfolio initiatives. It serves as the organizing structure for Chapters 3 through 7 of this book, each of which focuses on one sector of the *Framework*, analyzing effective practice and offering guided access to the strategies developed by leading ePortfolio campuses.

ePortfolio practice is not an end in and of itself. Rather, ePortfolio initiatives represent a rare opportunity, a way colleges and universities can meet pressing educational needs for student success and deep learning, institutional innovation and coherence, accountability, and the development of a campus-wide learning culture. An ePortfolio initiative requires leaders with grounded vision, informed design, and commitment to thoughtful, adaptive collaboration.

It is our hope that the *Catalyst Framework* will help new and experienced ePortfolio practitioners more effectively address what it takes for ePortfolio to make a difference. We believe this can be a powerful resource, helping us use ePortfolio to advance student, faculty, and institutional learning on campuses nationwide.

Notes

1. Randall Bass, "The Next Whole Thing in Higher Education," *Peer Review* 16, no. 1 (2014): 35.

2. Bret Eynon, "'The Future of ePortfolio' Roundtable," Academic Commons, accessed June 20, 2009, http://www.academiccommons.org/commons/essay/future-eportfolio-round table

3. George Kuh, *High-Impact Educational Practices: What They Are, Who Has Access to Them, and Why They Matter* (Washington, DC: American Association of Colleges and Universities, 2008).

4. David Kolb, *Experiential Learning: Experience as the Source of Learning and Development* (Englewood Cliffs, NJ: Prentice Hall, 1984).

5. "National Institute for Learning Outcomes Assessment: Making Learning Outcomes Usable and Transparent," accessed August 10, 2015, http://www.learningoutcomesassessment .org/

6. Mary Burns, Vicki Dimock, and Danny Martinez, "Action + Reflection = Learning," *TAP Into Learning 3*, no. 2 (2000): 1, http://www.sedl.org/pubs/tapinto/v3n2.pdf

7. Kathleen Blake Yancey, "Reflection and Electronic Portfolios: Inventing the Self and Reinventing the University," in *Electronic Portfolios 2.0: Emergent Research on Implementation and Impact*, ed. Darren Cambridge, Barbara Cambridge, and Kathleen Blake Yancey, (Sterling, VA: Stylus, 2009), 5–16.

8. "Integrative Learning," Association of American Colleges & Universities, accessed August 10, 2015, https://www.aacu.org/resources/integrative-learning

9. Association of American Colleges & Universities and Carnegie Foundation for the Advancement of Teaching, "A Statement on Integrative Learning," 2004, accessed August 10, 2015, http://gallery.carnegiefoundation.org/ilp/uploads/ilp_statement.pdf

10. Randall Bass, "Disrupting Ourselves: The Problem of Learning in Higher Education," *Educause Review* 47, no. 2 (March/April 2012): 23–33.

11. Bass, "Disrupting Ourselves," 32.

12. Ibid.

3

INTEGRATIVE ePORTFOLIO PEDAGOGY

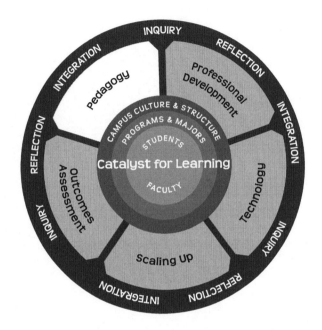

Integrative social pedagogy is the core of ePortfolio "done well." Collecting and reflecting on learning artifacts, ePortfolio practice prompts students to make their learning more visible. Connecting and making meaning from diverse learning experiences helps students develop more purposeful identities as learners. Reflecting in community—sharing and discussing their learning with others—adds depth and power to integrative learning. According to the three Catalyst value propositions, these processes can build student learning and success. To realize this potential, however, requires thoughtful guidance from faculty, staff, and mentors, informed by integrative social pedagogy. This chapter examines this high-impact ePortfolio pedagogy, identifies key theoretical frameworks, and spotlights faculty-generated practices that deepen student learning.

High-impact ePortfolio pedagogy is shaped, of course, by broader tenets of effective pedagogy. Whether or not they use ePortfolios, students learn best when learning is active, engaging, and collaborative, addressing their needs and prior knowledge.

ePortfolio-based activities are strengthened by clear directions and feedback as well as by logical sequence within broader course design. These and other facets of good pedagogy are applicable in ePortfolio and non-ePortfolio activities alike. What is particular to ePortfolio pedagogy is the centrality of integrative learning, supported by reflection, community, and connective ePortfolio technology.

Integrative learning has drawn wide recognition in higher education. Kuh and O'Donnell identify frequent opportunities to reflect and integrate learning as a salient characteristic of High-Impact Practices.[1] Mary Huber and Pat Hutchings wrote that "One of the great challenges in higher education is to foster students' abilities to integrate their learning across contexts and over time."[2] Noting that students often experience learning as fragmented, they call for strategies that help students make connections across courses and semesters, bridging disciplines and linking academic learning with co-curricular learning and life experience. "Learning that helps develop integrative capacities is important because it builds habits of mind that prepare students to make informed judgments in the conduct of personal, professional, and civic life."[3] Guiding students as they build new identities as learners, such strategies help students develop a stronger sense of meaning, motivation, and long-term purpose.

In "Only Connect," an often-cited essay on the guiding purposes of education, historian William Cronon chose one goal as most important. "More than anything else," he wrote, "being an educated person means being able to see connections that allow one to make sense of the world and act within it in creative ways."[4] Surveys published by the AAC&U show that employers highly value students' abilities to connect and transfer learning. Indeed, former AAC&U president Carol Geary Schneider set integrative learning at the top of the learning scale.

> Integrative learning is a shorthand term for teaching a set of capacities—capacities we might also call the arts of connection, reflective judgment and considered action—that enable graduates to put their knowledge to effective use. . . . It should also lead students to connect and integrate the different parts of their overall education, to connect learning with the world beyond the academy and, above all, to translate their education to new contexts, new problems, new responsibilities.[5]

Integrative learning addresses the link between the cognitive and affective aspects of learning, which has drawn new attention with discussions of grit and growth mind-set. As discussed later in this chapter and in Chapter 8, integrative pedagogy can help students not only engage more deeply with course content but also develop their inner voice, a stronger sense of identity and direction, or what Marcia Baxter Magolda and colleagues call "purposeful self-authorship."[6]

Designed to house a collection of multimedia materials, learning artifacts, and reflections created in diverse contexts, ePortfolio technology lends itself to these processes of connection, integration, and meaning-making. But the technology itself is insufficient to the task. Even the best ePortfolio platform cannot be a substitute for thoughtful teaching and guidance. Accustomed to fragmented learning, most students who are given an ePortfolio and simply told to use it are unlikely to find it meaningful or integrative. Taking effective advantage of ePortfolio's connective capacities requires intentional faculty design and action, guided by integrative pedagogy and practice.

The first section of this chapter explores a four-part framework for reflection, the active process at the heart of integrative ePortfolio pedagogy. It also draws on the work of C2L faculty and staff to showcase ways that pedagogical framework can be translated into practice. The examples of practice are drawn from multiple disciplines and diverse campuses such as San Francisco State University (SFSU), Pace University, Salt Lake Community College, and the University of Delaware, but they are by no means definitive. We encourage faculty and staff to use these activities as springboards for their own creativity, developing integrative practices that fit their own courses, students, and contexts.

The second section of this chapter focuses on one aspect of reflective learning that we call social pedagogy. We are pleased to include at the end of this chapter a discussion of social pedagogy for ePortfolio by C2L senior scholar Randy Bass.

Reflective ePortfolio Practice

If integrative learning is a key goal of student ePortfolio practice, then reflection is the vehicle, the active process for advancing toward that goal. Reflection is critical to helping students connect and make meaning from diverse learning experiences. Cognitive researchers such as John Bransford agree with a long line of theorists including John Dewey on the importance of reflection or metacognition in helping students focus on, retain, and take ownership of their learning.[7] As noted previously, Kuh and O'Donnell identify frequent opportunities to reflect on and integrate learning as defining features of high-impact learning.[8] Building the habits of reflection, students integrate specific learning experiences into a larger framework of education and purposeful self-authorship. As Dewey scholar Carol Rodgers has written:

> The function of reflection is to make meaning, to formulate relationships and continuities. . . . The creation of meaning out of experience is at the very heart of what it means to be human. It is what enables us to make sense of and attribute value to the events of our lives.[9]

ePortfolio has long been a vehicle for reflection. The slogan of early ePortfolio advocate Helen Barrett was "Collect, Select and Reflect."[10] Reflection can, of course, take place in other settings. But ePortfolio's technology, linking learning artifacts across time and boundaries, can support and extend reflective processes in ways that deepen integration. Kathleen Blake Yancey sees reflection as the centerpiece of powerful ePortfolio learning.[11] Reflective pedagogy transforms ePortfolio from a push-button technology into an engaging process of connection, integration of academic learning, life experience, and profound processes of personal growth.

What does meaningful reflection look like? How can faculty use it effectively? Some faculty are scornful of reflection as vague musings. Others are more interested but have difficulty designing effective ways to use ePortfolio to help students develop as reflective thinkers. "Teaching reflection is new to us," noted one faculty member in a C2L online chat. "I know how to teach biology, but I don't really know how to get students to reflect."

Campus teams in the Connect to Learning project spent many hours discussing reflection. We read the literature on reflective learning and developed a range of reflective ePortfolio strategies designed to help students bridge their inquiry into key academic topics with deeper and more integrative learning. The most helpful definition of *reflection* we found that shaped the pedagogy of many C2L teams came from the work of Carol Rodgers.

Rodgers identifies the following four principles for meaningful reflection:

- **Reflection as Connection:** Dewey saw experience and reflection as the essential elements of learning. As Rodgers writes, "Reflection is a meaning-making process that moves a learner from one experience into the next with a deeper understanding of its relationship with and connections to other experiences and ideas. It is the thread that makes continuity of

---

Getting Started
Seven Tips for Designing Effective Reflection

1. **Give students clear guidance:** Using language that students understand, design and scaffold prompts to focus students on key issues and help them build reflective skills.
2. **Design backward:** Think about what you want students to learn from reflection (and how that relates to course goals); design your prompt with that in mind.
3. **Strike the balance:** Make reflection a regular part of the course, but don't overwhelm students with reflection every day or week. Be judicious.
4. **Vary your approach:** Use reflection before, during, or after an activity. Planning forward is an important type of reflection. Have students reflect on different types of activities—assignments, experiential activities, and so on.
5. **Make the connection:** Reflection is about connection. Use it to help students see the relationship of the course or activity to the rest of their lives.
6. **Build student's learning mastery:** Use reflection to help students review the learning strategies they used in a given activity and identify what helped them succeed.
7. **Feedback matters:** Students want to know that someone is paying attention: you, advisors, classmates, or peer mentors. Make sure students get feedback that validates what they've done and encourages growing sophistication.

learning possible."[12] Reflection is critical to integrative learning, the ability of students to integrate learning across semesters and disciplines and to see connections between their coursework and their personal, family, and community lives.

- **Reflection as Systematic and Disciplined:** Many people think of reflection as vague and unstructured musing. But Rodgers, drawing on Dewey, argues that "Reflection is a systematic, rigorous, disciplined way of thinking, with its roots in scientific inquiry."[13] She lays out Dewey's structure for an ideal reflective process, moving from experience to description, then analysis and finally application of insight to the development of new, experimental actions.

- **Reflection as Social Pedagogy:** Our most familiar image of reflection is individual and solitary, a kind of meditation. But Dewey suggests that meaningful reflection often happens in community, in conversation, and in interaction with others.

- **Reflection as an Attitude Toward Change:** Reflection is not only cognitive but also affective, involving attitudes such as openness, curiosity, and a readiness to reconsider long-held ideas about oneself and the world. "Reflection" writes Rodgers, involves "attitudes that value the personal and intellectual growth of oneself and others."[14]

Rodgers' framework helped C2L teams design, test, and refine reflective strategies to enhance integrative learning. These principles do not delineate entirely distinct categories; many practices that highlight reflection in community, for example, can also be systematic and scaffolded. On the other hand, incorporating all the principles in a single reflective assignment could make it bulky and awkward. Ultimately, skilled C2L faculty selected the principles applicable to any given situation and used them in crafting their assignments and activities.

The following sections spotlight each principle, one by one, and provide examples of ways to translate these principles into meaningful ePortfolio practice with students.

Reflection as Connection

The idea that reflection builds meaningful connection is central to Dewey's theory of learning. According to Dewey, education is a "reconstruction or reorganization of experience, which adds to the meaning of experience."[15] Reflective learning is a process used to make sense of new experiences in relation to the individual, his or her environment, and a continuum of previous and subsequent experiences. According to Rodgers, reflection makes learning visible to the learner, making it available for connecting and deepening:

> The function of reflection is to make meaning: to formulate the "relationships and continuities" among the elements of an experience, between that experience and other experiences, between that experience and the knowledge that one carries, and between that knowledge and the knowledge produced by thinkers other than oneself.[16]

This principle underscores the critical role ePortfolio can play in integration, or integrative learning. Meaningful reflection is essentially integrative, helping students make powerful connections between different types of experiences.

Academic learning is often organized as a series of experiences in the classroom and beyond, such as reading books, engaging in research or community service, working with a faculty member, writing a paper, and so on. Reflection helps learners step back to see a larger picture, connect one experience to others, and consider their collective meaning. In so doing, reflection not only helps student sustain their focus on key course concepts and issues (a defining feature of High-Impact Practices) but also creates a sense of continuity between seemingly disjointed experiences. The meaning-making process can also include connections to prior learning and earlier reflections and can point forward to a projected future.

What does this look like in practice, using ePortfolio? As faculty guide students to use ePortfolio to engage with the connective aspect of reflection, what do they connect? Examining the work of C2L faculty, we found a variety of practices, including the following:

- Reflection that connects experiences in a course
- Reflection that connects experiences across courses, semesters, and disciplines
- Reflection that builds connection among academic, co-curricular, and lived experiences

Connecting Experiences in a Course
Students in ePortfolio-enhanced courses use reflection to examine their own learning, to explore the meaning of specific course activities, and to see how those activities add up to larger course goals and objectives. In this sense, ePortfolio cannot be separated from the rest of the course; it must be grounded in course content knowledge, skills, and competencies. For example, when teaching in the Geosciences Department of Salt Lake Community College (SLCC) Adam Dastrup asks students to reflect on particular assignments related to geospatial technology to inquire into their learning processes. In one activity, students use a professional interpretation framework to examine satellite imagery and then reflect in response to the following prompt:

> Outline the steps you took to analyze each image, and tell me about your thinking at each step. Describe any problems you had in trying to interpret these images. What aspects of the *Image Interpretation* framework were most helpful for you?[17]

Dastrup asks his students to reflect after a particular learning experience to examine their learning processes and make a connection to a key theoretical construct. This common reflective strategy sustains and extends student focus on key concepts. In other practices, rather than waiting until after the learning activity, faculty positioned reflection as a central element in the middle of the activity. For example, at Manhattanville College, students in Sherie McClam's first-year seminar,

Inquiry, Reflection, and Integration permeate students' *Learning for a Sustainable Future* ePortfolios. They were asked to explore and communicate their understandings of what is nature, what is culture, what is the economy and how these concepts connect in our daily lives. And, we ask, how does this new knowledge help them seek and interrogate solutions for the complex issues of creating a sustainable future.[19]

Sherie McClam,
Manhattanville College

"Sustainability: Creating a Future We Can Live With," create photographic essays with embedded reflections. Reflections connected personal responses to the images with larger questions about the course content, focusing on interrelated aspects of sustainability such as nature, culture, and the economy. McClam said, "As my students sought to capture, reflect on and share their interpretations of nature, culture, economy and the ways in which these concepts intersect, they were actively involved in reflection as a meaning-making process."[18]

Experienced ePortfolio faculty agree that reflection is most effective when it is a persistent or recursive element of the course rather than a one-shot experience dropped in (as is all too common) at the end of the course. Some faculty develop a sequence of staged prompts that scaffold reflection from the beginning to the end of their courses, connecting different processes at different points. Linda Anstendig, who teaches English 201, "Writing in the Disciplines," at Pace University, asks students to create six reflective postings in their portfolios. In their initial reflection, students preview the course syllabus and respond to prompts such as

- What assignments or activities look familiar and manageable, and why? What assignments or activities look more challenging or difficult for you, and why?
- What parts of your reading, writing, research background and skills make you confident about some parts of the course and hesitant about others?[20]

Here, reflection comes before the learning activity, helping students get their thinking started so they begin developing reflective skills right away. While reflecting is often discussed as looking backward, its forward-looking elements can be equally valuable.

Through the semester, students collect their work in their portfolios. Like Dastrup, Anstendig embeds task-specific prompts in the ePortfolio, asking students to reflect on challenges encountered and strategies used. Midterm and final reflections are more synthetic, asking students to connect their learning across the entire course. At the end of the course, Anstendig's prompts include

- What have you accomplished as a writer and learner? What activities, kinds of feedback and other support have helped you the most? How have your writing and research skills changed and improved? What kinds of research and revision strategies did you learn and use?

- What does this portfolio demonstrate about you as a writer, researcher and learner? Use an analogy, simile, and/or metaphor to describe yourself as one of these.[21]

Building on this reflective writing, Anstendig finally has students create three-minute videos, "digital stories" that express who they are as learners. The culminating writing and video process helps students to find meaning in the sequence of assignments enacted over the course of the semester. Reviewing the artifacts and reflections collected in the portfolio, the narrative construction process helps them recognize their own growth and identify strategies that can help them in future courses. As Anstendig writes, "In compiling their evidence and examining their own learning and development, [students] build their own academic story."[22]

Connecting Across Courses, Semesters, and Disciplines

Helping students make integrative connections across courses can be challenging for faculty, requiring them to address issues and settings they may know relatively little about. Similarly, students are not accustomed to focusing on connections across courses. However, this type of reflection is particularly valuable for helping students develop more integrative understandings of their education and the skills needed for lifelong learning.

First-year seminars and other High-Impact Practices may intentionally foster integrative learning across time and disciplines. Interdisciplinary learning communities provide a natural setting to invite students to reflect on different disciplinary ways of knowing. First-year and capstone courses support students as they make key educational transitions; ePortfolio practice can help students in such courses to think backward and forward across time. In first-year programs at Guttman Community College and Virginia Tech, for example, faculty embed prompts in the ePortfolio that ask students to reflect on prior learning experiences and to think about the skills, resources, and habits they bring to college. In LaGuardia's first-year seminar, students complete a wide-ranging skills inventory and respond to the following prompt: Where did you learn these particular skills? How do these skills help you as a student? How might they help you in your career? At times of transition, reflections that connect past and present can help students think more intentionally about the strategies, habits, and dispositions that can help them succeed in college and beyond. (For more on ePortfolio's link to first-year seminars and other HIPs, see Chapter 9.)

Capstone courses at Boston University, SFSU, LaGuardia Community College, and other C2L campuses provide a powerful opportunity to use the reflective ePortfolio to connect learning and make meaning from multiple courses. Here, the transition is different, but the reflective process is equally valuable. At SFSU, as students exit the Metro Health Academy, a two-year learning community, they review a statement they wrote in their ePortfolios in their first semester and then write a capstone reflective essay titled "Letter to a Future Self."

Letter to a Future Self

Imagine you're writing to yourself, years from now. What do you want to say to your future self? Think about the type of person you will be, your place in life, what you would have accomplished then, the kind of thoughts and feelings you will experience, and so on. What do you want your future self to be like?

- What are the different dreams and goals you would want to be realized by then?
- What do you hope to be doing or have achieved with respect to your education, career, or community?
- What specific steps will you need to take or obstacles will you need to overcome to achieve these goals?

Remind your future self of what you learned in your time in college, and think about what else you may want to do to reach your goals academically.[23]

This reflective assignment asks SFSU students to use the connective capacity of the ePortfolio to review artifacts from across the entire course of their educational experience and then make reflective meaning by distilling lessons from this experience that they want to remember for the rest of their lives. The "Letter to a Future Self" helps them think backward and forward in time and gives their lessons learned a sense of purpose and personal value.

Other capstone faculty use variations of this strategy. In the "Liberal Arts Capstone" course at LaGuardia, Max Rodriguez asks students to review artifacts and reflections from his and other courses to write a learning philosophy describing how they learn best.[24] In her business capstone at Tunxis Community College, Amy Feest has students review their collected artifacts and use reflection and ePortfolio technology to connect them with discipline-specific and general education competencies.[25] At Virginia Tech in the capstone of the dietetics major, students go over documents from four years of portfolio work and write a statement that spotlights "the connections between experiences" and "how you intend to transfer what you've learned to new complex situations beyond graduation."[26]

Connecting Learning In and Out of the Classroom
Across higher education, there is growing recognition that learning is not confined to the classroom, that it also takes place in co-curricular activities, advisement, and a range of other settings. Students can use a reflective ePortfolio to document these experiences and integrate them into a larger whole. Study abroad experiences, internships, professional practica, and community service activities lend themselves to reflection. Through reflection, students see how these learning instances fit with key academic concepts and competencies, and how their entire experience is shaping their growth as learners.

Many faculty use ePortfolio-based reflection to help students link course-based learning to learning in other settings. At Rutgers University's Douglass Residential College, students connect their academic courses to service-learning.[27] At Salt Lake Community College, students use ePortfolios to document their study abroad experiences and personalize the study of other countries, cultures, and times.[28] Similarly, in Global Guttman, Guttman Community College's study abroad program, Katie Wilson has students use the ePortfolio as a daily reflective journal. Upon returning home students use the following prompts to reflect on the overall impact of their experience:

1. Describe the similarities and differences between your own cultural heritage and the culture(s) you experienced while traveling with the Global Guttman program.
2. While traveling with the Global Guttman program, you were inevitably faced with a perspective other than your own. Briefly explain a particular example, how you dealt with it, and how that has changed your own thinking.
3. Think about a specific social problem that you learned about while traveling with the Global Guttman program. Describe how you can really take action in your community(ies), your city, your country or the global world to address that problem.
4. Describe the ways in which your day-to-day life is connected to global issues.
5. What is the most important thing you learned during your Global Guttman experience?
6. What did you learn about yourself on your Global Guttman trip?
7. In what ways has your Global Guttman experience changed your thinking about your academic goals and your professional future? [29]

In a second-semester nursing course at Three Rivers Community College (TRCC), faculty use ePortfolio and reflection to help students connect theory with practice, classroom learning with clinical application. One TRCC student used her portfolio to describe her care of an elderly woman and how the experience of care illustrated her growing understanding of geriatric care:

> I chose this patient . . . for a few reasons. She ties into my group's presentation of discharge planning and caregiver role strain as well as . . . polypharmacy. . . . As to polypharmacy, this patient, as is the case with many elderly patients, has been pre-scribed several different medications. Now, with the recent injuries and surgery, she has more pharmaceuticals added to her daily regimen.
>
> In completing the geriatric presentations, and watching the other groups present their topics, I was able to learn effectively about the care of the elderly. Caring for a geriatric patient in the hospital helped to reinforce this content since I feel that I learn best by actually seeing the situation in person.[30]

At Rutgers, Guttman, TRCC and elsewhere, the goal of ePortfolio practice is not only to help students assemble artifacts from diverse experiences but to use reflection to examine the connections among them and, in so doing, help students come to new understandings about key concepts and, perhaps more important, about themselves as learners.

C2L Core Survey data (discussed in Chapter 8) show that students in these types of classes develop new insights into such connections and into their own learning. For example, students were asked to use a four-part scale to agree or disagree with the statement, "Building my ePortfolio helped me to make connections between ideas"; 68.6% Agreed or Strongly Agreed. Similarly, 66.0% Agreed or Strongly Agreed with, "Using ePortfolio has allowed me to be more aware of my growth and development as a learner." The data suggest that guided by reflective pedagogy and practice, the ePortfolio experience helps students make integrative connections in and out of the classroom, and build more holistic self-portraits as learners.

Reflection as Systematic and Scaffolded Inquiry

Integrative reflection is central to ePortfolio pedagogy, but it does not always happen easily. "Students don't know how to reflect" is a common faculty complaint. Faculty who want students to engage in meaningful reflection must develop reflective scaffolding to help students connect their learning. As C2L faculty worked on this scaffolding they considered Rodgers' principle that effective reflection embodies a systematic and disciplined inquiry process.

Drawing on Dewey, Rodgers defines *reflection* as a structured, rigorous way of thinking. In reflection, she said that a thinker moves through a four-stage reflective

Figure 3.1. Carol Rodgers' Reflective Cycle.

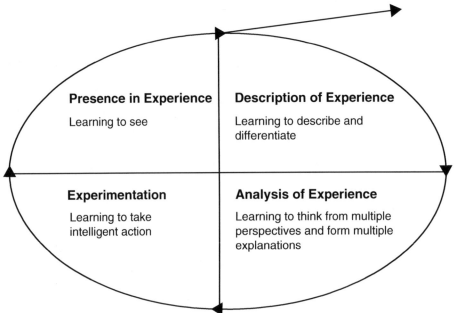

Source. Carol Rodgers, "Defining Reflection: Another Look at John Dewey and Reflective Thinking," *Teachers College Record* 104, no. 4 (2002). Reprinted with permission of Carol Rodgers.

cycle based on the scientific method (see Figure 3.1). Experience marks the first stage in the cycle; carefully prompted reflection moves from description to analysis, planning and implementing intentional experimentation, and back again to a new, more meaningful experience.

- **Presence in Experience:** The first stage is reflection and begins with experience, our physical, mental, or virtual interaction with the world. As we can perceive only that which we pay attention to, Dewey urges us to slow down and be more present in experience.
- **Description of Experience:** In the second stage, learners describe experience in detail, including affective responses. Careful and thorough observation is key. One of the most challenging aspects of reflection is to ensure that one continuously grounds thinking and description in specific evidence.
- **Analysis of Experience:** The third stage of the cycle is generating possible explanations while paying close attention to details and allowing the experience to emerge in all its complexities. In this stage the learner goes to sources of ideas beyond herself to deepen understanding of the experience itself. And at this stage, synthesizing information and deriving meaning from the interplay between theory and practice are essential tasks.
- **Experimentation:** The fourth stage in the cycle is experimentation. This stage cannot be overlooked, Dewey suggests, as reflection must include action. For him, the notion is that reflection must end in responsible action and experimentation.[31]

Rodgers spotlights reflection's potential for deepening students' inquiry into key academic concepts and problems. Moreover, supported by ePortfolio, the reflective process can help students engage in a recursive inquiry into the nature of learning and their own development as learners. Many C2L faculty adapted parts of Rodgers' reflective cycle, creating structured reflection prompts asking students to observe, describe, connect, and apply their learning.

In a service-learning project at Indiana University–Purdue University Indianapolis (IUPUI), for example, reflective self-assessment leads to action and then back to ePortfolio-based reflection. Guided step by step, students gain insight into career goals and learning processes.

IUPUI: Service-Learning Reflection at First-Year Psychology

Step 1. Students participate in a strengths assessment exercise, followed by reflection on it.

Step 2. Information about the service-learning project is distributed among the students, which leads to a class discussion about the students' goals for their education and career.

Step 3. A peer service-learning assistant leads a session utilizing the Bonner Leadership Compass, which is an exercise in learning about leadership styles and effective ways to work within groups.

(Continues)

(Continued)

Step 4. As the next step, students participate in their service experiences. Upon completing these tasks, they prepare written reflective essays about those experiences, connecting them with the leadership theory and their own self-assessment. Then they post their reflections in their ePersonal Development Plans (ePDPs) on their ePortfolios.

Step 5. Students then have a chance to meet with the faculty members to discuss their overall ePDP and how the service experience fit in it. Peers provide feedback on each others' reflective essays.

Step 6. Finally, each student creates a presentation using peer and instructor feedback and shares his or her ePDP with the other members of the class. They showcase how they connected their service to course materials and to their career goals and how they changed throughout this process.[32]

The scaffolded process begins with self-examination and introduction to relevant theory (Steps 1–3), helping students be more present in the service-learning experience. Describing and analyzing their experience in their ePortfolios (Step 4), students reflect on its implications. Sharing reflective learning in discussions with faculty and peers (Steps 5 and 6) provides a supportive social community that helps students consider implications for future action.

In Lehman College's graduate childhood education program, students create an ePortfolio with an educational philosophy statement and a set of artifacts linked to the national Interstate Teacher Assessment Support Consortium (INTASC) standards. Students select and describe artifacts (e.g., lesson plans, student work, and written assignments), reflect on learning tied to the artifact, and analyze its relationship to the standards. Instructions lay out the following step-by-step process:

- Describe (information gathering): What is the artifact? When was it collected? In order to ensure confidentiality, do not use student or teacher full names anywhere.
- Analyze (alignment): How does this artifact relate to the standard? Address the standard specifically.
- Appraise (evaluation): How does this artifact demonstrate your personal and professional growth? How does it demonstrate your impact on student learning? (if applicable)
- Transform (goal setting): Based on your answers to the first three reflection steps, are there specific ways you intend to use what you have learned in order to improve your teaching?[33]

The sequence of prompts guides students' reflective writing. Although students are provided with INTASC standards, they are not told which assignments to associate with a given standard. "The decision to place artifacts is determined wholly by the student," according to Alexandria Ross. The combination of structure and choice works well for Lehman faculty and students. "In this way," she continues, "they are able to affirm that they are indeed prepared for teaching in classrooms. The ePortfolio is a chance for students not only to reflect on their learning throughout the program but also to showcase their work and ability to think reflectively."[34]

Guided by Rodgers' reflective cycle, C2L faculty and staff carefully structured the reflective process. Sustaining students' attention to substantive course content, concepts, and learning processes, the process bolsters what Kuh identified as a defining HIP characteristic: significant investment of time and effort by students over an extended period of time.[35] C2L Core Survey data, discussed in Chapter 8, suggest the capacity of this approach to engage students and advance deep learning.

Reflection as Social Pedagogy

Reflection is often thought of as a quiet, meditative activity one does alone. And many practitioners treat the reflective ePortfolio as solitary and private. Some educators review the ePortfolio, some do not, and reviews often focus on whether assigned tasks are completed. The audience for the portfolio may be distant and unclear. Students hope employers will look at the portfolio after they graduate. Although this practice has value, it also has the following limits:

- It postpones active audience engagement with the portfolio for semesters or years.
- It scaffolds no intermediate stages where students can rehearse the process of engaging with an audience.
- It cuts off portfolio development from the power of social learning.

As social media use exploded, C2L faculty and staff were intrigued to find that Rodgers' principles of meaningful reflection included "reflection in community."[36] Drawing on Dewey, Rodgers suggests that reflecting in community deepens the impact of reflective learning. The process of communicating, she argues, can be understood to incorporate reflection. As Dewey notes, "the experience has to be formulated in order to be communicated,"[37] and the formulation process can be metacognitive. Moreover, when reflections are communicated, it creates the possibility for feedback. Rodgers lists three opportunities generated by reflection in community:

- First, collective reflection processes affirm the value of one's own experiences. Getting feedback from others validates our reactions and thoughts.
- Second, reflecting in a group can offer new ways to see things, present alternative meanings, or broaden our perspectives. The more people are involved, and the more diverse the group is, the better our chances are to be challenged, to be questioned, and to compare alternative perspectives.
- Third, collaborative reflection maintains the growth of the reflective practice. Reflecting within a supportive community serves as a testing ground for one's ideas and understanding, while helping all members of the community to grow and gain insight.[38]

> We define *social pedagogies* as design approaches for teaching and learning that engage students in authentic tasks that are communication-intensive, where representation of knowledge for an authentic audience is absolutely central to the construction of knowledge in a course.[39]
>
> Randy Bass and Heidi Elmendorf

As our collaboration began, C2L teams (like most in the ePortfolio field), were not in the habit of thinking about reflection as a social process. Discussing Rodgers prompted us to explore this possibility, first as theory and then in practice. We read an unpublished white paper by Randy Bass and Heidi Elmendorf on social pedagogy that complemented Rodgers' work. We then began to develop and test new strategies based on these ideas.

According to Bass and Elmendorf, social pedagogy can engage students in learning beyond the classroom via co-curricular activities and other informal learning environments. They point to the participatory culture of social media, which opens new dimensions for listening to, communicating with, and collaborating with people and groups that have different perspectives, values, and voices than students. The community aspect of social pedagogies provides a venue for formal and informal communication, a feedback loop that prompts students' intellectual growth. It broadens their viewpoints and opens doors for interdisciplinary exchange.[40]

C2L teams developed social pedagogy strategies for ePortfolio, positioning portfolios as collaborative spaces and platforms for interaction. They situated the portfolio as a liminal space, somewhere between entirely private and totally open to the public. They created intermediate reflective stages, where students rehearsed what it meant to use ePortfolios to connect with an audience and consider what their portfolio looks like to others. Based on C2L experimentation, we concluded that creating practices in which ePortfolios serve as sites for communication, collaboration, and exchange is a significant task for the ePortfolio field as a whole.

As a part of this process, Bass reviewed the work of C2L faculty and students and wrote an insightful essay about ePortfolio and social pedagogy, which is reprinted at the end of this chapter. Examining faculty-generated practices that combined reflection and social pedagogy, Bass found faculty using ePortfolio in a range of different approaches. Guided by faculty, students in C2L-related courses engaged in at least five types of dialogue and community through their ePortfolios:

- Sharing ePortfolios with and getting comments from faculty
- Sharing and engaging in interactive ePortfolio commentary with other students
- Sharing ePortfolios with and getting comments from external groups
- Linking ePortfolios to other students' ePortfolios
- Using ePortfolios as a site for collaborative projects with other students[41]

Bass reviewed each category and discussed activities that demonstrate this approach. His essay in this chapter offers an in-depth discussion of reflection in community.

It is worth noting here that data from our C2L Core Survey point to the effectiveness of using reflective ePortfolio practice for integrative social pedagogy. Data from the Core Survey (see Chapter 8) suggest that social pedagogy deepens the impact of students' reflective ePortfolio experiences. When ePortfolio is used with social pedagogy, students are more likely to report that ePortfolio deepened their engagement with ideas and course content, and that the course engaged them in integrative learning processes.

For example, Helen L. Chen's correlational analysis of responses from more than 3,000 students from 14 campuses found that among students who reported only a low level of peer feedback on their ePortfolios, 32.0% Agreed or Strongly Agreed with the statement, "Using my ePortfolio has allowed me to be more aware of my growth and development as a learner." In contrast, among students who reported a high level of peer feedback, 94.4% Agreed with the statement, which is a dramatic increase.

These data suggest that social engagement deepens the impact of the reflective ePortfolio, helping students understand connections and make meaning from their learning experiences. This is consistent with several of Kuh's key characteristics of High-Impact Practices done well, most notably "frequent, timely and constructive feedback," but also "interactions with faculty and peers about substantive matters" and, depending on the nature of the activity and the students involved, "experiences with diversity."[42] Chapter 8 provides a more extensive examination of the evidence, including more detail about the C2L Core Survey data and their findings related to ePortfolio and social pedagogy.

Collaborative Self-Authorship in Sophomore Writing Classes
Kati Lewis, Salt Lake Community College

In intermediate writing classes at Salt Lake Community College, student writers engage in authentic research, public writing, and multiple reflective practices to accurately represent diverse conversations taking place on public issues for external audiences. Students conduct field research that includes interviews with local leaders, activists, and others. Often their research leads to deeper discussions with interviewees and additional research.

The multimodal results of their field research, along with other research and writing activities, are presented in a section of their general education ePortfolios. This section then becomes a space for play—an artist's/writer's Web 2.0 studio—where students juxtapose their field research with more polished pieces.

The culminating project for this course is to design and publish a collaborative online magazine using a Web 2.0 platform (see Figure 3.2). Students re-envision multiple pieces from this section of their ePortfolios. Students work together in groups to workshop each other's pieces, revise and adapt those pieces, reflect on their research and writing processes, and publish their work.

(Continues)

(Continued)

Figure 3.2. eZine Example

HOME   TABLE OF CONTENTS   EDITORS' NOTE   WORKS CITED   MEET THE WRITERS

Editors' Note

Anne's Extended Note

Breeanna's Extended Note

Dear Reader,
Our magazine was created to inform people about voting, elections, improvements to our government, and what politicians view points really are. This magazine is a collection of our works created in our English 2010 class. We chose our articles from several assignments we wrote this semester. Among those assignments we had a profile, a memoir, a proposal, a position, a report, and an evaluation. Our writers consist of Breeanna ▆▆▆, Kiana ▆▆▆, Lynn ▆▆▆, and Anne ▆▆▆. Each writer chose the papers that they were the most passionate about and showcased their work. The collections have undergone numerous revisions and edits. Some of these revisions include, syntax, grammar, organization, fluidity, and new media. Along with major revisions we also adapted some of our works

Kiana's Extended Note

Lynn's Extended Note

Source. Reprinted with permission of Kati Lewis.

Students also craft two hypertext reflections for their magazine: an Editors' Note (a group reflection) and an individual course reflection. The Note (Figure 3.2) is a collaborative response to reflective prompts, which include the following:

Discuss the following:

- *The connectedness of the group members' political issues*
- *How the pieces demonstrate the personal as political and the political as personal*
- *How and why readers should use your magazine to understand the upcoming election through your issues and not only the candidates—Try to connect this to our discussions on and readings about the media.*

Describe what the group discovered about collaborative research and writing processes, using the following:

- *What did group members discover about their research and writing when making revision suggestions and choices as a group?*
- *What did the group learn about the research and writing process throughout the genres?*

(Continues)

(Continued)

- *Explain why specific essays were selected for revision over others for the project. Offer specific reasons for the group's choices, and explain those reasons with evidence from the work.*
- *Explain why specific adaptation choices were made for other essays or smaller projects.*
- *If appropriate, why were specific essays excluded from the magazine?*

While the Editors' Note connects individual pieces to the collaborative work process, the individual reflection asks students to examine their own research and writing processes with the following prompts:

- *Describe your own writing and research processes. Why did you select this issue? How did you go about forming your perspective? Did your perspective on the issue change over the course of the semester? How? Why? What specific sources helped shape/reshape your thinking and writing about the issue? Be specific.*
- *Why did you choose to write in the genres that you chose (e.g., why a profile over a memoir or vice versa; why a position over a proposal or vice versa; why a report over a review or vice versa)? Make connections among the different genres, and attempt to evaluate how effectively you made choices about genre and medium to communicate messages on your issue.*

This online magazine format and the accompanying reflections give audiences different ways of interacting with the magazine project. Built on integrative pedagogy, the project helps students locate their own space for entering public discourses on issues that matter to them as well as to make their carefully researched and collaboratively crafted messages public. They bring together work from multiple writers, situated in myriad complex personal and political contexts to consider the potential of their coursework to effect change far beyond classroom borders.

Reflection as an Attitude Toward Change

The last of Rodgers' four principles is reflection as an attitude toward personal change. In Rodgers' framework, this principle highlights the role of the affective in reflection as well as the integrative connection between reflection and personal change. Drawing on Dewey, Rodgers suggests that deep reflection shapes the learner's self-understanding. Being open minded toward change, having curiosity, and accepting the possibility of error are valuable aids to meaningful reflection. Conversely, reflective activities can help develop the learner's confidence and sense of self. The courage to face uncertainty and change is a cornerstone of the deepest reflective processes.[43] Dewey wrote that meaningful learning requires the learner "to consider the consequences." Learners must examine "the meaning of what they learn, in the sense of what difference it makes to the rest of their beliefs and to their actions."[44]

Change requires one to leave the comfort of the known. Reflection can play a valuable role in guiding students through changes: personal, academic, professional, or otherwise. Reflection can deepen the process of planning, helping students to critically examine past experiences; evaluate goals and options; make educated decisions about strategies to pursue; and get feedback from faculty, advisors, and peers. Reflective practices that incorporate planning, advising, or goal-setting often address this criterion.

Reflective activities focused on personal change are key elements of ePortfolio practice. Such activities aim to help students articulate their educational and career goals and to trace evolving educational plans. They prompt students to consider their personal relationship to learning and their changing identities as learners and emerging professionals. Some C2L teams incorporated the ePortfolio into formal advisement or peer mentoring; others strengthened the linkage of formal learning, co-curricular activity, work, and other life experiences.

Some practices discussed earlier in this chapter demonstrate this principle. The initial reflection in Pace's "Writing in the Disciplines" course asks students to examine their feelings about the course and its challenges; the final reflection focuses on how they've changed.[45] Nursing faculty at Three Rivers Community College ask students to observe their own attitudes and biases, building self-awareness as nursing professionals.[46] Manhattanville's first-year experience, LaGuardia's liberal arts capstone, and Lehman's early childhood education program have students consider the impact of their learning on their evolving sense of identity.[47]

At IUPUI, ePortfolio leaders have incorporated into their ePortfolio a reflective planning tool, the ePersonal Development Plan (ePDP). Used widely in IUPUI's first-year-experience program and beyond, the ePDP provides a fully realized structure for helping students engage in a sustained reflective inquiry into their goals and their learning (see Figure 3.3).

The ePDP includes seven major sections including About Me, Educational Goals and Plans, Campus and Community Connections, and My College Achievements. Each section includes prompts that guide students in considering their lives and developing a more purposeful approach to their education. Sample prompts completed in the initial semester include

- Describe yourself so that someone who doesn't know you gets a good sense of who you are as a person. Include information about your interests, skills, values, and personality.
- What is your major (or what majors are you considering)? Why did you select it?
- Give examples of the academic skills, strengths, and/or personal qualities you will need to be successful in this major. Considering your personal characteristics and strengths . . . why is this major (or possible major) a good fit for you? Or not?[48]

IUPUI uses the ePDP for advisement, helping students reflect to develop a clearer sense of purpose and pursue what they want from their college experience. As the student progresses, he or she gradually completes more of the ePDP. Each section asks students to include artifacts and provide descriptions of key learning experiences, as in the following example:

> What were the most important things you learned in this course? Be sure to think about and also beyond the course content; think about skills you may have developed, such as the ability to analyze complex problems or the ability to work in groups. Why is what you learned in this course significant or important to you? How does this learning contribute to your academic and career goals?[49]

Figure 3.3. IUPUI's ePersonal Development Plan (ePDP) Conceptual Model

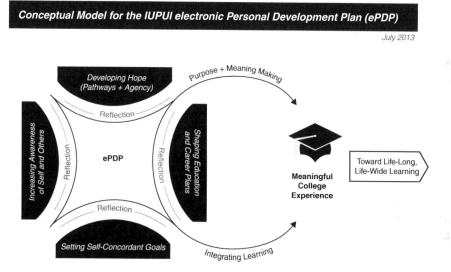

Source. Reprinted with permission of Indiana University–Purdue University Indianapolis.

As students complete the ePDP, writes Cathy Buyarski, "reflective prompts assist them in bringing narrative to their lives and aspirations."[50] IUPUI data on retention and GPA show that the ePDP is particularly beneficial for high-risk students, many of whom are first-generation college students. For all students, the content of the ePDP, Buyarski argues, is "in essence the students' understanding of self. . . . The student is firmly at the center of this narrative."[51] Conceptually, the ePDP resonates with the Rodgers framework.

> Students . . . use reflection as a form of connection in developing their capacity for integrative learning across curriculum, co-curriculum, and lived experience. Reflection in response to the ePDP prompts is systematic and inculcates a disciplined approach to reflection and learning. And certainly the ePDP uses reflection to support growth and personal change as a core element of student development.[52]

The Douglass Women's College at Rutgers University also uses reflective ePortfolio processes to help students develop a clearer sense of themselves and their direction. Guided by a feminist pedagogy, Douglass educators use ePortfolio to help their students develop a sense of identity, voice, and agency. They explicitly address life experiences and affective dimensions, helping students "write about and validate the kinds of personal experiences that are so often discouraged in 'objective' academic settings."[53]

The Douglass ePortfolio process starts in a required first semester mission course, "Knowledge and Power: Issues in Women's Leadership." Although the course had long been required, ePortfolio was first used in 2008–2009. As discussed more fully in Chapter 8, student learning immediately began to improve; the average grade for students in the course went up (from 3.2 in the two semesters prior to ePortfolio to an average of 3.5 in the next nine semesters in which ePortfolio was used). Student success in other first semester courses (as measured by cumulative GPA) also improved significantly. How did Douglass faculty and staff structure this effective ePortfolio practice?

In the Douglass mission course, initial assignments ask students to introduce themselves, define their interests, and articulate an issue that engages them. They also select "an object, piece of music, drawing, picture, spoken word or poem,"[54] put it into their ePortfolio, and discuss its relationship to their goals and interests.

For example, one Douglass student selected "The Mistress of Vision," a poem by Francis Thompson, and used it to highlight the role of connection in her learning—and in her emerging sense of self. "I find that a 'neuronal forest,' that is, the concept of the interconnected neurons in the nervous system, is an appropriate metaphor for the interdisciplinary nature of my academic interests," the student wrote. Discussing her family background, she noted that her "Chinese name literally means 'to admire the forest,'" and she used this to frame her interest in literature, biology, and quantum physics. "Essentially all studies are interdisciplinary," she wrote. "Similar to the neurons in the brain's forest, I am finding connections among my diverse interests so as to develop a cohesive plan of action for my education."[55] For this student, reflection helped her connect literature with her interest in science and to find metaphors that gave her studies a powerful personal meaning.

> **The Mistress of Vision**
>
> All things by immortal power,
> Near and Far,
> Hiddenly
> To each other linked are
> That thou canst stir a flower
> Without troubling a star
>
> Francis Thompson,
> "The Mistress of Vision"

In the first semester course at Douglass, students meet with advisors and peer mentors "to think more about the issues they care about, to connect those issues to academic pathways and to co-curricular programs . . . whether leadership, service-learning, study abroad, or research."[56] Moving forward, students develop a section of their ePortfolio called "My Path," where they track their experience, share artifacts, and consider the ways their experiences are shaping, changing, or deepening their goals and commitments. Sharing and discussing their learning with others, Douglass dean Rebecca Reynolds writes, helps them develop their voice and their identity, their ability to see themselves as individuals living and interacting within community.

> The ePortfolio becomes most compelling as students are asked to allow their inner lives to become outer lives—to incorporate their selves in their studies, their personal, subjective, social, academic, and disciplinary experiences—that is, to develop a public self.[57]

It is from that intersection or integration of inner and public self, Reynolds suggests, that students develop a more purposeful and empowered sense of themselves as learners, leaders, and agents of social change.

The work of C2L teams at Rutgers, IUPUI, and elsewhere suggest ways that reflective ePortfolio practice can not only build student success but also advance identity formation and what some prominent learning theories discuss as transformative learning and self-authorship. Richard Keeling, Jack Meizrow, Stephen Brookfield, and others have argued that reflective learning is transformative when it involves a fundamental questioning or reordering of how one thinks and acts.[58] The leading expert on purposeful self-authorship, Marcia Baxter Magolda, has explored the relationship between learning and the learner's evolving sense of self. She has developed a widely respected framework for helping learners develop "an internal set of beliefs that guide decision-making about knowledge claims, an internal identity that enables them to express themselves in socially constructing knowledge with others, and the capacity to engage in mutually interdependent relationships to assess others' expertise."[59] Her strategies for promoting self-authorship in the classroom include

- Providing opportunities for students to reflect on and express their learning experiences
- Having students reflect on *how* they learned in addition to *what* they learned
- Helping students set attainable but challenging goals, visualize and plan for potential obstacles, and reflect on outcomes[60]

As the activities discussed previously confirm, purposeful self-authorship can intersect with the integrative ePortfolio and extend beyond the academic realm, helping each student develop his or her inner voice and the internal commitments needed to function as an empowered individual. Building a stronger sense of self, the integrative ePortfolio can address a broad range of self-authorship dimensions, building capacities for initiative and self-direction, risk taking and resilience, critical empathy, and engagement with difference. Using ePortfolio to build these habits of heart and mind can not only help our students be more successful in college but also advance intentional lifelong learning and help our students' realize their potential for shaping society and their own lives.

Connections to the *Catalyst Framework*

Although reflection and integrative learning pedagogy are key elements of ePortfolio practice, they do not stand alone. Broad implementation of effective ePortfolio pedagogy depends on and helps shape work in other sectors.

Professional Development

Broad campus use of integrative ePortfolio pedagogy depends on effective professional development. Educators experienced in using reflection or integrative learning are rare. Gathering faculty and staff to review integrative theory and practice is crucial to helping them develop, test, and share reflective prompts. Professional development can sustain them as they try reflection with students, building their skills as they see what works. The most sophisticated professional development goes further to embed reflective social pedagogy practices into the professional development process, modeling the kinds of processes that work best with students and developing reflective practitioners.

Outcomes Assessment

The connection between pedagogy and assessment is also clear. It is vital for faculty and staff to effectively address established competencies in specific learning designs. Integrative social pedagogy helps students see the connections between specific activities and broader programmatic or general education competencies, empowering them to develop more cohesive understandings of their education experiences. Conversely, faculty skilled in integrative ePortfolio pedagogy can help campuses design outcomes assessment processes that value educating the whole student.

Technology

An effective ePortfolio platform can facilitate or obstruct integrative social pedagogy. An agile, well-designed platform supports faculty, making it easy to insert reflective prompts, comment on student work, and track connections across courses. To facilitate ownership and self-authorship, an ePortfolio platform should be easy to learn, and students should be able to customize their portfolios to reflect their evolving identities. A focus on functions that support reflection, integration, and social pedagogy should guide the selection of a campus ePortfolio platform.

Scaling Up

Integrative ePortfolio pedagogy, with its emphasis on connections and growth across courses and semesters, is most effective not in a single course but as a longitudinal and recursive process. To take full advantage of integrative ePortfolio pedagogy requires thoughtful attention to course sequences in a program or major as well as linkages with general education, co-curricular engagement, and experiential learning in relation to work, family, and community. For faculty to strengthen the integrative qualities of their programs, the institution must value teaching and a focus on holistic student learning. To be most effective, integrative ePortfolio pedagogy must be matched by integrative practice at multiple levels of campus life.

Conclusion

The C2L experience confirmed that integrative social pedagogy that engages students in regular opportunities to reflect and connect their learning stands at the core of what it means to do ePortfolio well. There are many ways to address this priority, as suggested in this chapter. Engaged with a growing body of cognitive research and learning theory, educators across the country are using reflective ePortfolio practices to help students bridge inquiry and integration, achieve greater success, and deepen their learning. Scaffolding a reflective activity into the ePortfolio-building process, they help students sustain their focus on learning, make integrative connections, and find larger meaning in their educational experiences. Incorporating social pedagogy, they use the ePortfolio to enhance feedback and structure interaction. Linking the cognitive to the affective and the social, their practices seek to address the needs of the whole student. Drawing on the work of thinkers and scholars from John Dewey to Carol Rodgers and Marcia Baxter Magolda, they aim not only to help students become more successful in individual classes but also to build vital capacities for integration and purposeful self-authorship, advancing students' potential for shaping society and their own personal lives.

Notes

1. George Kuh and Ken O'Donnell, *Ensuring Quality and Taking High Impact Practices to Scale* (Washington, DC: Association of American Colleges & Universities, 2013).

2. Mary Taylor Huber and Pat Hutchings, *Integrative Learning: Mapping the Terrain* (Washington, DC: Association of American Colleges & Universities, 2004), 1.

3. Huber and Hutchings, *Integrative Learning*, 1.

4. William Cronon, "Only Connect . . . The Goals of a Liberal Education," *American Scholar* 67, no. 4 (1998): 73.

5. Carol Geary Schneider, "Liberal Education and Integrative Learning," *Issues in Integrative Studies* 21 (2003): 1.

6. David C. Hodge, Marcia Baxter Magolda, and Carolyn A. B. Haynes. "Engaged Learning: Enabling Self-Authorship and Effective Practice," *Liberal Education* 95, no. 4, (2009): 16–23.

7. John D. Bransford, Ann L. Brown, and Rodney R. Cocking, eds., *How People Learn: Brain, Mind, Experience, and School* (Washington, DC: National Academies Press, 2000); John Dewey, *Democracy and Education: An Introduction to the Philosophy of Education* (New York, NY: Macmillan, 1916).

8. Kuh and O'Donnell, *Ensuring Quality and Taking High Impact Practices to Scale.*

9. Carol Rodgers, "Defining Reflection: Another Look at John Dewey and Reflective Thinking," *Teachers College Record* 104, no. 4 (2002): 848.

10. Helen C. Barrett, "Balancing the Two Faces of e-Portfolios," accessed August 5, 2016, http://electronicportfolios.com/balance/Balancing2.htm

11. Kathleen Blake Yancey, "Reflection and Electronic Portfolios: Inventing the Self and Reinventing the University," in *Electronic Portfolios 2.0: Emergent Research on Implementation and Impact*, ed. Darren Cambridge, Barbara Cambridge, and Kathleen Blake Yancey (Sterling, VA: Stylus, 2009), 5–16.

12. Rodgers, "Defining Reflection, 845.

13. Ibid., 845.

14. Ibid., 845.

15. John Dewey, *Democracy and Education: An Introduction to the Philosophy of Education* (New York, NY: Macmillan, 1916).

16. Ibid., 848.

17. Adam Dastrup, "Outcomes Reflection: Reflective Pedagogy in SLCC's GIS Program," *Catalyst for Learning: ePortfolio Resources and Research,* January 25, 2014, http://slcc.mcnrc.org/ref-practice-3/

18. Sherie McClam, "Learning for a Sustainable Future and Using Social Media for Social Change," *Catalyst for Learning: ePortfolio Resources and Research,* January 25, 2014, http://mville.mcnrc.org/soc-practice/

19. Ibid.

20. Linda Anstendig, "Reflective Thinking and Writing as Systematic Practice at Pace University," *Catalyst for Learning: ePortfolio Resources and Research,* January 25, 2014, http://pu.mcnrc.org/ref-practice/

21. Anstendig, "Reflective Thinking."

22. Ibid.

23. Alycia Shada, "Knowing Where You Are Going and Where You Have Been: Students Write a Letter to Their Future Self," *Catalyst for Learning: ePortfolio Resources and Research,* January 25, 2014, http://sfsu.mcnrc.org/ref-practice-1/

24. J. Elizabeth Clark, "Faculty Development Practices at LaGuardia: Capstone Courses, ePortfolios, and Integrative Learning," *Catalyst for Learning: ePortfolio Resources and Research,* January 25, 2014, http://lagcc.mcnrc.org/faculty-development-practices-laguardia-rethinking-the-capstone-experience-seminar/

25. Amy Feest, "The 'Business' of ePortfolios," *Catalyst for Learning: ePortfolio Resources and Research,* January 25, 2014, http://tcc.mcnrc.org/ref-practice-3/

26. Susan Clark, Marc Zaldivar, and Teggin Summers, "Reflective Process in the Dietetics: Human Nutrition, Foods and Exercise ePortfolio," *Catalyst for Learning: ePortfolio Resources and Research,* January 25, 2014, http://vt.mcnrc.org/ref-practice

27. Rebecca Reynolds, "Rutgers University—I Got It Covered: Reflection as Integrative, Social Pedagogy," *Catalyst for Learning: ePortfolio Resources and Research,* January 25, 2014, http://c2l.mcnrc.org/ru-ref-practice/

28. David Hubert, "Mixed Media Reflection: ePortfolios in an SLCC Study Abroad Program," *Catalyst for Learning: ePortfolio Resources and Research,* January 25, 2014, http://slcc.mcnrc.org/ref-practice-1/

29. Katie Wilson and Laura M. Gambino, "Guttman Global Badging Module," unpublished ePortfolio, New York, NY: 2016.

30. Three Rivers Community College, "Connecting Theory to Practice in Gerontology-Reflective Practice," *Catalyst for Learning: ePortfolio Resources and Research,* January 25, 2014, http://trcc.mcnrc.org/ref-practice-4/

31. Carol Rodgers, "Seeing Student Learning: Teacher Change and the Role of Reflection," *Harvard Educational Review* 72, no. 2 (Summer 2001): 230–253.

32. Cynthia Clark Williams, "Peer Reflective Feedback in First Year Service Learning," *Catalyst for Learning: ePortfolio Resources and Research,* January 25, 2014, http://iupui.mcnrc.org/soc-practice-1/

33. Alexandria Ross, "Reflective Pedagogy Practice: About Artifacts," *Catalyst for Learning: ePortfolio Resources and Research,* January 25, 2014, http://lc.mcnrc.org/ref-practice-2/

34. Ross, "Reflective Pedagogy Practice."

35. George D. Kuh, *High-Impact Educational Practices: What They Are, Who Has Access to Them, and Why They Matter* (Washington, DC: Association of American Colleges & Universities, 2008).

36. Rodgers, "Defining Reflection," 856.

37. John Dewey, *Democracy and Education: An Introduction to the Philosophy of Education* (New York, NY: Macmillan, 1916).

38. Rodgers, "Defining Reflection," 857.

39. Randy Bass and Heidi Elmendorf, "Designing for Difficulty: Social Pedagogies as a Framework for Course Design," Teagle Foundation White Paper, accessed August 5, 2016, https://blogs.commons.georgetown.edu/bassr/social-pedagogies/

40. Ibid.

41. Randall Bass, "Social Pedagogies in ePortfolio Practices: Principles for Design and Impact," *Catalyst for Learning: ePortfolio Resources and Research,* January 25, 2014, http://c2l.mcnrc.org/wp-content/uploads/sites/8/2014/01/Bass_Social_Pedagogy.pdf

42. Kuh, *High-Impact Educational Practices,* 8.

43. Rodgers, "Defining Reflection," 842–866.

44. John Dewey, *How We Think* (Buffalo, NY: Prometheus Books, 1933), 32.

45. Linda Anstendig, "Reflective Thinking and Writing as Systematic Practice at Pace University," *Catalyst for Learning: ePortfolio Resources and Research,* January 25, 2014, http://pu.mcnrc.org/ref-practice/

46. Three Rivers Community College, "Connecting Theory to Practice in Gerontology–Reflective Practice," *Catalyst for Learning: ePortfolio Resources and Research,* January 25, 2014, http://trcc.mcnrc.org/ref-practice-4/

47. Sherie McClam, "Learning for a Sustainable Future"; Elizabeth Clark, "Faculty Development Practices at LaGuardia: Capstone Courses, ePortfolios, and Integrative Learning," *Catalyst for Learning: ePortfolio Resources and Research,* January 25, 2014, http://lagcc.mcnrc.org/faculty-development-practices-laguardia-rethinking-the-capstone-experience-seminar/; Alexandria Ross, "Reflective Pedagogy Practice: About Artifacts," *Catalyst for Learning: ePortfolio Resources and Research,* January 25, 2014, http://lc.mcnrc.org/ref-practice-2/

48. Catherine Buyarski, "Reflection in the First Year: A Foundation for Identity and Meaning Making," *Catalyst for Learning: ePortfolio Resources and Research,* January 25, 2014, http://iupui.mcnrc.org/ref-practice/

49. Buyarski, "Reflection in the First Year."

50. Ibid.

51. Ibid.

52. Indiana University–Purdue University Indianapolis, *University College Program Review and Assessment Committee Annual Report 2013–2014*, accessed August 15, 2015, http://irds.iupui.edu/Portals/SDAE/Files/Documents/2013-14%20UCOL%20PRAC%20 Final.pdf

53. Reynolds, "Rutgers University."

54. Ibid.

55. Ibid.

56. Ibid.

57. Ibid.

58. Richard Keeling, ed., *Learning Reconsidered: A Campus-Wide Focus on the Student Experience* (Washington DC: National Association of Student Personnel Administrators and American College Personnel Association, 2004); Jack Mezirow, ed., *Learning as Transformation: Critical Perspectives on a Theory in Progress* (San Francisco, Jossey-Bass, 2000); Stephen D. Brookfield, "Using the Lenses of Critically Reflective Teaching in the Community College Classroom," *New Directions for Community Colleges* no. 118 (2002): 31–38.

59. Hodge et al., "Engaged Learning," 19.

60. Hodge et al., "Engaged Learning."

SOCIAL PEDAGOGIES IN ePORTFOLIO PRACTICES

Principles for Design and Impact

Randy Bass

In this essay, Randy Bass provides an introduction to social pedagogy and then reviews C2L social pedagogy practices, analyzing themes and patterns of use. "As these kinds of practices become more prevalent and developed," Bass writes at the end of this essay, they will "reshape what we think of as the purpose and nature of ePortfolios, as sites of student sense-making and 'learning to be.'"

Social Pedagogies in ePortfolio Contexts

In the *Catalyst Framework*, integrative social pedagogy is a foundational concept for the ways that ePortfolios make student learning visible. Utilizing ePortfolios in conjunction with social learning practices expands the boundaries of what we understand to be the potential and value of ePortfolios. By stressing ePortfolio practice as an integrative social pedagogy, we ask: What might it look like to take the social dimension of ePortfolios as seriously as integration—and to understand the importance of social learning for integration? What would it look like to put social learning at the heart of all the connections that we see as central to ePortfolio learning on our campuses?

Early in the history of C2L, we had a working assumption that social pedagogies are integral to fostering deep learning. Our C2L Core Survey findings (see Chapter 8) and the creative emerging practices on campuses bear this out. We take the term *social pedagogies* to mean "design approaches for teaching and learning that engage students in authentic tasks that are communication-intensive, where the representation of knowledge for an authentic audience is absolutely central to the construction of knowledge in a course."[1] This is the "social core" of these practices, an intricate interdependence among three key ideas: (a) *constructing understanding* (ways that students deepen their understanding of core concepts by engaging in the ways of thinking and practicing in a field), (b) *communicating understanding* (ways that students make their

65

Figure 3.4. Core Elements of the Social Pedagogy Model

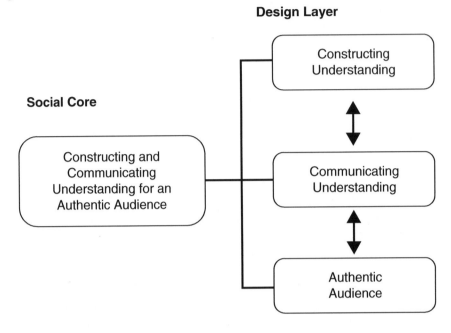

knowledge available for others), and (c) *authentic audiences*, (audiences other than the instructor), as seen in Figure 3.4.

Social pedagogies are most effective when undertaken by students through "iterative cycles of engagement, often with the most difficult material."[2] Similarly, "social pedagogies strive to build a sense of intellectual community within the classroom and frequently connect students to communities outside the classroom."[3] In the context of ePortfolios, social pedagogies are design approaches that help students deepen their reflections, build links across courses and semesters, and bridge formal curricular learning with co-curricular experiences.

Social pedagogies can be implemented using all kinds of technologies (as well as practices that involve no digital technologies). Social pedagogies are associated with a set of outcomes that help deepen and contextualize learning, strengthen students' sense of voice and agency, and find intellectual and personal significance in their learning (see Figure 3.5).

These outcomes, consonant with the kinds of learning associated with ePortfolios, are intensified when using social pedagogies with ePortfolios, where student work is lifted out of isolated assignments or bounded courses; learning processes can be archived and made visible; reflection is the norm; communities are developed, and courses and experiences, both curricular and co-curricular, are explicitly connected as part of a larger educational narrative.

And again in the C2L findings discussed in Chapter 8 when social pedagogies are being used, it suggests, students are more likely to report that ePortfolio deepened

Figure 3.5. Social Pedagogy Model With Associated Outcomes

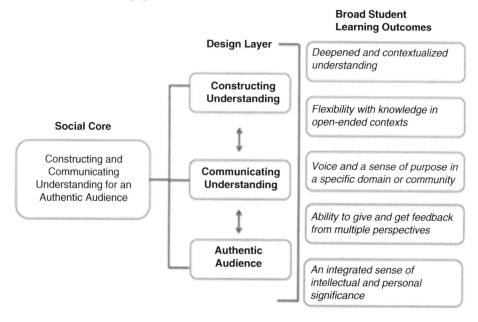

their engagement with ideas and course content, and that the course engaged them in higher order integrative learning processes.

C2L's fundamental premise is that deepening the integrative qualities of student learning makes learning more transformative and enduring; integration is promoted through reflection, by inviting students, in disciplined and systematic ways, to make connections that intensify their learning; and reflection is more meaningful when it makes learning visible to others. Integration, reflection, and social learning are at the heart of C2L's ePortfolio pedagogy "done well."

Early in the C2L project, we found few established practices involving ePortfolio and social pedagogies, especially with respect to the use of reflection in the context of community. Now there is a growing range of rich examples, as well as a sophistication and robustness around integrative social pedagogies in ePortfolio contexts. This essay describes some of the principles of design and characteristics of these exemplary practices in order to better promote social pedagogies within the ePortfolio community.

Principles for Design and Impact: Social Pedagogies in ePortfolio Contexts

In April 2013 we asked faculty on C2L campuses to share social pedagogy practices with these questions in mind: What makes these practices work? What might make them more successful? What else is taking place in ePortfolio practice that makes these particular practices effective (thinking about the larger ecology)? What prelimi-nary insights can we draw from these practices about the core principles of a social pedagogy for ePortfolio?

Here is some of what we've learned from these campus practices, grouped under three headings: Process and Audience, Purpose and Identity, and Learning Culture.

Process and Audience

ePortfolios enable social pedagogies, providing an intermediate space between pub-lic and private. ePortfolios are particularly well suited for social learning interactions because they can be situated as intermediate spaces, somewhere between entirely private and openly public. Guided by faculty, students rehearse what it means to connect with an audience and consider what their ePortfolio looks like to others. Inventing ways in which ePortfolios can serve as sites for communication, collabo-ration, and exchange is a significant task for the ePortfolio field as a whole. This intermediate space of ePortfolio learning and interaction enables students to engage in stages of reflection and layers of social learning. This helps students realize the impact of one of the principles of reflection—"reflection in community." Com-munity is critical to reflection—as Carol Rodgers stresses in her synthesis of John Dewey—because it allows for the affirmation of one's ideas, helps learners benefit from diverse perspectives and new ways to see, and provides a testing ground for ideas and understanding.[4]

Social pedagogy practices have at least four distinct layers or versions of "authen-tic audience" that can play out in ePortfolio contexts. Working with this idea of ePortfolios as an intermediate space, faculty at C2L campuses devised practices that engage at least four different kinds of audiences and interactions.

Faculty and peer feedback. The most common social pedagogy associated with ePortfolios is the use of faculty and peer response and social interaction to deepen individual work. Faculty feedback (frequent and targeted feedback) is one of the most important factors for improving learning in any context. C2L Core Survey findings corroborate this, showing that high levels of faculty feedback correlated with deeper engagement. Faculty feedback by itself is important, but it is not fully a *social pedagogy* in the way we use the term.

When peer feedback is introduced, it significantly enhances the experience. As argued in Chapter 8, the addition of peer feedback helps elevate this point to a broader understanding of the importance of the social element in student learn-ing. Examples on the *Catalyst for Learning* website are plentiful. For example, in an assignment at Guttman Community College connected with their integrative course, "Arts in NYC," students "respond to each other's comments via the course ePortfolio and use each other's ideas to generate insight and analysis into their own writing."[5] Northeastern's master's-level education courses use a layered, or staged, reflection approach, where "social pedagogy precedes individual reflection."[6] In both examples, ePortfolios provide a context for testing, refining and ultimately deepening understanding that then informs individual reflection and analysis.

Collaborative work. Another powerful form of audience and social learning is team-based work to create a collaboratively produced artifact. For example, in Boston University's College of General Studies' second-year capstone team projects, "students spend the last four weeks of their sophomore year working in groups of five to seven to research a contemporary problem and write a paper that describes the problem and its contexts and proposes a real-world solution."[7] ePortfolios play a crucial and unique role in the process by allowing students to "keep logs of their progress (what they read, who they interviewed, what they wrote), and they also archive all drafts they write on their portfolios."[8] This kind of sharing and archiving enables the students to make their thinking visible to each other (creating a more coherent end product) and to the faculty, who can better mentor the projects as a result.

At Lehman College, students preparing to become science educators "co-construct" a collaborative portfolio that "uses evidence to document and illustrate shared professional practices in the context of . . . an audience they select."[9] The emphasis in the collaborative process is to provide real evidence (baseline and post-baseline) of personal and professional development that integrates learning science with learning how to teach science.[10]

External audiences. Some social pedagogies make use of an external audience, which raises the stakes on production and intensifies the way students learn to be accountable for their thinking and communication. For example, at the University of Delaware "teacher candidate students" have a "defense of mastery presentation-style ePortfolio" that provides "a high stakes setting that replicates a position interview process."[11] At Hunter College, students in an "Advanced German Through Translation" course "develop their understanding of themselves as learners by posting in-depth reflections on the challenges they have faced as translators and the problem-solving strategies they have developed to meet those challenges."[12] In the end, the portfolios are public, and the instructor strives to "simulate an authentic audience for each translation that the students do, providing them with translation briefs based on 'real-life' commissions that translators receive."[13]

Knowledge communities. Another powerful kind of audience—one that builds on all the previous ones—is the formation of students into an expert-like "knowledge community of practice." For example, in a microbiology course, Pace University students spend eight weeks developing an "expertise" on a specific kind of bacteria, developing and presenting through an ePortfolio.[14] Peer commentary and hyperlinked cross-references generate networked, collaborative practice and product. In IUPUI's art history capstone, students engage in extensive "peer review . . . to begin to understand a singular paper as part of a wider research possibility" and "to understand research as a way of thinking rather than as a page and word limit."[15] At Northeastern,

In the EdD program, one faculty member who teaches Entrepreneurial Leadership involves groups of students in the development of ePortfolio case studies. Toward the end of the course, groups use Google Hangouts to broadcast and record a panel discussion with educational innovators about the case, and the recording is also embedded in the ePortfolio. These cases become part of a library that future students can draw upon in their learning.[16]

At Virginia Tech, they created a program called Zip Line to Success that quickly integrates transfer students in part by involving them in a final group research project "where students combine their interests and their disciplinary backgrounds to pursue a research topic from multiple perspectives. The students present their research through the medium of an electronic portfolio."[17]

The creation of a true knowledge community of practice has not been a common strategy in ePortfolio practices; yet, as social learning and networked knowledge play an ever greater role in higher education, these kinds of practices represent an important—if not profound—emergent area, in the development of integrative social pedagogies.

Purpose and Identity

Integrative social pedagogies contribute to giving students a sense of purpose.   Across the different activities, high-impact ePortfolio practice helps students find a sense of purpose in their learning. You can see it from the very first year—for example, at Manhattanville College, where Sherie McClam uses ePortfolio and social media to help her students work for "social action and social change."[18] And several master's-level ePortfolio practices use social pedagogies and ePortfolio assignments to galvanize their students' sense of agency in a given field.[19]

This primary objective—to develop a sense of purpose—helps remind us that social learning pedagogies are not only about process (peer review, revision, etc.) but also about learning processing. In particular, it is especially powerful to see how social pedagogies help students find new meaning in their learning experiences—by connecting and reframing them. It is a foundational premise of social pedagogies that helping to make sense of an idea or an experience for others is critical to making sense of knowledge and experience for oneself.

Social pedagogies help students "learn to be" in a discipline or professional area.   The role of social pedagogies in addressing learning outcomes is nowhere more evident than when practices make explicit connections between thinking in a field and learning to embody that field. This is captured, for example, in the description of the IUPUI art history capstone, where "the social pedagogy of peer feedback and subsequent discussion thus serves an important purpose of the course: strengthening students' professional identities by helping them learn to be peer reviewers of others' writing about art."[20] This connection—elsewhere expressed in the IUPUI case study as the synthesis of metacognition and professional-identity development—is one powerful way to articulate the relationship between "constructing understanding" and "communicating understanding," the core precepts of social pedagogies as laid out earlier in this essay.

Several of the social pedagogy practices shared on the *Catalyst for Learning: ePortfolio Resources and Research* website address the relationship among knowledge building, metacognition, and identity quite explicitly. What is especially powerful here is knowledge development through social pedagogies—where students understand how to translate their ideas for others, negotiate with peers around meaning, and internalize standards for quality and excellence that belong to communities of practice.

Learning Culture

Social pedagogies are typically integrative of multiple learning goals and outcomes. We usually talk about social pedagogies being integrative because they help students make connections across knowledge areas and connect disparate learning experiences (coursework, co-curricular, etc.). But it is also clear in these practices how social pedagogies often help students (and faculty) meet more than one learning goal for a course or a program—often meeting many at once. For example, at LaGuardia, students make video presentations on anatomy knowledge that "explicitly supports three core competencies: oral communication, critical literacy and technological literacy."[21] Or, to take an extreme case, the University of Delaware teacher candidate portfolios lead students to demonstrate the "application of all the competencies obtained throughout their academic program."[22]

Social pedagogies are especially powerful when they are distributed throughout the learning culture. Nowhere is social learning more pervasive than in Three Rivers Community College's use of integrative social pedagogy throughout its nursing program, from current students sharing letters of orientation with entering students, to information literacy assignments, to presentations on content and reflections on clinical growth. In assignment after assignment, horizontally and vertically across the curriculum, a social ethos permeates the program.[23]

Social pedagogies lead to a distinctive kind of evidence in ePortfolios themselves. In LaGuardia's practice outlining the anatomy video assignment, Preethi Radhakrishnan describes her experimental design, carried out in parallel sections, one with the social learning assignment and one without; a comparison of exam scores showed that "reflection and critical thinking does boost and deepen learning of 'hard concepts.'"[24] That's one compelling form of evidence of impact. A few practices speak directly about what the evidence looks like in the ePortfolios themselves. For example, in the Northeastern social pedagogy practices, "The ePortfolio helps the teacher see how a student distills and derives individual meaning from the large body of work generated in a fully online course, using that experience to negotiate the development of individual and professional identity. Sometimes this process is observed in the student's writing, but the evidence can also be visual."[25]

Social Pedagogies as a Growth Area for ePortfolios

Overall, social pedagogies intensify the impact of ePortfolios as sites for integrative student learning. As these kinds of practices become more prevalent and developed, they will also reshape what we think of as the purpose and nature of ePortfolios, as sites of student sense-making and "learning to be." Although still emerging on campuses, we are starting to see social pedagogies as a critical influence on the way that ePortfolio practices are evolving for a new paradigm of learning and knowledge-sharing at the heart of higher education and indeed our whole culture.

Notes

1. Randy Bass and Heidi Elmendorf, "Designing for Difficulty: Social Pedagogies as a Framework for Course Design," excerpt from a Teagle Foundation White Paper, accessed August 5, 2016, http://c2l.mcnrc.org/pedagogy-resources/, p. 2.

2. Ibid.

3. Ibid.

4. Carol Rodgers, "Defining Reflection: Another Look at John Dewey and Reflective Thinking," *Teachers College Record* 104, no. 4 (2002): 842–866.

5. Nate Mickelson, "Social Pedagogy: Using Comment Streams to Analyze Visual Art," *Catalyst for Learning: ePortfolio Resources and Research,* January 25, 2014, http://gcc.mcnrc .org/soc-practice-2/

6. Gail Matthews-DeNatale, "Zooming In and Out," *Catalyst for Learning: ePortfolio Resources and Research,* January 25, 2014, http://neu.mcnrc.org/ref-practice/

7. Robert Wexelblatt, "Social Pedagogy and General Education: The CGS Capstone Project," *Catalyst for Learning: ePortfolio Resources and Research,* January 25, 2014, http:// bu.mcnrc.org/bu-soc-practice/

8. Ibid.

9. Wesley Pitts, "Social Pedagogy: Engaging with Professional Colleagues," *Catalyst for Learning: ePortfolio Resources and Research,* January 25, 2014, http://lc.mcnrc.org/ soc-practice/

10. Ibid.

11. Lynn Worden, "Mastery ePortfolio Defense," *Catalyst for Learning: ePortfolio Resources and Research,* January 25, 2014, http://ud.mcnrc.org/soc-practice/

12. Lisa Marie Anderson, Gina Cherry, and Wendy Hayden, "Social Pedagogy in the Advanced Foreign Language Curriculum," *Catalyst for Learning: ePortfolio Resources and Research,* January 25, 2014, http://hc.mcnrc.org/soc-practice/

13. Ibid.

14. Andrew Wier, "Getting Social with Bio," *Catalyst for Learning: ePortfolio Resources and Research,* January 25, 2014, http://pu.mcnrc.org/soc-practice/

15. R. Patrick Kinsman, Susan Kahn, and Susan Scott, "Social Pedagogy: Working Together to Develop Metacognition and Professional Identity," *Catalyst for Learning: ePortfolio Resources and Research,* January 25, 2014, http://iupui.mcnrc.org/soc-practice-2/

16. Laurie Poklop, "Social Pedagogies Jam," (unpublished internal discussion board post), *Connect to Learning Project* (2012).

17. Jill Sible and Gary Kinder, "Social Pedagogy Practice: Zip Line to Success ePortfolio," *Catalyst for Learning: ePortfolio Resources and Research,* January 25, 2014, http://vt.mcnrc.org/soc-practice/

18. Sherie McClam, "Learning for a Sustainable Future and Using Social Media for Social Change," *Catalyst for Learning: ePortfolio Resources and Research,* January 25, 2014, http://mville.mcnrc.org/soc-practice/

19. Pitts, "Social Pedagogy"; Matthews-DeNatale, "Zooming In and Out."

20. Kinsman et al., "Social Pedagogy."

21. Preethi Radhakrishnan, "Video Presentations to Demonstrate Anatomy Theory and Oral Communication Skills," *Catalyst for Learning: ePortfolio Resources and Research,* January 25, 2014. https://lagcc-cuny.digication.com/eportfolio_sampler/Radhakrishnan_-_Video_Presentations_to_Demonstrate/published

22. Lynn Worden, "Mastery ePortfolio Defense," *Catalyst for Learning: ePortfolio Resources and Research,* January 25, 2014, http://ud.mcnrc.org/soc-practice/

23. Three Rivers Community College ePortfolio Leadership Team, "Who We Are—A Connect to Learning Campus ePortfolio," *Catalyst for Learning: ePortfolio Resources and Research,* January 25, 2014, http://trcc.mcnrc.org/

24. Radhakrishnan, "Video Presentations."

25. Matthews-DeNatale, "Zooming In and Out."

4

PROFESSIONAL DEVELOPMENT FOR HIGH-IMPACT ePORTFOLIO PRACTICE

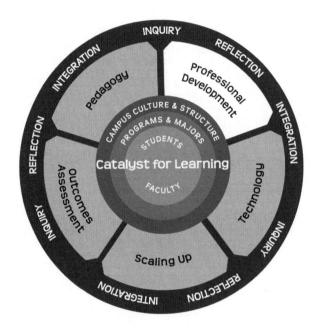

G uided by integrative social pedagogy, a sophisticated reflective ePortfolio practice can advance student success, deepen student learning, and help students develop more robust and resilient identities as learners.[1] In a fast-changing learning ecosystem marked by digital innovation and calls for unbundling, ePortfolio practice can help us build more integrative and adaptive universities.[2] But high-impact ePortfolio practice will never gain wide traction in higher education without effective professional development. This chapter examines effective professional development strategies for advancing and deepening ePortfolio practice.

Professional development is critical for advancing any educational innovation. To move beyond what Phil Hill has called the "purgatory" of pilot programs, colleges must support professional development with resources equivalent to those committed to developing new digital systems.[3] Although this priority is often acknowledged, robust support for faculty learning still lags. This is true even with digital courseware.

The Tyton Group found that 60% of faculty surveyed said that at their institutions, faculty "are encouraged to use digital courseware." However, "far fewer reported being trained (30%) or incentivized (15%) to do so effectively."[4]

Professional development is particularly critical for ePortfolio practice. ePortfolio technology can be simple to learn, but integrative ePortfolio pedagogy takes time and support to master. Because ePortfolio practice is most effective when students use it to connect learning across courses, disciplines, and semesters, ePortfolio projects must move beyond early adopters, engaging a broader group of faculty and staff to construct shared purpose and coordinated design.

Sophisticated integrative ePortfolio pedagogy is key to high-impact ePortfolio practice. But few faculty or staff are familiar with such pedagogy, and even experienced ePortfolio practitioners benefit from opportunities to deepen their craft. Studying our Connect to Learning (C2L) campuses, we found that the development of thoughtful, sustained professional development processes was perhaps the single most crucial indicator for success.

By *professional development*, we mean structured engagement of faculty and staff, focused on improved student learning. On some campuses, professional development means sending faculty to conferences to present disciplinary research. This can be valuable, but in this chapter we focus on sustained, pedagogy-centered engagement. Through professional development seminars, workshops, and online programs, faculty and staff develop and test new ideas, collaborate on projects, and reflect on professional growth. Professional learning can help faculty, peer mentors, and student life professionals integrate innovative pedagogies into their practice across settings. Working together in a structured process, professional development encourages collaboration; innovation; and productive, sustained engagement.

Figure 4.1. Engaging Faculty and Staff

Note. Professional development provides opportunities for faculty and staff to engage in collaborative conversations about teaching and learning.

Getting Started
Seven Tips for Effective
ePortfolio-Based
Professional Development

1. **Focus on pedagogy**: Technology is important to ePortfolio, but pedagogy is crucial.
2. **Form a partnership**: Work with your campus Center for Teaching and Learning, which can add experience, expertise, and continuity to your ePortfolio work.
3. **Build faculty leadership**: Faculty insight and faculty voice energize powerful professional development.
4. **Design for sustained engagement**: Changes in practice take time; integrative ePortfolio pedagogy can be particularly challenging.
5. **Model integrative ePortfolio pedagogy**: Help faculty experience the strategies you want to nurture.
6. **Connect with and across departments**: Respect discipline structures, but don't be limited by them.
7. **Support faculty engagement**: Recognize and reward faculty focus on ePortfolio innovation.

ePortfolio-related professional development can address issues from effective classroom teaching with ePortfolio to training on ePortfolio platforms; linkages with co-curricular learning or outcomes assessment; exploring disciplinary modes of inquiry and reflection; and making connections with other HIPs, such as first-year experience programs. It can build understanding of the broad usages of ePortfolio and connect faculty and student life professionals in a concerted focus on student learning and growth. Guided by the design principles of Inquiry, Reflection, and Integration, professional development can support powerful ePortfolio practice and build student, faculty, and institutional learning.

This chapter begins by spotlighting key points found in the professional development literature. Drawing on campus stories published on the *Catalyst for Learning* site, it reviews professional development structures used by different C2L teams. It then discusses ways that, across strategies, successful teams used Inquiry, Reflection, and Integration as design principles in planning and guiding effective professional development. Finally, it points to ways that professional development depends on thoughtful work done in other Catalyst sectors.

Drawing on the Literature

ePortfolio-focused professional development shares much with the broader professional development field, and the professional development literature is robust. We touch on four threads in this literature that proved helpful to C2L teams.

In C2L cross-campus seminars, teams discussed Thomas Angelo's essay in which he asked, "If producing high-quality student learning is American higher education's defining goal, how can faculty development best contribute to its realization?"[5] At the article's core, he lists seven guidelines for productive professional learning communities:

1. Build shared trust: Begin by lowering social and interpersonal barriers to change.
2. Build shared motivation: Collectively determine goals worth working toward and problems worth solving, and consider the likely costs and benefits.
3. Build a shared language: Develop a collective understanding of new concepts (mental models) needed for transformation.
4. Design backward and work forward: Work backward from the shared vision and long-term goals to determine outcomes, strategies, and activities.
5. Think and act systematically: Understand the advantages and limitations of the larger systems we operate in and seek connections and applications to those larger worlds.
6. Practice what we preach: Use what we have learned about individual and organizational learning to inform and explain our efforts and strategies.
7. Don't assume, ask: Make the implicit explicit. Use assessment to focus on what matters most.[6]

These guidelines, which directly apply to ePortfolio initiatives, highlight the importance of faculty engagement. Understanding faculty as active subjects who shape the professional development process, Angelo seeks to mobilize their creativity and expertise. He sees educational innovation as multilayered and suggests that careful professional development design must take into account not only goals and evidence of impact but also processes of professional inquiry and individual change. Thinking strategically, he points to the importance of contextualizing faculty practice in broader awareness of systems thinking and organizational learning.

In C2L, the importance of institutional context was emphasized when teams read an essay by Pat Hutchings.[7] Examining campuses that worked to advance integrative learning, Hutchings finds that professional development helps faculty study integrative learning concepts and begin to change their practice. However, she suggests, this is only one of the essential tasks accomplished by effective professional development. She also discusses the powerful role professional development can play in generating interdisciplinary community, a powerful component in motivating and supporting faculty doing the hard work of changing their practice. And she emphasizes the ways that professional development should also build a campus culture focused on learning and teaching, a key success factor for ePortfolio projects.

> Workshops on classroom approaches that promote connection-making, work on curriculum design, and exchange around assessment and the scholarship of teaching and learning are important contexts for getting smarter about the character of integrative learning and how to promote it. But just as important is the creation of a campus culture where the academic community faculty, staff, and, importantly, students is engaged in the hard but joyful work of integration.[8]

Getting Started
Tip 1: Focus on Pedagogy

ePortfolio-focused professional development should focus on helping faculty and staff understand, adapt, and test effective integrative pedagogy and practice with their students.

Helping practitioners learn the ins and outs of ePortfolio platforms can be important. If faculty and staff don't know what a platform can (and can't) do, and develop a level of comfort using it, their ePortfolio practice can be obstructed. But learning about the technology alone is unlikely to enrich student learning.

Professional development that focuses on integrative pedagogy helps educators connect ePortfolio to what they do every day: teach students and help them learn. A focus on pedagogy means exploring concepts and best practices related to reflection and integrative learning, but it also draws on and respects what participants already know. Positioning the classroom as a site for experimentation with new ePortfolio approaches, pedagogy-focused professional development helps faculty and staff explore the connection between the strategies they design and use and their ultimate goal: transformative student learning.

Mary Deane Sorcinelli and her coauthors have suggested that effective professional development depends on the ways that a college recognizes and supports it. "Successful programs," they argue, tend to demonstrate features that include "administrative support that encourages faculty development; a formal, structured, goal-directed program; connections between faculty development and the reward structure; faculty ownership; and collegial support for investment in teaching."[9] Reading Sorcinelli helped C2L teams recognize that all these factors play crucial roles in shaping the success of professional development and high-impact ePortfolio practice.

Finally, C2L teams reviewed scholarship that describes professional development leaders as active agents of institutional change. Debra Dawson and her coauthors discuss ways faculty developers increasingly manage institutional change, translating campus-wide goals and initiatives into classroom practice. Moving from the details of specific practices to a more macro level, they suggest, involves professional development leaders in shaping the "institutional approach to teaching and learning," and "shifting the teaching culture." Faculty developers, they conclude, "seem poised to take on a seminal role in the transformation of the university, given their strong skills in communication, team building and collaboration."[10]

Building on faculty expertise, generating community, changing the campus culture, attracting administrative support, linking to the reward structure, and consciously attending to issues related to systemic institutional transformation are best practices that can strengthen professional development related to ePortfolio. Educators seeking to build high-impact ePortfolio projects must attend to such issues as they envision, design, and guide their professional development programs.

Structures for ePortfolio-Related Professional Development

Professional development was a key component of the most effective C2L campus projects. Between 2011 and 2015, across our 24-campus network, C2L teams led professional development for more than 4,700 faculty and staff. Outreach events, such as presentations at department meetings, reached 6,700 faculty and staff.

Across the network, campuses employed a range of different professional development structures, often calibrating their strategies to campus-specific cultures, resources available to support professional development, and the institutional priority placed on teaching. Some C2L teams focused on workshops, and others developed summer institutes, teaching circles, and longer seminars. Some experimented with mini-grants, online professional development, and digital training modules. Before we examine ways that teams applied the Inquiry-Reflection-Integration design principles, it is helpful to understand the different structures they used.

> **Getting Started**
> **Tip 2: Form a Partnership: Work With Your Campus Center for Teaching and Learning**
>
> Growing numbers of colleges nationwide have established Centers for Teaching and Learning (CTLs) on their campuses. When they are robust, these professional development centers can be valuable partners for an ePortfolio initiative.
>
> CTLs are often led by faculty and staff with extensive experience leading professional learning processes. They are familiar with models, strategies, and mechanisms for offering meaningful professional development. They may or may not have specific ePortfolio experience, but their valuable skills can be adapted to address integrative social pedagogy. Connecting an ePortfolio initiative with the resources represented by a CTL can be a critical factor in determining its success.

Workshops and Institutes

A number of C2L campuses offered short two- to three-hour workshops for faculty and staff. Some workshops focused on ePortfolio technology, and others included introductory discussions on integrative pedagogy. Some workshops complemented more extended processes. The Hunter College C2L team described faculty workshops they ran for the master's program in literacy education in the following:

> Before the revamped ePortfolio was launched in the fall of 2011, the Literacy faculty met to learn about the design structure of the revamped ePortfolio and provide feedback and suggestions, and more importantly, to lend their support. This workshop was essential, as faculty need to understand the importance of building an organizational culture that values reflective and integrative learning. After it was launched, workshops were held for the Literacy faculty to navigate Digication, focusing more on empowering them as they learn to contribute to the ePortfolio process and experience the outcome of ePortfolio learning communities.[11]

Hunter and other C2L teams also sought to go beyond one-shot workshops. Most teams saw that a two- to three-hour workshop could, at best, introduce participants to an ePortfolio platform and point toward integrative ePortfolio pedagogy. A workshop offers little time for building community and thinking systemically. Consequentially, the most effective teams sought to extend the time span of the professional development process and move from introducing possibilities to supporting implementation. One approach was to create a workshop series, asking faculty and staff to commit to attending two or three sessions. An alternative approach was to hold an intensive, one-time-only, multi-day workshop. C2L teams at Norwalk Community College and Virginia Tech used this approach. The Norwalk team explained how it worked, recounting the following:

> Through experience, we have learned that the most effective structure for our faculty ePortfolio training is a two day "boot camp," which includes, later in the semester, one or two roundtable workshops where past/present users share successes and challenges as well as their student ePortfolios with the new practitioners. . . . The format is highly interactive, incorporating readings that provide the theoretical basis (distributed prior to the training), small and large group discussion, reflection, hands-on technical instruction, and some fun activities such as the "Digitective" virtual scavenger hunt, which requires that they search the Internet for key information about ePortfolios, and their own ePortfolio "mini" showcase.[12]

Teaching and Learning Circles and Seminars

One variation on this approach was to organize a workshop series called a Teaching and Learning Circle (TLC). A highly flexible structure, Teaching and Learning Circles tend to be small and relatively unstructured. Usually, in a TLC, a group of 8 to 10 faculty meet monthly for roughly an hour to informally discuss a teaching issue of common interest and share experiences. As the Manhattanville team tells us,

> TLCs were designed to strike a balance between having enough sessions and enough time on task to really get involved and engaged in the learning process, and not creating a program so intimidating that no one would willingly sign up. The balance we agreed upon was a four-session, face-to-face format of [90 minutes] each."[13]

In this "boot camp" approach, the emphasis was on faculty practice. Receiving a small stipend, every participant committed to using ePortfolio in his or her classes, often in the following semester. "We designed each session to include a mixture of discussion, based on a reading or readings focusing on new pedagogy, hands-on training utilizing the Digication platform, and sharing of results."[14]

The team from Pace University took a similar approach, saying

> We have continued to hold teaching circle seminars in fall and spring. Participants in the three-session seminars read about and discuss ePortfolio pedagogy and assessment and agree to incorporate ePortfolios into their courses the following semester. They earn stipends and get one-on-one support from the ePortfolio "e-terns" in building their ePortfolios and developing assignments. This is a very important means of expanding our ePortfolio program.[15]

The advantages of the Teaching and Learning Circle model are flexibility and low start-up costs. The disadvantage is that it does not provide structured support for faculty as they use ePortfolio with students. It can be a good step on a campus where an ePortfolio initiative is in its early phase.

Sustained Pedagogy Seminars

Seeking more sustained engagement, some C2L campuses offered professional development that combined intensive summer and midyear institutes with monthly seminars. One advantage of this approach is that it offers greater time for exploration, helping faculty and staff learn more deeply about ePortfolio and carefully redesign courses and co-curricular processes to integrate ePortfolio practice. Sustaining the community of practice while participants implement ePortfolio-enhanced courses and events offers opportunities for celebrating successes, troubleshooting problems, gathering evidence, and building reflective practice. Often organized with a campus Center for Teaching and Learning, most sustained seminars provide participants with incentives such as stipends or reassigned time.

Aiming to help faculty and staff plan, share, teach, and reflect on integrative ePortfolio practices, LaGuardia Community College has used a year-long seminar model for more than a decade with considerable success. LaGuardia's ePortfolio-focused seminars are part of a broader professional development effort, deeply embedded in LaGuardia's campus culture. Each year, the LaGuardia Center for Teaching and Learning offers 10 to 15 concurrent year-long seminars, focusing on different issues in teaching and learning, ranging from designing learning communities to strengthening advisement practice, global learning, and writing in the disciplines. Faculty

---

Getting Started
Tip 3: Build Faculty Leadership

Effective ePortfolio-related professional development depends on faculty engagement. It must respect faculty expertise, recognize faculty realities and concerns, and address faculty needs. Taking this seriously means involving faculty as partners in designing, leading, and assessing professional development processes.

There are meaningful professional development roles for staff. Professional development staff from a Center for Teaching and Learning, IT staff, advisement professionals, and ePortfolio specialists can all play key roles. But they cannot be a substitute for vocal faculty leaders who can mobilize their experiences using ePortfolio with students.

The most effective ePortfolio initiatives link faculty and staff as partners in leading professional development processes. The demands on faculty time make seminar leadership challenging. Faculty leaders need not only reassigned time but also staff partners who can handle logistics, ensure continuity, and provide additional expertise. A partnership model combines the vital contributions of faculty leaders with the sustained effort essential to ePortfolio success.

> **Getting Started**
> Tip 4: Design for
> Sustained Engagement
>
> Changes in practice take time and mastering integrative ePortfolio pedagogy can be particularly challenging. The most effective ePortfolio professional development unfolds over time, creating opportunities for faculty to carefully explore, consider, design, test, and reflect on new pedagogical strategies and practices.
>
> One-shot workshops can introduce faculty to ePortfolio practices. But they don't support faculty as they move from abstract exploration to concretely testing ePortfolio practices with their students. Putting new strategies into practice and observing the results can only take place over time. And bringing faculty back together to discuss what they did and what students learned in their ePortfolio assignments plays a critical role in helping faculty take ownership of ePortfolio practice.

and staff apply to take part and receive stipends for participation; they can report on their work in applications for promotion. Each year, more than 200 faculty and staff successfully complete a year-long seminar.

Over the past decade, one stream of LaGuardia seminars has focused on ePortfolio pedagogy. ePortfolio-related seminars have included "The ePortfolio Explorer"; "ePortfolio in the Professions"; "New to College: Rethinking the First-Year Seminar"; "The Art of Advisement"; "Rethinking the Capstone Experience"; and "Connected Learning: ePortfolio and Integrative Social Pedagogy." "Through participation in these seminars," the team noted, "faculty enjoy the opportunity to review, revise, experiment, and then implement new pedagogies in targeted courses to be taught in the Spring I semester of the academic year."[16] In its C2L portfolio, the LaGuardia team described the Capstone seminar, which served faculty teaching the capstone course in different disciplines and Connected Learning, open to faculty teaching any course college-wide, providing them with an introduction to the basics of ePortfolio practice.

> Connected Learning: ePortfolio and Integrative Pedagogy brings together faculty from across the disciplines to learn about ePortfolio and to develop new approaches to using it as an integrative tool in their classes. Faculty in the seminar create ePortfolios to document their professional growth, learning through this hands-on process and discovering new ways of implementing ePortfolio meaningfully and effectively with their students. The result is a greater attention to connections—between students and their classmates, between students and faculty, and between students and audiences outside of the classroom—made visible through the ePortfolio.

In Rethinking the Capstone Experience, the College's faculty take stock of existing capstone courses in their respective departments and redevelop them based on national best practices in the field. Faculty in this seminar strike a balance between the content and professional standards of their disciplines and established models for capstone learning grounded in integration, reflection, transition, and closure. In this setting, ePortfolio offers a useful medium through which students can represent the totality of their "capstone experience.[17]

Two notable trends have added new variations to LaGuardia's practice. The first is that the Center for Teaching and Learning has begun to offer more professional development for staff. Seminars on advisement bring faculty together with professional advisors and peer mentors to share expertise. At the same time, the Center has begun incorporating ePortfolio use as a subtheme in seminars that primarily focus on other topics such as advisement, as well as seminars focused on LaGuardia's new first-year seminar. In these seminars, ePortfolio practice is contextualized as one element in a complex combination of issues, tools, and pedagogies. The focus on ePortfolio is less intensive, but the new seminars assist faculty and staff in seeing new uses for ePortfolio and advance the process of making ePortfolio a pervasive part of the student experience at LaGuardia.

Hybrid/Online Training

Some C2L teams tested variations on these structures. Two campuses offered professional development resources and conversation online; others used a hybrid format, blending face-to-face and online activities. These formats were most attractive to campuses offering online courses and training adjunct faculty.

Offering most of its courses online, the City University of New York (CUNY) School of Professional Studies offers its professional development in a hybrid format, which reaches a wide audience, including part-time faculty. The process begins with a day-long face-to-face meeting, followed by an online discussion that spans two months and focuses on reflective pedagogy. Faculty examine extensive online ePortfolio resources as part of this structured conversation. The final session is, again, face-to-face, and serves as a celebratory reunion.[18]

Northeastern University offers fully online faculty development targeted to reach adjunct faculty. "Because many of our faculty teach online and/or are adjuncts, our faculty development has taken place virtually," the Northeastern team wrote. "We have offered several webinar workshops that have also been archived and made available to all faculty."[19] Despite the difference in delivery mode, Northeastern's goals are similar to those of other C2L programs.

> The core issue, when it comes to professional development, is to extend faculty vision beyond the technology (ePortfolio as tool) to perceive it as a driver for improvement of student learning and curricular integrity. Our core accomplishment is that professional development surrounding ePortfolios leads to faculty investment in improving the integrity of the program.[20]

Online professional development was also used as part of the C2L project itself, creating a hybrid community of practice linking our 24 campuses in ongoing conversation about ePortfolio practice. C2L's hybrid professional development structure effectively used ePortfolios to document and share practices, modeling for

Getting Started

Tip 5: Model Integrative
ePortfolio Pedagogy

Effective ePortfolio-focused professional development not only
addresses integrative pedagogy
but also models it for faculty,
embedding integrative practice
and experience into the professional development process itself.

Angelo suggests professional
development leaders must practice what they preach.[22] To get
faculty to learn how to use collaborative learning with students,
a PowerPoint presentation won't
work. A seminar that engages
faculty in collaborative learning
and helps them think about the
implications of their experience
will be much more powerful.

Similarly, professional development focused on integrative
ePortfolio practice must prompt
faculty to use reflection and
make connections, helping them
experience an integrative process. Having faculty plan, document, reflect on, and share their
teaching experience in their own
digital portfolio can be a valuable
professional learning experience.

participants professional development strategies they could implement on their campuses.[21]

Mini-Grants

Some C2L teams use professional development Mini-Grants. LaGuardia offers a Mini-Grant Program for out-comes assessment work, helping faculty use ePortfolio in programmatic learning and change. Professional development helps program faculty "close the loop" designing and implementing change based on analyzing data in their Periodic Program Review (PPR):

During the PPR process in the business program, students were found to be underachieving in oral communication. Using a CTL Mini-Grant, the business faculty paired with faculty from the communication area to revise introduction to business courses to incorporate activities to improve business-appropriate oral communication skills.[23]

The University of Delaware team offered Mini-Grants to programs to integrate ePortfolio into degree curricula. Faculty in the Mini-Grant program completed a reflective semi-structured faculty interview as part of this process."[24] Through these interviews, campus leaders obtained feedback on ePortfolios in academic programs and suggestions on institutional modifications. At the same time, these interviews helped faculty learn from their experiences: "Faculty participated enthusiastically and demonstrated deep reflection and thought in their responses. Many stated that they welcomed the opportunity to talk with us as it helped them deepen their understanding of the portfolio purpose, process, gains and challenges."[25]

Inquiry, Reflection, and Integration in Professional Development

As this survey suggests, C2L campuses shared a wide range of professional development practices, demonstrating a range of structures used to support faculty and staff learning and advance sophisticated integrative ePortfolio practice. Across all approaches and different levels of engagement and intensity, we found that effective professional development practices employed the design principles of Inquiry, Reflection, and Integration.

Professional Inquiry

In a professional development context, inquiry provides opportunities for participants to ask questions and explore their own teaching practices and their relationship to student learning. Inquiry-based professional development asks faculty and staff to use their classrooms and co-curricular events as laboratories for experiments with new pedagogies and practices. Inquiry approaches encourage participants to grapple with pressing questions and contrasting points of view on teaching and learning, pedagogy, curriculum design, and assessment. Inquiry helps to ground discussion of these questions in the real-life experiences of faculty, staff, and students.

ePortfolio-related professional development incorporates inquiry by asking participants to explore ePortfolio pedagogy, consider how to fit ePortfolio into their own practice, and investigate the impact on student learning. While serving as the subject of inquiry, the ePortfolio can also make changes in student learning visible for examination in the professional development space. Shared

> **Getting Started**
> **Tip 6: Connect With and Across Departments**
>
> Departments are powerful centers of campus life. Disciplinary concepts and habits of mind shape faculty practice. The department is where faculty spend most of their time on campus and is often the site of promotion and tenure processes as well as everyday interaction. Connecting to departments, recognizing their significance, and helping them adapt ePortfolio practice to their needs can deepen the impact of ePortfolio initiatives.
>
> At the same time, it is valuable to engage faculty in cross-disciplinary professional development. Linking faculty across disciplines can spark pedagogical creativity and build the cross-campus community often missing in higher education.
>
> Powerful ePortfolio initiatives connect student learning across semesters, linking discipline courses with first-year seminars, general education, internships, co-curricular learning, and capstone experiences. To realize the potential of integrative ePortfolio practice, professional development designers must bring faculty and staff together to build cohesive vision and connected practice.

review of students' ePortfolios creates opportunities to consider the complex dynamic between teaching and student learning. Using ePortfolio to contextualize pieces of student work with an understanding of the student's broader experiences can help faculty and staff think in new ways about students.

Most C2L teams combine individual and collective inquiry in the professional development process, asking faculty to jointly explore relevant literature, generate

Getting Started
Tip 7: Support Faculty
Engagement

When faculty engage in ePortfolio-related teaching and professional development, they are committing precious time and attention. To sustain that commitment, institutions must find ways to reward faculty focus on ePortfolio innovation.

There are many ways to support faculty engagement in the professional development process. Stipends or honoraria for participation in sustained processes are common. Recognition in departmental or collegewide communications are welcome. Creating faculty showcases at the end of seminars where faculty can share and discuss their work with the broader campus can help faculty feel that their time is valued.

The most powerful way to recognize faculty participation in ePortfolio-related professional development is through the tenure and promotion process. When these reward processes recognize faculty commitment to improving teaching and learning, faculty are much more likely to take the risk of trying out new approaches.

questions, experiment in their classrooms, and return to the group for shared conversation. For example, a group of faculty in a seminar might consider ways to use social pedagogy with ePortfolio, help each other plan experiments in their courses, and then meet to discuss findings. Or faculty and staff might, through professional development linked to assessment, explore the types of student learning taking place in a particular program. Through this process, faculty and staff can identify gaps in curriculum and instruction.

Collective inquiry is sometimes directly connected to outcomes assessment. An authentic outcomes assessment process that involves guided inquiry on student learning outcomes often becomes an opportunity for professional learning. When this process generates recommendations for change in programmatic practice, professional development is often needed to implement the recommendations.

Manhattanville College uses collaborative, cross-disciplinary inquiry to shape their ePortfolio-focused Teaching and Learning Circles. Driven by an inquiry-oriented design process, they reported the following:

> We ask faculty and staff to participate in a needs assessment process in which they are first asked to identify their instructional/programmatic goals and outcomes. With goals and outcomes in place, participants are asked to reflect on the degree to which their current practices work to meet those goals. Identifying gaps between where they want to be and where they are sets up an inquiry process in which they can ask genuine questions about the ways in which ePortfolio can be used as a pedagogical tool to help bridge that gap or to transform ineffective strategies/practices.[26]

Sophisticated inquiry requires focused time. Investigative teams may start with a set of questions about teaching and learning and systematically explore them together; alternatively, the inquiry structure could be more exploratory and self-directed, as participants review relevant research and develop their own research questions. Year-long professional development seminars at LaGuardia use a model of extended inquiry, slowly unfolding inquiry processes across several months or semesters.

Professional development sometimes incorporates professional portfolios as a space for documenting inquiry and supporting reflection. Faculty in LaGuardia's programs often build a seminar portfolio where they share initial designs for teaching with ePortfolio. They use the commenting functions of the ePortfolio platform to give each other feedback and help sharpen draft plans. And as students create portfolios, faculty can link to their students' ePortfolios, using evidence to deepen the inquiry process.[27]

This type of inquiry can connect with the scholarship of teaching and learning (SoTL), a systematic inquiry into one's practice. Spurred by the Carnegie Foundation for the Advancement of Teaching, SoTL has gained wide currency in higher education. Rigorous SoTL helps faculty gain deeper understanding of their craft and publish their findings.[28] Linking ePortfolio to SoTL opens new possibilities for deepening practice and advancing the field.

Reflective Practice

Reflection is fundamental to powerful professional development. Building directly on inquiry, reflection helps participants make meaning out of their own experiences and those of their students. Reflective professional development deepens faculty and staff learning and helps them develop as practitioners. As Dewey scholar Carol Rodgers explains:

> The power of the reflective cycle seems to rest in the ability first to slow down teachers' thinking so that they can attend to what is, rather than what they wish were so, and then to shift the weight of that thinking from their own teaching to student learning.[29]

As discussed in Chapter 3, Rodgers outlined a four-stage cycle for scaffolding reflection: (a) being present in the experience, (b) describing the experience, (c) analyzing the experience, and (d) shaping plans for new experiences (see Figure 4.2). When used in professional development, this inquiry process grounds reflection in faculty's own classroom experiences. At the same time, it can help participants move past presenting lesson plans and highlighting successes to engaging in a more productive professional learning process.[30] "I have two goals when using the reflective cycle in my work with teachers," Rodgers notes:

> The first is to develop their capacity to observe skillfully and to think critically about students and their learning, so they learn to consider what this tells them about teaching, the subject matter, and the contexts in which all of these interact. The second goal is for them to begin to take intelligent action based on the understanding that emerges.[31]

In a professional development context, reflective activities help participants document and share their learning, becoming more reflective practitioners. Reflections

Figure 4.2. Carol Rodgers' Reflective Cycle.

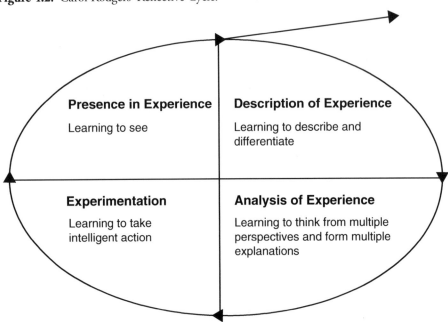

Presence in Experience

Learning to see

Description of Experience

Learning to describe and differentiate

Experimentation

Learning to take intelligent action

Analysis of Experience

Learning to think from multiple perspectives and form multiple explanations

Source. From Carol Rodgers, "Defining Reflection: Another Look at John Dewey and Reflective Thinking," *Teachers College Record* 104, no. 4 (2002). Reprinted with permission of Carol Rodgers.

can be written, oral, artistic, or multimedia in form, taking place individually or in a community. Reflection allows participants to connect experiences and integrate new knowledge. Through reflection, participants think in new ways about High-Impact Practices, integrative pedagogies, and classroom-based ePortfolio assignments.

Professional reflection can take different forms. Workshops often use brief reflective activities such as an open-ended post-seminar survey. Longer, more intensive professional programs allow for staged written and oral reflections, giving faculty and staff time to make meaning of their successes and challenges. The common process of lesson sharing creates possibilities for reflective thinking, particularly when the process is scaffolded to encourage faculty to move from "what I did" to "what students did," from pedagogical design to the complex realities of classroom implementation, and from a description of teaching to an analysis of student learning and grounded consideration of implications.

Peer mentorship programs and retreats can also create opportunities to reflect. Reflection in community can move beyond making meaning at the course level to spotlighting broader challenges, such as gaps in disciplinary curricula, college-wide approaches to new technologies, and cross-disciplinary strategies to address general education and integrative learning goals.

C2L teams used a variety of reflective professional development practices. Teaching and Learning Circles are often reflective by design. The Pace University team notes, "Reflection and Integration are two key principles of the TLC curriculum. Regarding reflection, we highlight Mahara's [Pace's ePortfolio platform] journal feature. Participants create their own journals to reflect on each session."[32]

Reflection is also an important component in Northwestern Connecticut Community College's professional development seminars. To allow enough time for richer and more meaningful reflections, Northwestern's team extended the seminar program to span the entire academic year. According to one member of the team, "if utilizing ePortfolio can help faculty become more effective reflective practitioners, then they will be able to both model and guide students in meaningful reflection to enhance learning."[33]

Guttman Community College uses institution-wide collective reflection to strengthen professional development and outcomes assessment. At two-day-long meetings built into the College's annual calendar, faculty and advisors work together to assess student achievement and reflect on the alignment of outcomes at the assignment, course, and program level. The Guttman team reported:

> The Assessment Days reflect Guttman's commitments to using ongoing assessment to guide professional development and improve institutional practice and to maintaining student learning as the driver for all decisions made throughout the institution. The Days have three main purposes: 1) assessing student achievement of learning outcomes in their work on integrated assignments; 2) reflecting on the alignment of assignment, course, program, and institutional outcomes; and 3) evaluating student progress as a guide for planning and revising curricula and determining course offerings for subsequent semesters.[34]

Reflection deepens ePortfolio-focused professional development. Linking reflective professional learning with the power of ePortfolio to make student learning visible, ePortfolio-based professional development can not only help participants become more proficient with ePortfolio pedagogy; done well, it can also help them become more focused on students, develop as reflective practitioners, and support transformative student learning campus-wide.

Integrative Learning

Integration, or integrative learning, helps students make connections and transfer knowledge across disciplines, semesters, and experiences. In a professional learning context, integration takes on new meaning. Here it helps faculty and staff transfer specific knowledge from a particular experience to broader contexts, extending to sustained practice, adaptation to other courses, and changes in departmental or college practice. Integration is operative when faculty and staff apply insights from one experience to another, deepening innovations and turning creative, one-shot experiments into broadly adopted changes.

Integration as backward design is a feature of Manhattanville's teaching circles. Participants discuss integrative learning strategies and ways to apply these strategies in their classrooms and curriculum.

Integration is one of the most important goals of the teaching circle. Rather than simply use ePortfolio as an add-on, we encourage participants to think about how they might re-envision their curriculum, possibly do some "backward design" in order to incorporate the ePortfolio as both a space for students to process their learning (do the "intermittent thinking" that Randy Bass refers to), and to showcase the products of their learning (and develop some rubrics).[35]

Cross-disciplinary programs provide an opportunity for integration as faculty and staff build interdisciplinary communities of practice for change at the departmental or institutional level. These communities allow participants to critique each other's assignments, course designs, and assessments in a collegial manner, integrating new learning into their practices. Integration provides an opportunity to implement pedagogical innovations in broader classroom contexts.

Integration that fosters interdisciplinary collaborations between faculty and staff can spur institutional change by deepening the learning that takes place beyond the classroom. LaGuardia's year-long professional development seminar, "Art of Advisement: Learning and Implementing Holistic Advisement Skills," creates a professional learning community consisting of faculty and student affairs staff. The community explores ePortfolio's role in helping students integrate their curricular and co-curricular learning and the use of ePortfolios for improved advisement. Faculty and staff work together to apply their shared learning to advance a meaningful and effective advisement structure for students. According to the LaGuardia team, "The integration of faculty and staff in this seminar stresses the idea that it takes an entire college community to support a meaningful and effective advisement structure for students."[36]

Integration is key to developing a broad and effective ePortfolio initiative. Faculty and staff are expert learners; they have mastered the ability to transfer knowledge from abstract to specific in their own disciplines. Professional development can leverage these expert learning skills to help faculty and staff connect theories about integrative, reflective ePortfolio pedagogy to their courses and co-curricular experiences. Conversely, integration encourages faculty and staff to transfer lessons learned to new settings. Insights developed through classroom-based inquiry can be extended when faculty apply them to new courses. Taking those insights into broader conversations about programmatic curricula and institutional policy creates opportunities to design for coherence and create more integrative learning experiences for students.

Connections to the *Catalyst Framework*

Pedagogy

Professional development and pedagogy are mutually dependent. To build a high-impact ePortfolio initiative, faculty need guided opportunities to explore integrative ePortfolio pedagogy and incorporate it into their practice. At the same time, integrative pedagogy should inform the design of ePortfolio-related professional development, or "practicing what we preach."[37] Modeling integrative processes in the professional learning context adds depth and resonance to the professional learning process.

Outcomes Assessment

On campuses with robust ePortfolio initiatives, we found that professional development substantially overlapped with outcomes assessment. Meaningful professional development incorporates attention to evidence, helping faculty think about learning as well as teaching. Building a culture of evidence, in which faculty think about the impact of their designs, professional development can help faculty value outcomes assessment. Meanwhile, dynamic outcomes assessment programs often use professional development as a key step in closing the loop. Grounding assessment in artifacts of student learning can facilitate this linkage, making it easier for faculty to use professional development processes to identify and design the changes needed to improve student outcomes.

Technology

ePortfolio-focused professional development must significantly focus on pedagogy. But it must also address technology. If faculty aren't comfortable with an ePortfolio platform, they cannot guide students in using it. Faculty need to be comfortable not only designing ePortfolio activities but also reviewing and commenting on students' ePortfolio work. Having faculty build their own ePortfolios and use them for sharing, commentary, and exchange is one way of helping faculty become increasingly familiar with the platform they and students will use.

Scaling Up

Professional development advances the broad faculty and staff engagement that is crucial to scaling an ePortfolio initiative. At the same time, the success of professional development is in many ways dependent on the broader campus context. Professional development requires a commitment of resources to compensate leaders and incentivize participants. A campus culture that values teaching and rewards faculty who focus energy on learning-centered innovation can facilitate the effective professional development needed for ePortfolio success.

Conclusion

Professional development is a critical component in the cultivation of a robust campus ePortfolio initiative. C2L research shows that effective ePortfolio-related professional development activities are guided by the design principles of Inquiry, Reflection, and Integration. These principles come to life when collective classroom-based inquiry and recurring reflections help faculty and staff generate deeper understanding about teaching and learning. Thoughtful professional development, in combination with attention to the other Catalyst sectors, can advance the development of vibrant learning organizations. When that happens on a broad scale across higher education, the potential of ePortfolio practice for building student learning and transformative change will begin to be realized.

Notes

1. Bret Eynon, Laura M. Gambino, and Judit Torok, "What Difference Can ePortfolio Make?: A Field Report from the Connect to Learning Project," *International Journal of ePortfolio* 4, no. 1 (2014): 95–114.

2. Randy Bass and Bret Eynon, *Open and Integrative: Designing Liberal Education for the New Digital Learning Ecosystem* (Washington, DC: Association of American Colleges & Universities, 2016).

3. Phil Hill, "Pilots: Too many ed tech innovations stuck in purgatory," *e-Literate,* August 12, 2014, http://mfeldstein.com/pilots-many-ed-tech-innovations-stuck-purgatory

4. Emily Lammers, Gates Bryant, Adam Newman, and Terry Miles, "Time for Class: Lessons for the Future of Digital Courseware in Higher Education," accessed August 20, 2015, http://www.onlinelearningsurvey.com/reports/EGA009_CourseWP_Upd_Rd7.pdf

5. Thomas A. Angelo, "Doing Faculty Development as If We Value Learning Most: Transformative Guidelines from Research to Practice," *To Improve the Academy* 19 (2001): 225.

6. Angelo, "Doing Faculty Development," 225–237.

7. Pat Hutchings, "Fostering Integrative Learning Through Faculty Development," 2006, http://gallery.carnegiefoundation.org/ilp/uploads/facultydevelopment_copy.pdf, 6

8. Hutchings, "Fostering Integrative Learning," 6.

9. Mary Deane Sorcinelli, Ann E. Austin, Pamela L. Eddy, Andrea L. Beach, *Creating the Future of Faculty Development: Learning From the Past, Understanding the Present* (San Francisco, CA: Jossey-Bass, 2005), 28.

10. Debra Dawson, Joy Mighty, Judy Britnell, "Moving From the Periphery to the Center of the Academy: Faculty Developers as Leaders of Change," *New Directions for Teaching and Learning* (2010): 69–78. doi:10.1002/tl.399

11. Gina Cherry, "Connect to Learning Annual Report: Hunter College," (unpublished annual report, 2014).

12. "Norwalk CC—Reflecting to Learn: Professional Development Practice at NCC," *Catalyst for Learning: ePortfolio Resources and Research,* January 25, 2014, http://c2l.mcnrc.org/ncc-pd-practice/

13. Alison Carson, Jim Frank, Gillian Greenhill Hannum, Kate Todd, and Sherie McClam, "Professional Development Practice—Teaching and Learning Circles," *Catalyst for Learning: ePortfolio Resources and Research,* January 25, 2014, http://mville.mcnrc.org/pd-practice/

14. Carson et al., "Professional Development Practice."

15. Beth Gordon, "Connect to Learning Annual Report: Pace University," (unpublished annual report, 2014).

16. J. Elizabeth Clark, "Faculty Development Practices at LaGuardia: Capstone Courses, ePortfolios, and Integrative Learning," *Catalyst for Learning: ePortfolio Resources and Research,* January 25, 2014, http://lagcc.mcnrc.org/faculty-development-practices-laguardia-rethinking-the-capstone-experience-seminar/; Howard Wach, "Faculty Development Practices at LaGuardia: Connected Learning Professional Development Seminar," *Catalyst for Learning: ePortfolio Resources and Research,* January 25, 2014, http://lagcc.mcnrc.org/pd-practice-3/

17. J. Elizabeth Clark, "Faculty Development Practices at LaGuardia: Capstone Courses, ePortfolios, and Integrative Learning," *Catalyst for Learning: ePortfolio Resources and Research,* January 25, 2014, http://lagcc.mcnrc.org/faculty-development-practices-laguardia-rethinking-the-capstone-experience-seminar/; Howard Wach, "Faculty Development Practices at LaGuardia: Connected Learning Professional Development Seminar," *Catalyst for Learning: ePortfolio Resources and Research,* January 25, 2014, http://lagcc.mcnrc.org/pd-practice-3/

18. CUNY School of Professional Studies "Hybrid/Online Professional Development Practice," *Catalyst for Learning: ePortfolio Resources and Research,* January 25, 2014, http://sps.mcnrc.org/pd-practice/

19. Gail Matthews-DeNatale, "Connect to Learning Annual Report: Northeastern University," (unpublished annual report, 2014).

20. Ibid.

21. Bret Eynon, Laura M. Gambino, and Judit Torok, "Connect to Learning: Using e-Portfolios in Hybrid Professional Development," *To Improve the Academy* 32 (2013): 109–126.

22. Angelo, "Doing Faculty Development."

23. Stacy Provezis, "LaGuardia Community College: Weaving Assessment Into the Institutional Fabric," June 2012, http://www.learningoutcomeassessment.org/documents/LaGuardiaCC.pdf, 7.

24. Kathleen Pusecker and Nancy O'Laughlin, "Connect to Learning Annual Report: University of Delaware," (annual report, 2014).

25. "Faculty Development via Reflective, Semi-Structured Interviews," *Catalyst for Learning: ePortfolio Resources and Research,* January 25, 2014, http://ud.mcnrc.org/ud-pd-practice/

26. Sherie McClam, "Faculty Development Offered With a Lot of 'TLC'," *Catalyst for Learning: ePortfolio Resources and Research,* January 25, 2014, http://mville.mcnrc.org/pd-story/

27. Wach, "Faculty Development Practices."

28. Pat Hutchings, Mary Taylor Huber, and Anthony Ciccone, *The Scholarship of Teaching and Learning Reconsidered: Institutional Integration and Impact* (San Francisco, CA: Jossey-Bass: 2011).

29. Carol Rodgers, "Seeing Student Learning: Teacher Change and the Role of Reflection," *Harvard Educational Review* 72, no. 2 (Summer 2001): 231.

30. Rodgers, "Seeing Student Learning," 231.

31. Ibid, 231–232.

32. Pace University, "Professional Development Practice: ePortfolio Teaching Circles," *Catalyst for Learning: ePortfolio Resources and Research,* January 25, 2014, http://pu.mcnrc.org/pd-practice/

33. Catalyst for Learning, "Northwestern Connecticut Community College—Professional Development in Action—Building Opportunities for Habitual Reflective Practice," *Catalyst for Learning: ePortfolio Resources and Research,* January 25, 2014, http://c2l.mcnrc.org/nccc-pd-story/

34. Laura M. Gambino, "Putting Students at the Center of Our Learning: Connecting Assessment and Professional Development," *Catalyst for Learning: ePortfolio Resources and Research,* January 25, 2014, http://gcc.mcnrc.org/pd-practice/

35. Alison Carson, "Connect to Learning Annual Report: Manhattanville College," (unpublished annual report, 2014).

36. Craig Kasprzak, "Advising With ePortfolio: Professional Development," *Catalyst for Learning: ePortfolio Resources and Research,* January 25, 2014, http://lagcc.mcnrc.org/pd-practice-2/

37. Angelo, "Doing Faculty Development," 225.

5

OUTCOMES ASSESSMENT THAT CLOSES THE LOOP

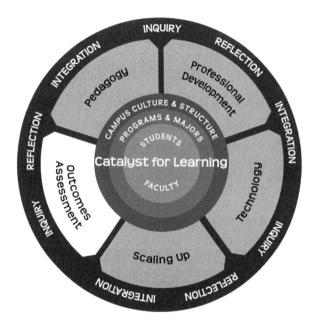

Done well, guided by integrative pedagogy and sustained professional development, ePortfolio practice can deepen student learning. But ePortfolio practice can also advance faculty and institutional learning, helping colleges engage in iterative cycles of improvement. This chapter examines the ways high-impact ePortfolio practice supports authentic assessment and helps build what we will call "learning colleges."

Focused on the Outcomes Assessment sector of the *Catalyst Framework*, this chapter begins by setting the stage, contextualizing assessment in the currents of change sweeping higher education and explaining what we mean by authentic assessment and learning colleges. We then look at examples of effective ePortfolio-based assessment practice, drawn from C2L campuses, that illuminate the power of the Inquiry, Reflection, and Integration (I-R-I) design principles, and the ways these principles can guide the development of meaningful assessment processes. Throughout the chapter, in our Getting Started boxes, we discuss key steps campuses can take to launch and sustain an effective ePortfolio-based assessment program.

Outcomes assessment is, of course, a charged topic in higher education. Legislators, federal agencies, and accreditation bodies push colleges to assess and report on the quality of the education they provide. Faculty often associate assessment with standardized testing, something done for others that has no value for their own practice. But assessment can be entirely different; a meaningful way for educators to deepen their understanding of their craft. High-impact ePortfolio practice can play an important role in helping shift the ways educators approach assessment.

Based on national surveys, the National Institute for Learning Outcomes Assessment (NILOA) released a report that pointed to significant progress on key mechanisms of outcomes assessment: identification of outcomes, development of rubrics, and communication of findings.[1] The vital next step, NILOA found, is the need to more effectively engage faculty in the assessment process:

> First and foremost, attention needs to be directed to involving more faculty in meaningful ways in collecting student learning outcomes data and using the results. . . . Indeed, if there is one matter on which almost everyone agrees—administrators, rank-and-file faculty members, and assessment scholars—it is that faculty involvement is essential both to improve teaching and learning and to enhance institutional effectiveness.[2]

ePortfolio-based outcomes assessment work can help colleges not only meet accountability needs but also engage faculty and staff in powerful professional and institutional learning processes. Using ePortfolio can help campuses ground assessment in the authentic work of students. Examining student work in an ePortfolio can help faculty and staff take part more fully in the assessment process, connecting institutional learning outcomes to everyday practice and considering curricular (and co-curricular) improvements based on assessment findings. Done well, ePortfolio-based outcomes assessment creates a transformative learning cycle, spurring improvement for students, faculty, programs, and the entire institution. Connecting ePortfolio to assessment is critical to realizing the full potential of high-impact ePortfolio practice.

Accountability, Assessment, and Institutional Learning

At least since the 2005 Spellings Commission on the Future of Higher Education,[3] outcomes assessment has been shadowed by debate over *accountability*. In higher education, accountability involves the pressure put on colleges to prove they are effective. According to the National Council of State Legislatures,

> States are looking at ways to increase the efficiency and productivity of their postsecondary institutions. . . . States are setting goals for higher education, creating metrics to measure performance, and holding colleges and universities accountable for meeting state goals. Some states are taking their accountability system a step further and are awarding state higher education funding based on institutional performance.[4]

This pressure grew under President Barack Obama. In July 2015 Secretary of Education Arne Duncan spoke about the need to pay more deliberate and increased attention to accountability in higher education. He argued that educators should continue to "concentrate on boosting student success through shared responsibility and accountability for outcomes."[5]

Many accountability advocates call for standardized national examinations and so-called "institutional report cards" that require colleges to report on outcomes such as graduation or job acquisition. Assessment that focuses narrowly on accountability is sometimes referred to as *assessment OF learning*. Faculty and staff who see assessment as a means of satisfying accountability demands often resist it, seeing no benefit to their everyday work with students. In part, as a result, assessment remains a conflicted activity on some campuses.

Other assessment leaders argue for more authentic forms of assessment.[6] Rather than focus on standardized tests, this type of assessment practice engages faculty and staff in an examination of classroom-generated student work in relation to institutional learning outcomes. Faculty and staff can then learn from this examination and consider the implications of the assessment for their own practice, making changes to improve student learning. We refer to this type of assessment as *assessment FOR learning*.

> **Getting Started**
> Seven Steps to Effective ePortfolio-Based Assessment
>
> 1. **Identify outcomes**: Develop clear, measurable outcomes at the course, program, or institutional level.
> 2. **Develop rubrics for each outcome**: Create a set of criteria and levels of achievement for each learning outcome.
> 3. **Complete a curriculum mapping process and organize assignment design workshops**: Identify which learning outcomes are assessed in each course and work with faculty to design assignments that address those outcomes.
> 4. **Identify mechanisms and structures for assessment**: Consider who, what, where, and when in relation to assessment.
> 5. **Create a pilot process that engages faculty and staff**: Start with a small group of interested participants.
> 6. **Showcase successes**: Build broad understanding, acceptance, and engagement by sharing what you learn with others on campus.
> 7. **Develop an assessment plan and timeline**: Create an assessment plan that aligns with institutional goals and plans and share with campus stakeholders to ensure buy-in.

Assessment *for* learning helps move institutional improvement to a more central place in faculty and staff work. According to Linda Suskie, assessment for learning "engage[s] faculty and staff, so the assessment becomes a useful part of the fabric of campus life."[7] Done well, this type of assessment engages participants in a process of Inquiry, Reflection, and Integration. There is a shift from thinking solely about "my course" to considering how a course or program is situated in a larger institutional context. As Peggy Maki explains, when "driven by internal curiosity about the nature of our work, assessment becomes a core institutional process, embedded into definable processes, decisions, structures, practices, forms of dialogue, channels of communication, and rewards."[8]

ePortfolio practice is an effective method for involving faculty and staff in assessment for learning, and its use in such assessment is growing. A study showed that the number of campuses using ePortfolio for programmatic and general education assessment has exploded, more than tripling between 2009 and 2013.[9] As Kuh and colleagues wrote, "Portfolios are a form of authentic assessment that draw on the work students do in regular course activities."[10]

Moreover, because integrative ePortfolio pedagogy encourages deep learning and holistic thinking, ePortfolios can offer richer artifacts for authentic assessment. As Suskie notes, the combination of ePortfolio pedagogy and ePortfolio-based outcomes assessment "encourages students, faculty, and staff to examine student learning holistically—seeing how learning comes together—rather than through compartmentalized skills and knowledge."[11]

Done well, ePortfolio-based outcomes assessment meets the needs of external and internal stakeholders, complementing student success data with assessment evidence grounded in authentic student work. It helps engage faculty and staff in the assessment process, connecting institutional outcomes to classroom and co-curricular practices. Guided by the I-R-I principles, ePortfolio-based outcomes assessment can spur student, faculty, and institutional learning, helping colleges develop a culture of learning and advance as learning organizations.

ePortfolio and the Learning College

The concepts of learning organizations, organizational learning, and learning cultures are well documented in the research literature. Peter Senge discusses organizational learning, identifying the need to make learning a social process integrated into institutional culture.[12] Organizational learning, according to Argyris and Schön, takes place when members of an organization act for it and learn for it, pursuing an inquiry process that leads to organizational knowledge. That learning and knowledge then become part of the organization's culture.[13]

How does this concept of a learning organization translate to higher education? In a learning college, student learning has to be the central, enduring focus of attention; yet, students are not the only ones who learn. Faculty, staff, and executive leadership are also learners, engaging in an ongoing examination of what can be done to advance student learning and success. According to Central Piedmont Community College,

A learning college places learning first and provides educational experiences for learners any way, anywhere, anytime. Its mission is not instruction, but to produce learning with every student by whatever means work best. The college itself is a learner, continuously learning how to produce more learning with each entering student.[14]

In a learning college, student learning is the subject for recursive cycles of Inquiry, Reflection, and Integration at the student, faculty, program, and institutional levels. This ongoing process creates a culture of learning. High-impact ePortfolio practice can play a key role in supporting this process. It can help colleges become more agile learning organizations, better able to navigate today's changing higher education landscape.

To become true learning organizations, colleges must focus outcomes assessment on authentic student work, connected to real classroom and co-curricular activity. ePortfolio practice helps campuses collect and organize student work for general education and programmatic competencies. Reviewing student ePortfolios, faculty and staff can more easily make concrete recommendations to improve curriculum and pedagogy. This makes it easier to close the loop and implement changes that improve student learning. As these processes are woven into the fabric of an organizational culture, institutions move toward becoming true learning colleges.

Challenges of an ePortfolio-Based Assessment Structure

Developing an ePortfolio-based assessment process can be challenging. In the Getting Started boxes throughout the chapter, we share a set of strategies that will help campus leaders get started on the path to effective ePortfolio-based outcomes assessment.

Using authentic student work in assessment creates opportunities to see inside courses and programs and to

---

Getting Started
Step 1: Identify Outcomes

The first step toward building an ePortfolio-based assessment process is to identify at what level you will conduct your initial assessment—course, program, or institutional—and the outcomes you will assess.

Campuses often build an ePortfolio-based assessment structure by beginning at the individual course level, using Inquiry, Reflection, and Integration processes to identify curricular needs in classroom teaching and learning practices. ePortfolio and assessment leaders then look for opportunities to connect these course-level efforts to broader program or general education outcomes assessment efforts.

Other institutions begin work at the program or major level, engaging small groups of faculty and staff in assessment using program-level outcomes. Many of these schools also incorporate development or collection of student ePortfolios for assessment in a capstone course.

Some schools begin with assessment of institution-level student learning outcomes. Getting started at the institution level can be challenging. In this case, we recommend assembling a small group of participants to begin working with and scaling up assessment efforts over time.

No matter which option you begin with, you will want to ensure that learning outcomes are clear and measurable.

look closely at student learning. Although valuable in many ways, this experience can be uncomfortable for faculty used to working in isolation. It is important to acknowledge concerns and build in time and space—through professional development and other opportunities—to help faculty and staff see the value in this work for their own teaching and learning practices.

Overcoming faculty and staff resistance to assessment doesn't happen overnight. Creating a meaningful assessment process takes time—time to build the mechanisms; engage student, faculty, and staff in assessment activities; and integrate improvements. There is much work involved as well. Assessing portfolios, reflecting, and designing recommendations takes effort. College leaders must value the time and effort required to do authentic assessment and close the loop.

Effective assessment requires a whole college effort. It cannot be relegated to a single assessment leader or small group of faculty. ePortfolio-based outcomes assessment, when done well, engages all areas of an institution, connecting faculty and staff across disciplines and departments; it encompasses curricular and co-curricular student learning experiences and connects academic affairs, student affairs, Centers for Teaching and Learning, and institutional research in a sustained conversation about learning. To manage this requires careful attention as well as ongoing connection and coordination between campus ePortfolio and assessment leaders.

ePortfolio-Based Outcomes Assessment and Learning

Most campuses in the Connect to Learning project used ePortfolio to integrate the review of authentic student work into outcomes assessment. Some focused on assessment of particular programs, others on general education. On some C2L campuses, this work was in a rudimentary stage; on others, it was advanced, attracting support from administrators along with participation from key faculty and program leaders. We found that the C2L campuses doing the most effective assessment work used the following practices that embodied the design principles of Inquiry, Reflection, and Integration:

- Framing assessment as an *inquiry* into student learning highlights its scholarly nature, making it more engaging and rewarding.
- Incorporating *reflection* helps transform assessment into an individual and collective learning opportunity and moves the focus from findings to recommendations for change.
- In an assessment context, *integration* involves closing the loop, applying the recommendations emerging from reflective assessment to the active processes of changing pedagogy and practice, curriculum, and even institutional structure.

If we think of assessment as an ongoing cycle, these three principles align with a cyclical assessment process of gathering and evaluating data, recommending action,

Figure 5.1. LaGuardia Community College's Core Competency Assessment Cycle.

Assessment Cycle

Faculty Development
Faculty design assignments addressing competencies in specific courses.

Classroom Implementation
Faculty test new competency-focused assignments with students.

Integration

Inquiry

Core Competency Assessment Cycle

Gathering Evidence
Students deposit work that demonstrates learning in ePortfolio.

Designing Change
Programs use CTL mini-grants to design change processes.

Analysis & Recommendation
Faculty analyze data, identify needs and recommend changes in curriculum and pedagogy.

Assessment of Student Work
Faculty review student work against rubrics.

Reflection

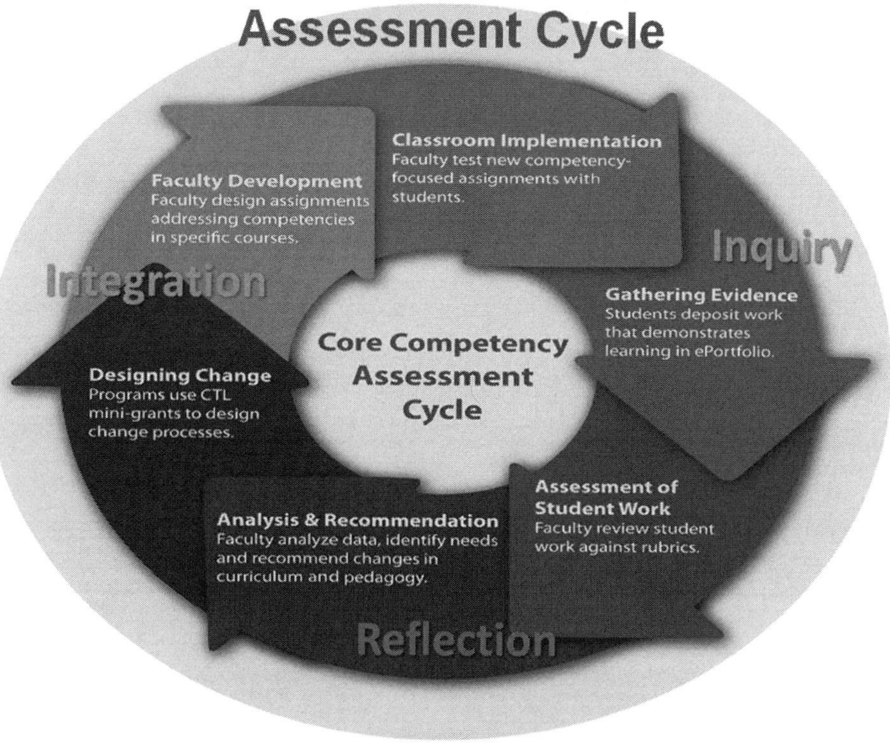

Source. Reprinted with permission of LaGuardia Community College (CUNY).

and implementing changes based on evaluation findings (see Figure 5.1). Let's more closely examine the ways inquiry, reflection, and integration support the assessment cycle, looking at practices from some of the C2L schools.

Inquiry

Inquiry is central to effective, learning-focused outcomes assessment implementation. Assessing for learning, according to Maki, "is a systematic and systemic process of inquiry into what and how well students learn over the progression of their studies and is driven by intellectual curiosity about the efficacy of collective educational practices."[15]

On C2L campuses where ePortfolio-based assessment is well established, assessment is understood as a structured inquiry process, focused on questions related to student learning and improvement. Assessment leaders engage faculty in an inquiry process, based on evaluating student work. The ePortfolio functions as the vehicle to provide access to specific artifacts of student work; in some cases, the ePortfolio itself serves as evidence for evaluation. Groups of faculty and staff examine and score student work in relation to either program or institutional outcomes using assessment rubrics.

The C2L network offers multiple examples of this inquiry process. At Boston University, ePortfolio-based assessment takes place in the College of General Studies,

---

Getting Started
Step 2: Develop Rubrics for
Each Outcome

To effectively assess student learning, most institutions create rubrics for their learning outcomes. Some schools use the Association of American Colleges & Universities VALUE Rubrics, others modify those rubrics, and some develop their own rubrics.

Rubrics are most effective when they are clear, concise, and easy to use. The best rubrics are developed through iterative processes of development and testing against authentic student work.

---

a two-year program. Using ePortfolio to gather student work, college leaders launched an assessment process to evaluate how well students achieved program outcomes. The university's C2L team worked with a small group of faculty in an inquiry process: "The assessment committee in charge of this project, made up of 11 faculty members, met once a month for a year to assess student ePortfolios as a group."[16] As part of an ongoing process, faculty members now assess student ePortfolios each summer.

Similarly, in the nursing program at Three Rivers Community College, ePortfolio practice is integrated across the curriculum, helping students articulate and illustrate their development as twenty-first-century nursing professionals. Using these rich portfolios, faculty and staff analyze student work using standardized rubrics to measure attainment of program outcomes as well as qualitative statement analysis. Data are shared, reviewed, and discussed at faculty retreats.[17]

At IUPUI, "most, if not all, of the approximately 40 programs that have adopted ePortfolio are making some use of it for assessment," using rubrics and practices calibrated to programmatic needs.[18] IUPUI's C2L team notes that assessment is conceptualized as "a faculty-led inquiry into student learning. . . . A key value that ePortfolios add to common practice is that they can support nuanced understandings of strengths and areas for improvement."[19]

LaGuardia uses ePortfolio-based artifacts for assessment of college-wide general education and its majors. LaGuardia has collected more than 130,000 artifacts of student learning, which are sampled and examined against rubrics by faculty teams that identify recommendations and action plans for improvement. In the assessment process, faculty explore key questions such as, "What do we want students to learn, why, and how can we measure that learning?" The philosophy for outcomes assessment at the college is one of "appreciative inquiry" that asks the questions, "What do you do well? What can you do better?"[20]

At Guttman Community College, where ePortfolio is used with all students across their curricular and co-curricular experiences, all faculty and staff take part in mid- and end-of-semester Assessment Days, built into the academic calendar. On these days, faculty and staff use ePortfolios to assess the Guttman Learning Outcomes (GLOs), following a systematic, intentional inquiry and reflection process: "Our Assessment Days provide the community ample opportunities to use ePortfolio-based outcomes assessment as a point of inquiry for asking the larger questions about student learning."[21]

On all these campuses, framing assessment as an inquiry into student learning and then using ePortfolios to examine authentic student work creates an engaging environment for faculty and staff. This process connects institutional assessment to everyday classroom and co-curricular practices and sets the stage for the reflection phase of the assessment cycle.

Reflection

Once faculty have analyzed student work for evidence of learning, they turn to interpretation. Reflection is critical in this process, helping faculty to make meaning from their findings and identify recommendations for curricular and pedagogical change. The reflection phase of ePortfolio-based outcomes assessment spurs faculty and campuses to move beyond accountability, deeply reviewing assessment findings and their implications. Reflection on evidence and findings can help transform outcomes assessment into professional and institutional learning, and support change in practice at multiple levels.

Following Rodgers' framework, we find reflection conducted in the assessment cycle is systematic and disciplined, carefully scaffolded, and takes place on a regular basis at the course, program, and

> **Getting Started**
> **Step 3: Complete a Curriculum Mapping Process and Organize Assignment Design Workshops**
>
> If you are assessing program or institutional learning outcomes, creating a curriculum map is a key step for aligning courses and artifacts with learning outcomes. A curriculum map is a matrix that identifies the learning outcomes that are assessed in each course in a program or major. Some institutions identify the particular assignment that aligns with the outcomes identified for each course.
>
> Once the mapping process is complete, organize assignment design workshops. These workshops can help faculty and staff develop and revise assignments to address the outcomes identified in the curriculum map. Led by Pat Hutchings, NILOA has developed an assignment design charrette workshop model[22] that can be useful for this effort. Charrettes provide a structure that is collaborative and reflective, with opportunities for participants to discuss and receive constructive feedback on their assignments.

institutional levels.[23] We also see campuses reflecting in community, as groups of faculty, staff, and administrators join in a collective conversation. When fully realized, the process embodies an attitude toward change, often generating organized efforts to implement new curricula and pedagogy.

At Guttman, every Assessment Day includes time for reflective conversation. Based on data and observations from the ePortfolio assessment, faculty and staff discuss strengths and areas for improvement. GLO assessment teams, subsets of the

Valid Assessment of Learning in Undergraduate Education
Terry Rhodes, AAC&U

One of the most widely examined and used assessment instruments in the United States currently is the Valid Assessment of Learning in Undergraduate Education (VALUE) rubrics. As the Spellings Commission called for educational accountability and generated resistance from multiple higher education organizations and institutions, the AAC&U received a grant from the Fund for the Improvement of Post-Secondary Education to create the VALUE rubrics as an alternative to standardized tests.[24]

Available for free download at www.aacu.org/value-rubrics, the 16 VALUE rubrics address key competencies for higher learning, including Inquiry and Analysis, Creative Thinking, Written Communication, Quantitative Literacy, Problem Solving, Civic Engagement, Global Learning, and Integrative Learning.

The rubrics were created by teams of multidisciplinary faculty from a wide array of institutional types, tested through three rounds of campus-based faculty assessing their own students' authentic work, revised based on the feedback, and finally released in fall 2009.

The VALUE rubrics were premised on the following five primary suppositions:

1. Faculty (absent in the focus of the Spellings report) share expertise and a broadly based consensus on the key components of learning outcomes for undergraduate students essential for success as civically engaged, global citizens and productive contributors to the economy;
2. Learning is enhanced when faculty articulate for themselves and their students their expectations for learning on all the shared outcomes, such as with rubrics and performance descriptors;
3. Learning is not something that occurs once and is done but rather is an iterative and progressively more complex process that occurs over time and in multiple instances;
4. The best demonstration of student learning is most likely to occur in response to assignments from faculty in the student's formal curriculum and co-curriculum; and
5. Assessment is about formative improvement for learning, which, when done well, also can provide necessary evidence for summative accountability purposes without additional testing or work for students or faculty.

Since their release in the fall of 2009, the rubrics have gained wide campus use. As of December 2015, the rubrics have been accessed by more than 42,000 individuals from more than 4,200 unique institutions, including more than 2,800 colleges and universities.

AAC&U is now engaged in a new phase of the VALUE initiative. With support from major foundations, AAC&U is strengthening the psychometric reliability of the rubrics and partnering with state education systems to advance comprehensive use of the VALUE rubrics in authentic assessment.

larger group, are then responsible for harvesting that conversation and creating recommendations for improvement.[25]

Similarly, Northeastern University faculty in the Graduate School of Education held an all-day reflective retreat to discuss the ePortfolios they assessed. This became an opportunity for faculty to express concerns about what they observed in the portfolios, specifically discussing "observations that could not be gleaned from the demographic data typically gathered about students."[26] They wrestled with the implications of their findings in relation to the following questions:

> Did we need to reconsider program admittance and/or realign the curriculum to the needs of pre-professional students? Were we missing the mark in achieving integrated program learning outcomes? Was there a problem with the ePortfolio requirement implementation? The consensus was that it was a combination of all three, and this informed subsequent reformulation of the program.[27]

This reflective retreat gave faculty the time and space to consider what they learned from their ePortfolio review and identify next steps for their collective work in the program.

LaGuardia engages faculty in annual collegewide Benchmark Readings for general education and organizes majors into sustained three-year conversations for Periodic Program Reviews. Both processes build in reflection: faculty "examine artifacts of learning, reflect on the teaching and learning process, and consider changes in pedagogy and curriculum needed to close the gap between what students already know and what they need to learn."[28]

The assessment committee at BU's College of General Studies reflects as a community on its assessment data. They discuss how to interpret these data and translate the information into improvements in the program.[29] They have also considered their student learning findings in relation to other national studies of student performance.[30]

As shown by these C2L examples, ePortfolio-based assessment processes incorporate reflection and encourage

---

Getting Started
Step 4: Identify the Mechanisms and Structures for Assessment

Before conducting any sort of assessment, ePortfolio and assessment leaders must work together to identify the mechanisms for gathering ePortfolios and distributing them to faculty and staff conducting the assessment. Many ePortfolio platforms have assessment systems that automate this process and help faculty access rubrics as well.

It is always helpful to think about the who, what, where, and when questions in relation to assessment. Will faculty and staff be doing this outside their everyday responsibilities? If so, how will that work be recognized by the institution?

Thinking through the steps of the assessment process will help eliminate potential roadblocks. Addressing potential questions ahead of time will also result in smoother implementation.

Getting Started
Step 5: Create a Pilot Process That Engages Faculty and Staff

Many schools introduce ePortfolio-based outcomes assessment as a pilot activity. Pilots build experience with the use of ePortfolio in a holistic assessment process, demonstrating the effectiveness of the process before systematizing a long-term implementation plan. Are programs interested in assessment or ePortfolio or both? Schools often begin with programs that already use assessment as part of an external accreditation process, such as allied health, business, or engineering, as they are more familiar with assessment activities.

It's important for leaders to consider how the I-R-I design principles help systematize a learning-based practice and develop a process to

- bring faculty together to examine ePortfolios,
- reflect in community about what they learned,
- recommend curricular improvements, and
- integrate those recommendations into practice.

This process can prepare the ePortfolio team and other key stakeholders for scaling up your campus assessment work as outlined in Steps 6 and 7.

grounded, collective conversation about student learning. As faculty and staff consider the implications of assessment findings and recommend specific curricular and co-curricular changes, the process supports individual and institutional learning and change.

Integration

The integration and application of new understandings emerging from inquiry and reflection advances the assessment cycle. In outcomes assessment, integration is associated with closing the loop, taking action based on evidence-based recommendations. Designing and implementing new curricula or pedagogical strategies to improve student learning is central to assessment that emphasizes integration. Integration can also require addressing institutional structure, steps that involve campus leaders, budgets, and governance. Assessment that emphasizes integration is part of a continual process of institutional improvement.

Across the country, most outcomes assessment programs fall short of closing the loop, failing to turn assessment findings into effective educational change. In 2009, Trudy Banta examined the assessment programs of 150 colleges and found that only 6% provided evidence that their processes advanced student learning.[31] On C2L campuses where ePortfolio practice was done well, we found a number of campuses successfully taking this step.

On some C2L campuses, the most fully realized assessment work tends to take place in a specific major. At Three Rivers Community College, the nursing program integrated ePortfolio practice into its curriculum and its assessment process. "Examining students' artifacts, reflections and ePortfolio designs, we found validation for our work—but also surprises," the C2L team wrote. "This important process added life and meaning to student learning and engaged faculty in the effort to deepen our curriculum and our teaching."[32] They go on to tell us that

> Our outcomes assessment process integrated General Education Core Values and program outcomes. Using rubrics calibrated to our scaffolded assignments, we reviewed student work, assessing for critical thinking, information literacy, communication, professionalism, reflective and integrative learning. This inquiry process supported faculty reflection that highlighted areas where change was needed, and development of integrative action plans. In one semester, for example, when we assessed the process recordings stored in student ePortfolios, we found the scores did not reach therapeutic communication levels. Meanwhile, in student reflections, we found that students had expressed discomfort with patient communication. Reflecting on these findings, we decided that students needed additional experiences to develop their communication skills. To "close the loop," we implemented a set of interventions: faculty development related to process recordings; student exercises in class; and the development of a new clinical experience in a senior center. Similarly, information literacy reviews led us to generate an online module for constructing annotated bibliographies.[33]

> **Getting Started**
> Step 6: Showcase Successes
>
> What did you learn from your pilot? Did faculty and staff make improvements to their courses or programs based on assessment data? Showcasing successes and sharing what was learned is a key step in building acceptance and support. Encourage pilot participants to remain involved in the assessment process, helping to define an assessment plan and to lead and engage their colleagues.

Northeastern University's graduate education faculty engaged in a similar process. Focusing on their master's program, they moved from examining student ePortfolios and reflecting on the implications to taking integrative action. According to Gail Matthews-DeNatale, faculty engaged in comprehensive curriculum redesign and "transformed the program from a collection of courses into an intentionally designed learning experience. Features of the new program include: co-designed cognitive apprenticeship, orientation to the professional context, integrated opportunities for connected experiential learning, variation nested within continuity, and looking back to look ahead." The impact on curriculum integration was particularly striking:

> The first three to four courses in each concentration have been co-designed by faculty as an integrated suite that takes students through a 'cognitive apprenticeship' in the skills, understandings, and capabilities of professionals within the field. They are designed to foster connected learning, in which each course builds upon and complements the rest, and the faculty have a clear understanding of how "their" courses intersect with and reinforce other courses in the program.[34]

Engaged in a similar process on a college-wide scale, LaGuardia was recently commended by the Middle States Commission for Higher Education for its exemplary outcomes assessment process that closed the loop:

> As the faculty in a major complete their PPR [Periodic Program Review] Report, they can apply for an ePortfolio/Assessment Mini-Grant to help them implement their own recommendations for program-wide pedagogical and curricular improvement. The Mini-Grants are often used to support curricular change and faculty development, refining and implementing pedagogies and assignments that build students' General Education Core Competencies.[35]

LaGuardia's outcomes assessment team provided multiple examples of how mini grants support closing the loop, such as this from the business department:

> When Business Administration and the Business Management programs assessed student work around the general education oral communication competency in 2010, they found that students did not perform well. Using a Mini-Grant, they partnered with faculty from Communication Studies to revise the Introduction to Business courses to address oral communication skills. Students gave an initial oral presentation, which was taped and deposited into the ePortfolio. Then, a faculty member from Communications Studies did a one-hour intervention about how to conduct more effective presentations. Students reviewed their presentations and redid them taping them a second time for a pre/post comparison. 60% of students showed improvement on oral communication, and overall scores improved from 3.05 to 3.675. As a result, this intervention is mandated in all Introduction to Business courses, and the program plans to extend it to other courses as well, making it a more sustained and scaffolded effort. Other Business-related programs are learning from their efforts and making efforts to include more oral communications assignments in their business-specific courses.[36]

In spring 2013, LaGuardia's assessment leaders took another step toward greater transparency and shared learning. At a college-wide faculty meeting, six programs that had recently completed ePortfolio-based PPRs reported on their work, sharing findings, recommendations, and action plans. This public discussion of concrete examples of closing the loop is another key step in the ongoing efforts to cultivate a culture of learning at LaGuardia.

At Boston University, faculty and staff engage in the reflection process with their faculty and identified areas of improvement specifically related to the College of General Studies' quantitative reasoning outcome. Based on their findings, they refined the curriculum to more intentionally integrate quantitative reasoning in courses across the program (see Figure 5.2).[37] Taking the lessons learned from this assessment process one step further, ePortfolio leaders at BU now have an assessment framework that can be applied to other curricular and co-curricular programs.

As these examples illustrate, C2L teams that have been most successful at implementing ePortfolio-based outcomes assessment build the I-R-I design principles into

Figure 5.2. Boston University's College of General Studies Assessment Results.

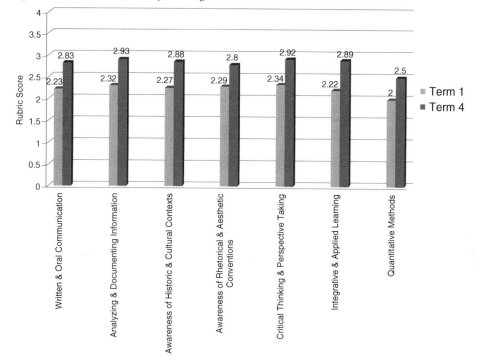

Source. Results from Boston University's ePortfolio assessment comparing first-semester student work with fourth-semester student work. Reprinted with permission of Boston University.

specific campus practices. The employment of these strategies as part of an integrative, high-impact ePortfolio practice spurs institutional change, leading to a culture of institutional learning grounded in authentic student work.

Connections to the *Catalyst Framework*

The power of the *Catalyst Framework* emerges from the interconnection of the five sectors, as well as the I-R-I principles. On its own, ePortfolio-based outcomes assessment has value. Connections to other *Framework* sectors can enhance the power of assessment to inform student, faculty, and institutional learning, helping institutions become adaptive learning organizations.

Pedagogy

Used with the I-R-I design principles, ePortfolio-based outcomes assessment enables faculty and staff to identify and implement recommendations for curricular and pedagogical improvements. Often these recommendations encourage the use of integrative, reflective, and social pedagogies to deepen student learning. Using ePortfolio in

Transforming Teaching Culture With Integrative Outcomes Assessment
Gail Matthews-DeNatale, Northeastern University

ePortfolios provide a window into student meaning-making and self-perception. Viewed as a whole, an ePortfolio is a construct of identity created by the student. Viewed as a collection, ePortfolios depict a community of learners, making it possible to spot patterns that are not readily apparent in enrollment statistics.

This process of discernment is best positioned as an evidence-informed conversation among students, faculty, and administrators about the impact of program design on learner growth, and about opportunities for improvement (assessment *for* learning as opposed to assessment *of* learning). The conversation is intentional and leads to decisions about next steps, but it is also an ongoing process and not a one-time evaluative task.

This is the philosophy that informed the master of education program's process for curriculum revision in 2011. We kicked off the redesign with a faculty retreat. Prior to that gathering each person was given a set of ePortfolios for review. The inquiry prompt for discussion was simple: What do you observe in the ePortfolios?

The faculty retreat provided an opportunity for community reflection. There were many surprises. For example, our curriculum was designed for education professionals who had at least several years of experience, but many of our students were fresh out of college or career changers. The content of some portfolios revealed deep misconceptions about systems for education, and many were not presenting themselves in a professional manner.

These insights increased our sense of direction and purpose as we integrated recommendations from the retreat into the curriculum redesign process. We created a mission statement and articulated outcomes, the aspirations that we held for our students. We revised and developed new courses designed to enculturate students into the profession of education. Each course in the new curriculum includes one or two signature assignments, authentic work that maps to program outcomes. Students incorporate these assignments into their ePortfolios, and the eLearning and Instructional Design Program also requires its students to include a final reflection for each course.

This program redesign process is in accordance with the Inquiry, Reflection, and Integration design principles that are central to the learning of students, educators, and organizations. What can we learn from a review of the ePortfolios generated by our students (inquiry)? What insights do we gain from the review about the strengths and opportunities for improvement in our work (reflection)? How can we leverage those insights to improve our course, curriculum, program design, and facilitation (integration)?

(Continues)

(Continued)

The revised curriculum launched in fall 2013. Students complete the program in one to two years, and so we had our first in-depth review of the postrevision ePortfolios in spring 2015.

We were happy to see that student portfolios from the revised curriculum are more polished and represent a much deeper understanding of education as a profession. However, we also noted that students are still not making as many connections across courses as we would like. Following the meeting we revised the capstone course to guide students through an intentional process of mining their ePortfolios to look for connections across coursework. The signature assignment for that class is to author an integrative professional portfolio, a showcase site for public readership that makes explicit connections between the author's strengths in life, learning, and work.

There is an energy and excitement to doing something new. However, provisions must be made to engage newcomers, people who weren't there when the innovations were instigated. Dialogue about the purpose of ePortfolio also needs to be shared and ongoing, or over time the I-R-I process can be perceived as top-down and routinized.

For example, during a review, faculty found it more difficult to assess program impact when students' signature work was not accompanied by reflection. The master's program includes four concentrations; some stress reflection more than others. The review discoveries sparked a discussion about the value of embedding reflection in all ePortfolio work, such as prompting students to reflect on curricular connections and their development in relation to program outcomes.

If the assessment conversation is grounded in inquiry, in genuine curiosity, then gaps can be perceived as opportunities instead of failures. Insights, however challenging, are an opportunity to take programs to the next level of excellence, with the shared goal of invigorated learning.

the assessment process can also allow faculty and staff to see models of these practices in action.

Ironically, the twin power of ePortfolio pedagogy and assessment can create a dilemma for campus ePortfolio leaders. Is it better to focus first on working to integrate ePortfolio pedagogy into courses and programs? Or is it better to have assessment drive the ePortfolio initiative, hoping that it will, in turn, spur interest in pedagogy? Is it possible to tackle both at once?

There is no one right answer to such questions. The decision will depend on a number of factors related to institutional situation and context. From our work with C2L campuses, we've seen that any of these approaches can be successful.

Some schools begin their ePortfolio work focused on reflection, integrative learning, and student success and introduce ePortfolio-based assessment later. LaGuardia's ePortfolio team emphasized pedagogy first and began with assessment after several years.

Getting Started
Step 7: Develop an Assessment
Plan and Timeline

As you scale up your assessment work, you will need a plan
and timeline to guide the assessment process. A plan should
consider details such as overall
goals, stakeholder expectations, necessary resources, and
training and support structures.
Additionally, outline the steps
of the assessment process and
the ways results will be used to
guide change and improvement.
    It will be helpful to engage
key stakeholders in the development of the assessment plan to
get their buy-in before sharing it
institution-wide. Some schools
use their governance structures
for formal endorsement of the
assessment plan. Other campuses build assessment activities into the college's strategic
planning process, signifying
institutional recognition of the
importance of assessment.
Whether or not you use either of
these routes, having a plan and
sharing it broadly will help support the series of steps needed to
scale up a high-impact ePortfolio-
based assessment initiative.

As they did so, they were able to draw on the expertise and the faculty leadership developed in the earlier phases.[38]

In contrast, Salt Lake Community College's ePortfolio work began with an institutional mandate to use it for general education assessment. ePortfolio and assessment leaders focused initially on having students use the ePortfolio to document their learning in their general education courses. Once that process was established, ePortfolio leaders began working with faculty to understand the ways ePortfolio pedagogy could enhance student learning.[39]

Professional Development

Professional development is critical to the success of an ePortfolio-based outcomes assessment process. Assessment activities can be a professional learning process in and of themselves, particularly when faculty and staff come together to reflect on their review of student portfolios. But, professional development is also critically important to the integration phase of the assessment cycle. Professional development can help faculty and staff to close the loop and integrate course, curricular, and co-curricular improvements. Professional development workshops such as assignment design charrettes can also help faculty and staff improve assignments and activities, making outcomes more transparent to students.[40] As discussed in Chapter 4, using ePortfolio in the professional development process can model pedagogies that enhance student learning and support an effective outcomes assessment process.

Technology

ePortfolio-based assessment is difficult without an effective ePortfolio platform. Highly functional ePortfolio technology not only provides the space for students to connect, reflect, and self-assess on their "whole" student learning experience but also serves as a vehicle for faculty and staff to evaluate student work. Many ePortfolio platforms also provide the technological mechanisms to organize ePortfolios for assessment, distribute those portfolios to assessment participants, and facilitate data tracking. Assessment leaders can then use the ePortfolio platform to analyze assessment data.

Scaling Up

Institutional stakeholders are much more likely to endorse an ePortfolio project if it supports effective outcomes assessment, in part because of growing pressures around accreditation. But assessment also supports other aspects of Scaling Up. Effective assessment processes involve the whole college, encouraging cross-campus connections. ePortfolio-based outcomes assessment can generate collective conversation about learning, helping faculty and staff break out of traditional silos. And successful assessment processes can encourage additional faculty, majors, and programs to adopt ePortfolio practice, adding breadth to campus ePortfolio use. Using student ePortfolios in the assessment process makes learning visible across campus boundaries, builds connections among different areas, and supports shared attention to changes that improve student learning.

Conclusion

C2L findings highlight the important role ePortfolio practice can play in outcomes assessment at the course, program, and institutional level. ePortfolio practice not only offers students the ability to integrate disparate student learning experiences but also provides an institution with a holistic picture of the ways learning takes place across the different sectors of their college. Our findings suggest that ePortfolio's capacity to make student learning visible can play a major role in facilitating authentic assessment. Used in conjunction with an I-R-I framework, effective ePortfolio-based outcomes assessment has the potential to spur learning and improvement at the course, program, and institutional levels, enabling campuses to move beyond accountability as they focus on becoming learning colleges.

Notes

1. George D. Kuh, Natasha Jankowski, Stanley O. Ikenberry, and Jillian Kinzie, *Knowing What Students Know and Can Do: The Current State of Student Learning Outcomes Assessment in U.S. Colleges and Universities* (Bloomington, IN: National Institute for Learning Outcomes Assessment, 2014).

2. Kuh et al., *Knowing What Students Know and Can Do*, 34.

3. Margaret Spellings, *A Test of Leadership: Charting the Future of U.S. Higher Education.* (Washington, DC: U.S. Dept. of Education, 2006), http://www2.ed.gov/about/bdscomm/list/hiedfuture/reports/final-report.pdf

4. Brenda Bautsch, "Higher Education Accountability: Briefing Document Prepared for the California Legislature," December 3, 2012, http://www.ncsl.org/documents/educ/AccountabilityBrief.pdf

5. Arne Duncan, "Toward a New Focus on Outcomes in Higher Education" (speech, University of Maryland-Baltimore County, Baltimore, Maryland, July 25, 2015). http://www.ed.gov/news/speeches/toward-new-focus-outcomes-higher-education

6. Linda Suskie, *Assessing Student Learning: A Common Sense Guide* (San Francisco: Jossey-Bass, 2009); Trudy W. Banta and Catherine A. Palomba, *Assessment Essentials Planning, Implementing, and Improving Assessment in Higher Education* (San Francisco: Jossey-Bass 2015); Peggy L. Maki, *Assessing for Learning* (Sterling, VA, Stylus, 2010).

7. Suskie, *Assessing Student Learning*, 37.

8. Maki, *Assessing for Learning*, 29.

9. Kuh et al., *Knowing What Students Know and Can Do.*

10. George D. Kuh et al., *Using Evidence of Student Learning to Improve Higher Education* (San Francisco, Jossey-Bass, 2015), 36.

11. Suskie, *Assessing Student Learning*, 204.

12. Peter M. Senge, *The Fifth Discipline: The Art and Practice of the Learning Organization* (New York: Doubleday/Currency), 1990.

13. Chris Argyris and Donald Schön, *Organizational Learning: A Theory of Action Perspective* (Reading MA: Addison-Wesley, 1978).

14. Central Piedmont Community College, "About the Learning College," accessed, August 20, 2015, https://www.cpcc.edu/learningcollege/about-the-learning-college

15. Maki, *Assessing for Learning*, p. xix.

16. Natalie McKnight, John Regan, Amod Lele, and Gillian Pierce, "Assessing General Education at Boston University's College of General Studies," *Catalyst for Learning: ePortfolio Resources and Research,* January 25, 2014, http://bu.mcnrc.org/bu-oa-story/

17. Lillian A. Rafeldt et al., "Reflection Builds 21st Century Professionals: ePortfolio and Nursing Education at Three Rivers Community College," *Peer Review* 16, no. 1 (Winter 2014).

18. Susan Scott and Susan Kahn, "Assessment Is Everyone's Business," *Catalyst for Learning: ePortfolio Resources and Research,* January 25, 2014, http://iupui.mcnrc.org/oa-story/

19. Scott and Kahn, "Assessment Is Everyone's Business."

20. Howard Wach, "The Story of a Learning College: The Evolution of Outcomes Assessment at LaGuardia," *Catalyst for Learning: ePortfolio Resources and Research,* January 25, 2014, http://lagcc.mcnrc.org/oa-story/

21. Laura M. Gambino, Chet Jordan, and Nate Mickelson, "Outcomes Assessment: Making Student Learning Visible," *Catalyst for Learning: ePortfolio Resources and Research,* January 25, 2014, http://gcc.mcnrc.org/oa-story/

22. Pat Hutchings, Natasha A. Jankowski, and Peter T. Ewell, *Catalyzing Assignment Design Activity on Your Campus: Lessons from NILOA's Assignment Library Initiative* (Urbana, IL: University of Illinois and Indiana University, National Institute for Learning Outcomes Assessment [NILOA], 2014). http://www.learningoutcomesassessment.org/documents/Assignment_report_Nov.pdf

23. Carol Rodgers, "Defining Reflection: Another Look at John Dewey and Reflective Thinking,' *Teachers College Record* ,104, no. 4 (June 2002): 842–866.

24. Margaret Spellings, *A Test of Leadership.*

25. Gambino et al., "Outcomes Assessment."

26. Gail Matthews-DeNatale, "Are We Who We Think We Are?" *Catalyst for Learning: ePortfolio Resources and Research,* January 25, 2014, http://neu.mcnrc.org/oa-story/

27. Matthews-DeNatale, "Are We Who We Think We Are?"

28. Wach, "The Story of a Learning College."

29. McKnight et al., "Assessing General Education."

30. Ashley Finley, *Making Progress? What We Know About the Achievement of Liberal Education Outcomes* (Washington, DC: Association of American Colleges & Universities, 2012).

31. Trudy Banta, *Designing Effective Assessment: Principles and Profiles of Good Practice* (San Francisco, CA: Jossey-Bass, 2009).

32. Lillian A. Rafeldt, Heather Jane Bader, Nancy Lesnick Czarzasty, Ellen Freeman, Edith Ouellet, and Judith M. Snayd, "Reflection Builds 21st Century Professionals: ePortfolio and Nursing Education at Three Rivers Community College," *Peer Review*, 16, no. 1 (Winter 2014).

33. Ibid.

34. Gail Matthews-DeNatale, "Are We Who We Think We Are? ePortfolios as a Tool for Curricular Re-design," *Journal of Asynchronous Learning Networks* 17, no. 4 (2014): 10.

35. Wach, "The Story of a Learning College."

36. Paul Arcario, Bret Eynon, Marisa Klages, and Bernard A. Polnariev, "Closing the Loop: How We Better Serve Our Students Through a Comprehensive Assessment Process," *Metropolitan Universities Journal* 24, no. 2 (2013): 21–37.

37. McKnight et al., "Assessing General Education."

38. Wach, "The Story of a Learning College."

39. David Hubert, "Assessing General Education Outcomes With ePortfolios at SLCC," *Catalyst for Learning: ePortfolio Resources and Research,* January 25, 2014, http://slcc.mcnrc .org/oa-story/

40. Hutchings et al., *Catalyzing Assignment Design Activity.*

6

THE "e" IN ePORTFOLIO

ePortfolio as Digital Technology

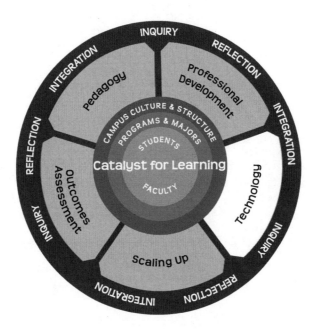

"What ePortfolio platform will be best for our campus?" This question inevitably arises at regional and national ePortfolio-related events. Beneath this seemingly simple question, however, lays a range of complex questions, such as, "What features of a platform are most important in supporting high-impact ePortfolio practice? How is ePortfolio technology different from other educational technologies, such as learning management systems? What's a smart process for selecting a platform and engaging students and faculty with its use?" This chapter explores such questions and clarifies the ways the Technology sector connects to the other sectors of the *Catalyst Framework*.

ePortfolio platforms are not new to higher education. Emerging in the late 1990s, ePortfolio platforms have since become more sophisticated with the integration of Web 2.0 functionality and are now easier for students and faculty to use. Our understanding of ePortfolios' role and purpose has also become more sophisticated. But even in those early days, some saw that their potential went beyond a simple digital storage device. As Trent Batson wrote, "[ePortfolio is] not a simple add-on to existing courses; if it is, students may not see the value. Indeed, if ePortfolio tools become just a simpler way to log student work, we've missed the boat."[1]

Most experienced ePortfolio users now understand ePortfolio as much more than a technology add-on. We have a much clearer sense of ePortfolio's potential in terms of improving student, faculty, and institutional learning. As Randy Bass argued, "ePortfolios are at heart a set of pedagogies and practices that link learners to learning, curriculum to the co-curriculum, and courses and programs to institutional outcomes."[2] Because of these linkages, ePortfolio technology is not a "plug and play solution" but one that requires collaborative planning.[3]

Although an effective ePortfolio project takes more than a platform, there are specific ways the technology shapes high-impact ePortfolio practice. How does an ePortfolio platform help engage students with Bass' set of interconnected pedagogies and practices to demonstrate a full range of contextualized, connected learning experiences? And how can it help them take ownership of their learning and develop richer conceptions of themselves as learners? In other words, what difference does the *e* make? We argue that the *e* in ePortfolio is vitally important to a successful ePortfolio initiative and must be included as one of the five key sectors of the *Catalyst Framework*. An awkward platform can frustrate users and stall an ePortfolio initiative. Conversely, an effective platform helps students leverage many elements of a high-impact ePortfolio practice. It does this in two salient ways.

First, effective ePortfolio technology helps make student learning visible. Making learning visible to students themselves, ePortfolio platforms enable students to reflect on and take ownership of their learning, becoming constructors of knowledge and active agents of their learning experience. Meanwhile, ePortfolio technology enhances faculty, staff, and institutional learning by making student learning visible to the entire institution as well as to viewers outside the walls of the academy. Families, external education providers, transfer institutions, and potential employers can all examine parts or wholes of a student's ePortfolio in order to better understand, contextualize, validate, support, and build on the learning they see in a student's ePortfolio. As the boundaries of higher education become more permeable, this latter capacity may take on new importance.

The second value of the *e* in ePortfolio technology is the way it creates a space for students to make connections among their different learning experiences inside and outside of classrooms. Most traditional demonstrations of learning focus on isolated, course-level learning experiences. A student's ePortfolio, on the other hand, has the potential to exist outside a single course experience, spanning courses and semesters. It can create a space for students to link academic and life experience and shape new identities as learners. Having a sustained, holistic learning space makes it easier for students to see and make connections among diverse learning experiences, in and beyond the classroom. It helps students to more easily connect, reflect on, and share diverse elements of their learning, bringing together curricular, co-curricular and experiential learning across the breadth and depth of their academic experience.

ePortfolio practice engages a student's learning over time across semesters, and an ePortfolio platform must effectively facilitate this. It is this fundamental capacity of ePortfolio technology that distinguishes it from a learning management system (LMS). An LMS can help make learning visible for connection and interaction, but it does so within the confines of a course. While connecting to courses, ePortfolios live outside a course environment. They are student-centric rather than course-centric; as such, they can span a student's entire learning experience from entry through graduation and beyond. This unique capability creates opportunities for students to evaluate and connect their learning across course, co-curricular, and lived experiences.

When these two capabilities—making learning visible and making connections—work in combination, students are able to see the ways they have grown and changed over time as they progress to earning their degree. The co-joined ability of an ePortfolio technology platform to make learning visible and serve as a comprehensive and connective space for learning helps to make ePortfolio powerful and in some ways unique in today's higher education digital ecosystem.

The Evolution of ePortfolio Technology

Before we examine the ways ePortfolio technology supports high-impact ePortfolio practice, it helps to briefly review the evolution of ePortfolio platforms. At the beginning of this century, platforms provided basic functionality—the ability to upload, reflect on, and organize artifacts of student work. Many of these initial platforms also provided the ability to share ePortfolios with different audiences: faculty, students, and external viewers. They were difficult to use, however, for students and faculty and offered little if any interactive capacity.

As Web 2.0 functionality emerged, ePortfolio vendors began to incorporate new features. In addition to uploading artifacts, students could create and embed photos and videos. Enhanced formatting and customizing an ePortfolio became more common; connections to social media tools and capacity for commenting slowly emerged. Many ePortfolio vendors also integrated assessment management systems, providing a powerful combination for institutions.

> **Getting Started**
> Five Steps for Making Your ePortfolio Platform Work
>
> If you're launching an ePortfolio initiative, following are five early, platform-related steps you can take that support a high-impact ePortfolio practice:
>
> 1. Collaborate with stakeholders to establish goals and needs.
> 2. Design and configure your ePortfolio platform.
> 3. Conduct pilot testing; develop an implementation plan.
> 4. Offer professional development that links technology and pedagogy.
> 5. Develop support structures for students, faculty, and staff.

Aligning with new understandings of ePortfolio practice, today's ePortfolio platforms have growing capacity for customization and interaction along with the ability to create multiple ePortfolios and to hide different sections of a portfolio. New assessment management systems streamline and simplify outcomes assessment. Many platforms integrate with LMSs or provide basic LMS capabilities. Some platforms can also connect to institutional student information services and other digital systems, although full integration with degree planning tools and other technology services is still on the horizon.

Which Platform Should We Choose?

Selection of an ePortfolio platform must go beyond examination of technical specifications and involve faculty, staff, and students, as well as information technology experts. Campuses must evaluate platforms in relation to their key pedagogical and learning priorities. No platform does everything well; the challenge is to find an ePortfolio platform that balances a range of priorities. To strike that balance, campuses with successful ePortfolio initiatives engage multiple stakeholders in a collaborative process that considers campus goals for learning, teaching, and assessment as well as the overall campus technology environment.

Collaboration

The process of selecting an ePortfolio platform requires collaboration among an array of campus stakeholders, including key faculty and staff, assessment leaders, IT managers, and other campus administrators. Reports from C2L campuses suggest that a collaborative process for selecting an ePortfolio platform not only improves the chances of selecting an effective platform but also helps these stakeholders focus on

Getting Started
Step 1: Collaborate With Stakeholders to Establish Goals and Needs

As you consider platform options, do your best to establish campus goals and needs for your ePortfolio work. What are you trying to accomplish? Who are the different users? What do you hope they'll do?

You'll need to get input from a broad range of stakeholders and potential users. It helps to have a selection committee that includes a range of perspectives, such as faculty, students, and assessment leaders, as well as IT. Agreement with campus leaders on a preliminary set of goals for ePortfolio is important.

A clear sense of goals and needs will help your campus review the range of possible platforms. Develop criteria, share them with your review committee, and actively use them in interviewing vendors and reviewing platforms. You won't find any one platform that does everything well. But your chances of getting a platform that's right for your institution increases if you can articulate and agree on your goals.

student learning. Such a process can help deepen pedagogy, professional development, and outcomes assessment, and it can lay groundwork for broader institutional change.

At Pace University, for example, after experimenting with several different ePortfolio tools, the ePortfolio leadership team wanted to select a single platform to use across the institution. The ePortfolio team reports they

> formed an ePortfolio advisory board and under the guidance of our CIO, created a "bucket list" of what we wanted our ePortfolio tool to do and look like. . . . The advisory board consisted of about 25 faculty and staff from across the institution.[4]

Guttman Community College also "convened a task force including faculty and administrators to review and recommend ePortfolio platforms."[5] Tunxis Community College, LaGuardia, and Virginia Tech used similar processes. The value of this collaborative process goes beyond the task of identifying an effective platform. It can also spark a productive conversation about technology, pedagogy, and student learning. At its best, this process engages all participants in thinking about the role technology plays in supporting and enhancing teaching and learning. Putting student learning at the center of technology-focused conversations can help campuses develop a broader, learning-centered culture.

Goal Setting and Evaluation

In addition to involving the right people in decision-making, it's important to conduct a needs assessment and then prioritize essential technology features. To advance this process, many C2L campuses created lists or rubrics, what the Pace team called a "bucket list." At Manhattanville College, ePortfolio leaders began the selection process by

> developing a matrix of features that we thought were important and examin[ing] these features in the products of a number of different vendors. These features included: ability to support accreditation reporting, ADA compliance, cost and cost structure, compatibility with our Student Information System and existing LMS (Blackboard), assessment capabilities including rubrics and reports, ease of use, flexibility in the interface, portability capabilities, social networking/media integration, storage allotment, training and support for faculty and students, the visual look and feel of the interface, and file management and organization capabilities. We then prioritized these features for Manhattanville.[6]

In 2012, IUPUI joined other campuses in the Indiana University system in considering their next generation of learning technologies. A committee on ePortfolio platform review worked to prioritize ePortfolio technology needs and review potential platforms. As the largest user of ePortfolios in the system, IUPUI was well represented, and the committee was cochaired by one of the C2L project directors.

The committee produced a detailed list of requirements, ranging from basic functionalities for document management to those that support social and reflection-based pedagogies and those that enable assessment management. Improved user experience and ability to integrate with other enterprise systems were also high priorities.[7]

Criteria for ePortfolio platforms must address issues of teaching and learning. An effective ePortfolio platform helps students to document, connect, reflect on, and share diverse elements of their learning. As discussed later, it builds student engagement by offering opportunities for customization and interaction. An effective platform also helps faculty and staff examine ePortfolios and focus on student learning. Facilitating the integration of ePortfolios and related artifacts into professional development and outcomes assessment processes, effective platforms help deepen faculty, staff, and institutional learning. On C2L campuses with thriving ePortfolio initiatives, these complex goals guide the selection and management of an ePortfolio system. For example, ePortfolio leaders at San Francisco State University (SFSU) report,

> First [we] conducted a needs assessment, polling the Chairs of departments in 2006 to discern how widespread the use of portfolios for formative/summative assessment of student work was. . . . We had a small committee comprised of 2 faculty, 1 department chair and academic technology manager who began experimenting with a variety of platforms.[8]

Getting Started
Step 2: Design and Configure Your ePortfolio Platform

Once you've selected your platform, ePortfolio leaders should work closely with IT administrators to configure your system. Many platforms integrate with student information systems to automate the creation of student and faculty accounts. In addition, platforms with assessment management features also allow you to automatically import course enrollment information, learning outcomes, and rubrics.

Your campus ePortfolio team will want to consider whether and how to structure students' ePortfolio experiences. Some campuses ask students to use templates as a starting point when they create their ePortfolios. Educators disagree on how much to structure a student's experience with technology. Some argue that students should have total control over sharing and showcasing information. Proponents for this suggest that ownership and creativity will enhance learning. Others believe that structure not only supports students and helps them develop the technological literacies they need but also enables faculty to more easily integrate effective technology-rich pedagogies into their courses and practices. If you opt for the latter, it will be important to design templates before launching your ePortfolio project.

IUPUI's Platform Selection Process
Susan Kahn and Susan Scott
Indiana University–Purdue University Indianapolis

In fall 2012 after more than a decade with the Sakai LMS, Indiana University technology leaders decided the time was ripe to explore new possibilities for supporting teaching and learning at the university's eight campuses. At the same time, a search was begun for a successor to the open source portfolio in Sakai that IUPUI and several other Indiana campuses had been using.

A Joint Committee on ePortfolio Platform Review was charged with the task of developing ePortfolio platform recommendations for the University Information Technology Services unit (UITS). Carefully composed to represent a range of roles (faculty, staff, program leaders, learning technologists, IT administrators) and of ePortfolio uses and priorities (assessment, student development, integrative learning, academic and career advising), the committee was cochaired by a member of the UITS learning technologies unit and the director of the ePortfolio initiative at IUPUI, the campus with the most use of ePortfolios across academic and co-curricular programs.

Work proceeded in several overlapping stages over the next 18 months.

- Committee members reviewed online demonstrations of leading ePortfolio platforms archived on the AAEEBL website as premeeting homework and attended live or webinar-style demonstrations of several other platforms. Using a shared online document, individual members noted the strengths and weaknesses of each platform, then discussed these as a whole group.
- As the work was proceeding, the UITS cochair developed a detailed functional requirements matrix including such categories as reflection, Web presentation, assessment, reporting, collaboration, social networking, and mobile support. Committee members suggested, discussed, and reached consensus on additions and changes. The final matrix document was shared online. Each committee member individually rated each requirement as *must have, should have, nice to have,* or *not needed*; the whole committee then discussed and voted on final ratings for all requirements.
- UITS issued a request for information in June 2013, and seven vendors sent detailed responses.
- Committee members individually rated each response, using the shared requirements matrix document. The full committee then discussed the ratings and voted to narrow the pool to four finalists.
- With committee input, the UITS cochair and a committee member from IUPUI developed two scenarios drawn from real-life IUPUI projects, one geared to learning outcomes assessment and the

(Continues)

(Continued)

other to student reflection and development. UITS invited the finalists to offer two-hour online presentations that were recorded and archived. All committee members either participated in or viewed all four archived sessions.

- Committee members individually scored the vendor presentations, again using the shared requirements matrix. The full committee then discussed and agreed on a rank-ordered platform recommendation to UITS, which issued a final request for proposals, negotiated the vendor contract, and announced the selection in August 2014.

Most of these steps will no doubt sound familiar to those acquainted with evaluating and selecting learning technologies for large institutions. We believe that two aspects of our process were especially important and distinctive.

- Committee leaders and members clearly understood ePortfolios as a set of pedagogical practices, not as just technology tools.
- The two scenarios we developed enabled us to base our evaluation of the finalist platforms on customized responses to our teaching and learning needs, rather than canned demonstrations.

Although the committee work demanded significant time from committee members—and several did fade away over the course of the lengthy process—a core group of faculty, staff, and administrators remained committed and engaged throughout. We believe it was time well spent; we now have a platform we expect to serve our needs for some years to come.

Factors such as ease of use, customization, cost, vendor support, and assessment tools were among the criteria used in the selection process at SFSU and other C2L campuses. Knowing the goals of the ePortfolio project and the needs of the faculty, staff, and student users allows teams to select the most appropriate platform for an institution.

Connecting to the Field

External resources can assist campuses in their platform selection process. The Electronic Portfolio Action Committee community of practice maintains an active list of ePortfolio-related tools and technologies.[9] The Association for Authentic, Experiential and Evidence-Based Learning (AAEEBL) regularly hosts webinars where ePortfolio providers and educators discuss current ePortfolio platforms.[10]

More informal resources can also be useful. C2L teams found it helpful to draw on the insights of experienced campuses. City University of New York's School of Professional Studies and Lehman College worked with colleagues at Bronx Community College when evaluating different platforms. C2L leaders at Northwestern Connecticut Community College report that it was helpful to learn that two of their "sister community colleges in Connecticut were using Digication and seemed to be particularly pleased with the platform."[11]

Selecting an ePortfolio platform is a critical campus decision. An effective platform that aligns with campus needs and goals will help position a project for success. A platform that is not a good fit undermines broad acceptance and use by students, faculty, and other stakeholders. C2L campus stories suggest that the best way to select an effective ePortfolio platform is an inclusive process involving stakeholders from across the institution. Working collaboratively and learning from other campuses are key steps. These steps help generate acceptance for ePortfolio, which can, in turn, advance the growth of an ePortfolio initiative across a program, college, or institution.

Connections to the *Catalyst Framework*

Meaningful ePortfolio practices involve a complex interplay among teaching, learning, and technology. The technological aspect of ePortfolio plays a critical role in supporting high-impact ePortfolio pedagogy. Effective technology also facilitates work taking place in every Catalyst sector, and work in those sectors must in turn incorporate a thoughtful understanding of the technology. As the C2L team from Northeastern University noted,

> It's important to embed conversations about technology into all other dimensions of the Catalyst (e.g., Pedagogy, Outcomes Assessment, Professional Development, and Scaling Up). It's also important for technology specialists to develop sophisticated understanding of the other domains, so that they can participate as collaborators and partners in the process.[12]

Pedagogy

Asking students to demonstrate their learning through activities, experiences, and assignments is an essential aspect of the college experience. Ineffective technology, or a poor fit between technology and pedagogy, can distract users and impede the digital advancement and demonstration of learning. Supporting thoughtful pedagogy with effective ePortfolio technology can enhance the demonstration of learning, making that learning visible to students themselves across multiple learning experiences and providing opportunities for integration.

C2L campuses understood ePortfolio technology as a way to support reflection and integration. At IUPUI students use ePortfolio in their first-year seminar course to create a personal development plan (PDP); a campus team recognized the pedagogical value of making the PDP digital.

> The PDP was originally developed as a paper binder; one of the reasons for pursuing an alternate strategy was that students often perceived the plan as a series of discrete exercises, rather than a unified, coherent document, and were thus not particularly invested in the resulting plan.[13]

Similarly, at Guttman where ePortfolio pedagogy is integrated throughout its curriculum, "reflective pedagogy is central to student learning . . . . The ePortfolio makes learning visible; students and faculty are able to see 'change over time' as students progress through their first year at the college and beyond."[14]

Fostering an integrative experience where students see their own learning improve over time, effective ePortfolio platforms support ongoing reflection and recursive revision. Nearly all ePortfolio platforms allow students to create longitudinal ePortfolios, spanning multiple semesters and existing outside of any single course or co-curricular activity. This gives students the ability to continue to revise their ePortfolios as

> **Getting Started**
> Step 3: Conduct Pilot Testing;
> Develop an Implementation Plan
>
> It is vital that key stakeholders collaborate to develop a clear and manageable initial implementation plan. An important component of this initial plan will be piloting the system with a small control group, making sure that it is operating smoothly. Feedback from this group can help sharpen the implementation plan and increase the platform's effectiveness in meeting the needs of students, faculty, and staff.

they move through their educational experiences, sustaining attention to key concepts, skills, and content. Curating an ePortfolio is not a once-and-done assignment but an ongoing process. ePortfolio leaders at Pace argue

> the most important reason for advocating for the electronic use of portfolios is that it can be continually reviewed and revised. A paper portfolio gives the impression of being complete once submitted, whereas an electronic portfolio is always ready to be enriched and changed.[15]

Feedback from faculty and peers is a key characteristic of HIPs and an invaluable element of ePortfolio pedagogy. Effective ePortfolio platforms provide flexible, easy-to-use commenting features for students and faculty, opening opportunities for feedback and interaction. As discussed in Chapter 8, C2L data show that engagement increases when students know that faculty and peers are commenting on their ePortfolios. At CUNY's School for Professional Studies, an online institution that relies on Blackboard's LMS, ePortfolio leaders see benefits in creating opportunities for interaction outside an LMS.

> ePortfolio can be seen as a way to extend conversations beyond and across individual courses and sections. . . . ePortfolio also allows students to pull other artifacts and interests into a space they can share with others, promoting authorship, ownership, and metacognition.[16]

ePortfolios can be used by students for the collaborative construction of knowledge. Through project ePortfolios, students work together to develop a shared demonstration of learning. At Virginia Tech, transfer students in the College of Science participate in a ZipLine to Success Program:

> The final project for the course is a group research project, which is presented in the ePortfolio. For the research, students combine their interests and their disciplinary backgrounds to pursue a research topic from multiple perspectives. The various perspectives are represented throughout the organization of the portfolio, including a bio for each contributing member of the group; three or more secondary pages representing each of the different perspectives of research on their topic; three or more reflections on each of the research perspectives; resources for each of the perspectives; and a Works Cited section for each of the perspectives.[17]

Some ePortfolio platforms integrate with other social media applications, such as Twitter and YouTube. LaGuardia faculty link social media technologies with ePortfolio.

> Unlike a paper-based format, an ePortfolio allows students to connect social media with social pedagogy practices. Through this, students are equipped with the necessary knowledge and tools to make relevant connections between the learning that is happening in their academic, professional, and personal lives.[18]

ePortfolio technology supports High-Impact Practice behaviors, facilitating public demonstration of competence and making learning visible to authentic audiences, including other students, family, potential employers, and transfer institutions. In a typical course setting, or with a paper portfolio, the demonstration of learning is a private exchange between instructor and student. The ePortfolio extends that learning to a broader audience. As one C2L team noted, "The *e* factor provides a wider and more authentic audience, one that goes beyond simply the teacher."[19]

Using ePortfolio technology in conjunction with effective pedagogies help students take ownership of their learning and become more active agents in the learning process. With many ePortfolio platforms, students technically own their ePortfolio; they have rights to its content and can take it with them when they graduate or leave the campus. But ownership has other, subtler aspects. Do students really feel that their ePortfolio is theirs? Does it visually express their personality and how they see themselves? Helping students develop a sense of ownership is a critical way that effective ePortfolio technology can enhance student learning.

At Boston University, Tunxis, LaGuardia, Salt Lake Community College, and other C2L campuses, students are encouraged to customize their ePortfolio using color, images, and design to express their identities in visual form. The capacity to customize a portfolio can be a meaningful consideration in platform selection. Visual customization allows students to use color and images to express who they are as learners and as individuals. It also encourages a sense of ownership, not just of the visual aspects of the ePortfolio, but of the content itself, and, in turn, the student's entire learning experience. As the IUPUI team explains:

One of the main reasons for digitizing the electronic Personal Development Plan (ePDP), the focus of our C2L project, was to support not only the literal ownership of a presentation style portfolio, but more importantly to foster students' sense of agency, self-authorship, and ownership of learning from the start of their undergraduate experience.[20]

Customization can pose challenges for campuses. Customizable ePortfolios are often more difficult to manage than standardized ePortfolios. Training and technical support can also become more difficult with these additional features. Campus teams often work to strike a balance between standardization and customization, balancing the ability to easily manage an ePortfolio system with student autonomy and ownership.

Thoughtful discussion of ePortfolio ownership must consider the public/private dimensions of digital learning environments. Some ePortfolio platforms allow students to choose which sections of their portfolios will be public and which will remain private. Students can often create multiple portfolios for different public audiences. As Gail Matthews-DeNatale from Northeastern University states, "ePortfolios make it possible to share, but to share within limits. This combination of privacy and sharing could not be accomplished in a paper-only format."[21]

Using ePortfolio practice to help students examine their own learning has long been a major focus of LaGuardia's ePortfolio initiative. As the LaGuardia C2L team explains,

> For students, being able to see learning and the process of learning are key ingredients that can lead to change and success. At LaGuardia, students take pride in who they are, what they have learned, and who they want to be. Digication allows students the opportunity to learn, create, share, and own a roadmap for their success—academic, career, and personal.[22]

Effective ePortfolio platforms help students situate their learning in more visible, holistic, and longitudinal contexts. They help ePortfolio practice extend beyond course and co-curricular boundaries spanning the entire student learning experience. And they help students take ownership of their learning and become active agents in the learning process. Used this way, ePortfolio technology supports a practice that requires a "significant investment of time and effort by students over an extended period of time."[23]

Professional Development

The linkage of ePortfolio technology to professional development starts with the necessary training on the platform. Learning the ins and outs of a platform is important, yet it is only the beginning. It is equally, if not more, valuable to support faculty as they learn how to use the platform with integrative social pedagogy and figure out how to incorporate reflective ePortfolio practices into their curricula.

Getting Started
Step 4: Offer Professional Development That Links Technology and Pedagogy

As with any new technology, professional development is essential for building high-impact ePortfolio practice. Connecting technology and pedagogy in this process can help make it more effective, particularly for faculty.

Simply showing faculty where to click has limited value. Discussing pedagogy and giving faculty time to think about how and why they might use the technology to enhance teaching and learning can make a much bigger impact.

This kind of professional development usually means going beyond one-shot workshops. Recursive opportunities to plan, test classroom use, and reflect on the experience can make it more likely that faculty will use the platform effectively. Join forces with your Center for Teaching and Learning!

Some faculty developers see a tension between emphasizing technology and exploring pedagogy. Others see the introduction of new technology as an opportunity to spur faculty and staff learning. Engaging faculty in exploring the capacities of ePortfolio technology is a process they can use to spark conversation about pedagogy and purpose. A shift from "How do I do this?" to "What do I want to do in my class—and why?" focuses faculty and staff on the ways to rethink the teaching and learning process. At SFSU, professional development that began as technology workshops evolved to focus increasingly on pedagogy and design:

Most of our professional development work is now focused on pedagogy. Through our grant program from 2006–2011 we grew to understand the extent to which we were asking faculty to transform their practice. In almost every case, faculty begin with the idea of learning how to use a technology tool to accomplish their goal. Through consultations, symposia, and support of travel to present at inter/national conferences, we worked to help them move beyond focusing on the technology to emphasize curriculum design, pedagogy, and assessment principles.[24]

ePortfolio technology can help bring student work into professional development processes, connecting discussion of teaching strategy to examination of student work. Some campuses also use ePortfolio to host discussions of professional development topics. At CUNY's School of Professional Studies, for example, leaders "created a workshop ePortfolio to house support materials and information. . . . we also created a shared ePortfolio 'sandbox' where each workshop participant completed a number of tasks."[25] Similarly, Guttman ePortfolio leaders work to integrate ePortfolio into professional development practices, using ePortfolio to

practice what we preach. For example, we developed professional development ePortfolios for our "ePortfolio and the Arts" and "ePortfolio Peer Mentor/Grad Coordinator Bootcamp" workshops. While sharing materials, participants engage in social pedagogy, commenting and engaging with each other via the ePortfolio before and during workshops.[26]

Some campuses model effective ePortfolio pedagogy through portfolio building; professional developers ask participants to maintain a professional ePortfolio. In ePortfolio-related seminars, participants build their portfolios, showcase best teaching practices, describe research projects, and reflect on classroom experiments. Professional portfolios can then be shared with colleagues, serving as spaces for feedback. Building an ePortfolio helps faculty and staff not only become familiar with the technology itself but to also understand more deeply the power of making learning visible for students.

Outcomes Assessment

The most effective ePortfolio platforms provide mechanisms to gather, save, and use artifacts of student work or entire ePortfolios for outcomes assessment. Platforms with assessment management components also allow institutions to upload learning outcomes and rubrics. Stored artifacts or portfolios are linked to these outcomes and distributed to faculty and staff to assess, using the rubrics. Data from this assessment are aggregated and analyzed. ePortfolio platforms can facilitate this process and provide a streamlined system to manage the entire assessment process.

For campuses that use ePortfolio for outcomes assessment, these features can help engage the institution in a conversation about learning. Examining ePortfolio-based evidence of student learning and reflecting on ways to improve pedagogy and curriculum is a powerful process. When the use of ePortfolio in this process becomes part of institutional practice, it strengthens an institutional learning culture.

Scaling Up

Building an ePortfolio platform into a college's technology infrastructure brings with it challenges and opportunities. One challenge is cost. Most ePortfolio platforms calculate costs based on enrollments or the number of students using the system. As campus ePortfolio use grows, so will the cost for maintaining that ePortfolio solution. Campus leaders must plan for the ongoing costs of an ePortfolio platform, thinking about sustainability.

Another challenge is the integration of ePortfolio technology with the campus technology suite. Some ePortfolio platforms integrate with institutional LMSs. Platforms also use

> **Getting Started**
> **Step 5: Develop Support Structures for Students, Faculty, and Staff**
>
> Professional development can only go so far in helping address technical training needs. Both faculty and students will need help as they actually begin using your ePortfolio platform. Consider how you will build and offer support structures for students and faculty, including videos and other tutorials, peer mentor support, and/or ePortfolio labs.

Students as ePortfolio Mentors

Using students as technology mentors can help address some of the technology challenges related to ePortfolio. Student mentors spur student engagement with ePortfolio by supporting their peers. At many C2L campuses, ePortfolio consultants and student technology mentors work in ePortfolio labs and provide personal assistance to students. As Arcario, Eynon, and Lucca explained, at LaGuardia,

> We had previous experience with students as technology teachers—in our Student Technology Mentor (STM) program, specially trained students worked with interested faculty, helping them learn the tools needed to integrate Web-based resources into their courses. We took this concept (and some of our successful STMs) and created a cohort of ePortfolio consultants, who would run a dedicated computer lab, the "ePortfolio Studio." The ePortfolio consultants and the ePortfolio studio not only provide students with drop-in assistance but also come to classes and provide workshops, based on faculty requests.[27]

Student mentors also work with faculty members. Pace, Manhattanville, and LaGuardia assign peer mentors to assist faculty in teaching their first-year experience courses, where students are introduced to the ePortfolio. At Manhattanville, eTerns—ePortfolio student interns—support faculty as they participate in the college's teaching and learning circles, with an eTern assigned to each cohort. At LaGuardia, Arcario and colleagues reported that their ePortfolio consultants "play an even larger role in some classes, which have an attached weekly hour in the studio—the 'Studio Hour'—where consultants are responsible for guiding an in-depth ePortfolio construction process."[28]

In addition to formal peer mentors, informal student mentoring takes place as well. C2L ePortfolio leader Lili Rafeldt reported that in the nursing program at Three Rivers Community College: "The students actually have been able to mentor themselves. . . . There's not a formalized peer mentor program, but there is an informal peer mentor program in that sense, that they do help each other."[29]

Whether their role is formal or informal, student mentors help increase acceptance and participation from other students. In addition, when students work with and support faculty, they support advancement of the project by encouraging faculty interest and engagement in using ePortfolio at the course and/or program level.

data from student information systems to automate the creation of student and faculty accounts. At some institutions, such as Tunxis and Guttman Community Colleges, IT staff created login portals for students and faculty, providing a single sign-on and authentication solution for their ePortfolio platforms.

Yet another challenge is providing necessary support for students and faculty. While ePortfolio platforms have become increasingly user friendly, teaching students how to use the platform still requires attention. Few faculty want to spend significant class time teaching students the nuances of any ePortfolio platform. Some C2L campuses, such as Pace, Manhattanville and LaGuardia, address this issue by hiring student mentors to run workshops and provide one-on-one guidance, helping other students become comfortable using their ePortfolio platforms. Student mentors not only support the technological elements of portfolio build, but also help their peers reflect on their experiences and develop future plans.

C2L campuses used other strategies as well. Tunxis and many other C2L campuses have dedicated ePortfolio labs where students can seek help building their ePortfolios. CUNY's School of Professional Studies created online tutorial materials and videos. Many teams, such as Salt Lake Community College (SLCC), tell us they combine these approaches. At SLCC students have had the option of choosing from multiple open source ePortfolio platforms. To support these choices the ePortfolio leadership team reports that they "have online tutorials for all three platforms. The second support structure consists of free introductory workshops for students. . . . We've added a third support structure, . . . two ePortfolio labs."[30] Campuses must provide necessary resources to intentionally design and build appropriate support structures into their ePortfolio scaling process.

While challenges inevitably arise, the technological aspect of scaling an ePortfolio initiative can bring opportunities for college-wide collaboration. An effective platform selection process must bring together faculty, advisors, IT staff, and administration. Once a platform is selected, launching and supporting its use will benefit from close collaboration between IT staff and ePortfolio leaders. Integrating ePortfolio practice into curricular and co-curricular learning experiences provides valuable opportunities for faculty and staff collaboration across disciplines, majors, departments, and programs. Through professional development and outcomes assessment, ePortfolio can bring distinct areas of a campus together. Collaborative platform planning, professional development, and assessment can all blossom into shared conversations about student learning goals and realities. These conversations can bear long-term fruit, in the form of an increasingly cohesive college-wide learning culture.

Conclusion

ePortfolio technology, because of its longitudinal capacity, plays a unique educational role. Unlike learning management systems, ePortfolios exist outside of a single course experience, spanning courses, experiences, and semesters. Effective ePortfolio technology, used well, has the potential to enhance student, faculty, and institutional learning in significant ways.

The *e* makes a difference across the various layers of an institution—for students, faculty, staff, and administrators—in two key ways. First, it makes student learning visible to students themselves, as well as to their peers, faculty, and other audiences. Students are able to see a holistic picture of their academic learning experience and the ways they have developed from entry to graduation. Second, ePortfolio serves as a space for students to make connections among their different learning experiences, turning a set of disparate courses and co-curricular activities into a cohesive whole that spans the breadth and depth of their time at an institution.

To realize this potential, campus leaders must pay attention to the digital aspects of ePortfolio—and at the same time, understand that effective ePortfolio practice goes well beyond the technology itself. Building cross-divisional partnerships and carefully weighing the ways platform technology can address campus goals is critical to success. Understanding the connections among Technology and the other sectors of the *Catalyst Framework* will enhance the likelihood of building and scaling high-impact ePortfolio practice.

Notes

1. Trent Batson, "The Electronic Portfolio Boom: What's It All About?" *Campus Technology,* November 22, 2002, https://campustechnology.com/articles/2002/11/the-electronic-portfolio-boom-whats-it-all-about.aspx

2. Randall Bass, "The Next Whole Thing in Higher Education," *Peer Review*, 16, no. 1, (Winter 2014): 35.

3. Bass, "The Next Whole Thing," 35.

4. Pace University, "Mahara: From Bucket List to Implementation," *Catalyst for Learning: ePortfolio Resources and Research*, January, 25, 2014, http://pu.mcnrc.org/tech-story/

5. Laura M. Gambino, Tracy Daraviras, Chet Jordan, and Nate Mickelson, "Using Technology to Connect Our Learning," *Catalyst for Learning: ePortfolio Resources and Research*, January, 25, 2014, http://gcc.mcnrc.org/tech-story/

6. Alison Carson, Jim Frank, Gillian Hannum, and Sherie McClam, "Our Technology Story," *Catalyst for Learning: ePortfolio Resources and Research,* January 25, 2014, http://mville.mcnrc.org/tech-story/

7. Susan Kahn and Susan Scott, "Technology: There Are No Silver Bullets," *Catalyst for Learning: ePortfolio Resources and Research,* January 25, 2014, http://iupui.mcnrc.org/tech-story/

8. San Francisco State University, "eFolio Platform Since 2005: Accessible and Economical," *Catalyst for Learning: ePortfolio Resources and Research,* January 25, 2014, http://sfsu.mcnrc.org/tech-story/

9. "Evolving List of ePortfolio-Related Tools," January 5, 2015, http://epac.pbworks.com/w/page/12559686/Evolving%20List%C2%A0of%C2%A0ePortfolio-related%C2%A0Tools

10. Association for Authentic, Experiential and Evidence-Based Learning, "Screen-Side Chats; AAEEBL ePortfolio Webinars 2015, 2015," accessed August 20, 2015, http://www.aaeebl.org/?page=2015_SSChats

11. Northwestern Connecticut Community College, "Northwestern Connecticut Community College—Technology and Pedagogy," *Catalyst for Learning: ePortfolio Resources and Research,* January 25, 2014, http://c2l.mcnrc.org/nccc-tech-story/

12. Gail Matthews-DeNatale, "The Ecology of Support," *Catalyst for Learning: ePortfolio Resources and Research,* January 25, 2014, http://neu.mcnrc.org/tech-story/

13. Catherine Buyarski, "Reflection in the First Year: A Foundation for Identity and Meaning Making," *Catalyst for Learning: ePortfolio Resources and Research,* January 25, 2014, http://iupui.mcnrc.org/ref-practice/

14. Gambino et al., "Using Technology."

15. Pace University, "Mahara."

16. City University of New York School of Professional Studies, "Technology Story," *Catalyst for Learning: ePortfolio Resources and Research,* January 25, 2014, http://sps.mcnrc.org/tech-story/

17. Virginia Tech, "Social Pedagogy Practice: Zip Line to Success ePortfolio," *Catalyst for Learning: ePortfolio Resources and Research,* January 25, 2014, http://vt.mcnrc.org/soc-practice/

18. Craig Kasprzak, "The Evolution of ePortfolio Platforms at LaGuardia: Our Technology Story," *Catalyst for Learning: ePortfolio Resources and Research,* January 25, 2014, http://lagcc.mcnrc.org/tech-story/

19. Norwalk Community College, "'The Awkward Age': The Technology Story at NCC," *Catalyst for Learning: ePortfolio Resources and Research,* January 25, 2014, http://c2l.mcnrc.org/ncc-tech-story/

20. Catherine Buyarski, "Reflection in the First Year: A Foundation for Identity and Meaning Making," *Catalyst for Learning: ePortfolio Resources and Research,* January 25, 2014, http://iupui.mcnrc.org/ref-practice/

21. Matthews-DeNatale, "The Ecology of Support."

22. Craig Kasprzak, "The Evolution of ePortfolio Platforms at LaGuardia: Our Technology Story," *Catalyst for Learning: ePortfolio Resources and Research,* January 25, 2014, http://lagcc.mcnrc.org/tech-story/

23. George Kuh and Ken O'Donnell, *Ensuring Quality & Taking High Impact Practices to Scale* (Washington, DC: Association of American Colleges & Universities, 2013), 8.

24. Ruth Cox, "Connect to Learning Annual Report: San Francisco State University," (unpublished annual report, 2014).

25. City University of New York School of Professional Studies, "Technology Story."

26. Gambino et al., "Using Technology."

27. Paul Arcario, Bret Eynon, and Louis Lucca, "The Power of Peers: New Ways for Students to Support Students," in *Making Teaching and Learning Matter Transformative Spaces in Higher Education,* eds. Judith Summerfield and Cheryl C. Smith (New York, NY, Springer: 2011): 197.

28. Arcario et al., "The Power of Peers," 197.

29. Lili Rafeldt, interview by Judit Torok, March 8, 2012.

30. Salt Lake Community College, "Variety and Student Choice: SLCC's Technology Story," San Francisco State University, http://slcc.mcnrc.org/tech-story/

7

SCALING UP!

Six Core Strategies for Effective ePortfolio Initiatives

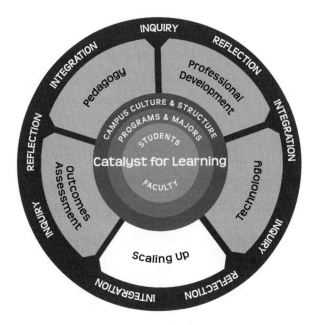

hat does it take to build a large, robust campus ePortfolio initiative? Most ePortfolio projects start small, with a few faculty, staff, or administrative leaders. What strategies do these innovators use to expand and deepen, or scale, their work? When we use the terms *scaling* or *scaling up*, we refer to the process in which ePortfolio projects begin in small segments of an institution and then expand, as additional faculty, courses, and programs begin to work with ePortfolio. This chapter draws on the experiences and scaling up stories of Connect to Learning (C2L) campuses to spotlight effective scaling strategies.

Scaling any technology-based innovation in higher education is challenging. As Phil Hill wrote:

> Getting a new idea adopted, even when it has obvious advantages, is difficult. Many innovations require a lengthy period of many years from the time when they become

available to the time when they are widely adopted. Therefore, a common problem for many individuals and organizations is how to speed up the rate of diffusion of an innovation.[1]

Everett Rogers discussed the notion of diffusion, or scaling, arguing that organizations go through a five-phase innovation-decision process: knowledge, persuasion, decision, implementation, and confirmation.[2] Hill suggested that in higher education, most innovations are stuck in the persuasion stage and never achieve mainstream adoption across an institution. Colleges and universities often have great difficulty moving innovations, even ones that appear to be working well, past the pilot or early implementation stage.[3]

The challenge of innovation diffusion holds true for ePortfolio initiatives. Evidence of the benefit of ePortfolio practice is growing, and the latest Campus Computing Survey shows that 64% of U.S. colleges use ePortfolio at their institution, yet very few of them have most or all of their students using ePortfolios.[4] Many ePortfolio projects remain at the pilot stage and never fulfill their promise. What do the most effective campus ePortfolio leaders do to broadly diffuse or scale up ePortfolio practice, moving from pilot adoption to mainstream integration? And, how can that scaling up be "done well?"

Scaling is particularly essential to a high-impact ePortfolio initiative. Based in longitudinal and integrative processes, ePortfolio practice is most beneficial for student, faculty, and institutional learning when it has a strong, well-established cross-campus presence. Using ePortfolio in the context of a single course or program has benefits, but it is only when it is scaled broadly across the entire student learning experience that ePortfolio's true potential can be realized.

The *Catalyst Framework* can guide campus efforts to expand and deepen high-impact ePortfolio practice. Campuses that want to scale their ePortfolio initiatives must support faculty and staff's use of integrative ePortfolio Pedagogy. They must use their Centers for Teaching and Learning to offer Professional Development that supports ePortfolio Pedagogy and Outcomes Assessment. There must be a Technology platform that meets pedagogical and assessment needs, and adequate support for students, faculty, and staff. To work in these *Framework* sectors, scaling also requires attention to issues of institutional culture and structure, leadership, evaluation, planning, and resources.

Having previously discussed the four other *Framework* sectors, here we introduce six additional strategies for scaling an ePortfolio initiative, developed from our research with the C2L network. These strategies range from developing an effective leadership team to making use of evidence and aligning with institutional planning. Together with the *Catalyst Framework*, these strategies provide a powerful tool kit for ePortfolio and institutional leaders to advance broad use of high-impact ePortfolio practice.

To understand these strategies, it's helpful to first visualize the scaling process. In the next section, we offer a set of vignettes from C2L campuses that have scaled their ePortfolio initiatives. This is followed by a detailed description of each of the six scaling strategies. Following this chapter, Randy Bass discusses the transformative potential of a scaled ePortfolio initiative.

What Does Scaling Look Like?

All C2L campuses have addressed the process of scaling in one way or another. Some campuses, such as LaGuardia Community College and IUPUI, have robust, well-established ePortfolio projects involving hundreds of faculty and serving thousands of students across their campuses each year. They started with small ePortfolio pilots; over time, they successfully scaled their initiatives to where they are today. It's helpful for all of us to understand these success stories as well as the stories of other campuses at different points on the scaling pathway, considering where they began, how they grew, and the challenges they encountered along the way.

No two scaling stories are exactly the same. We've seen that some ePortfolio initiatives start in a single course or set of courses, focusing on ePortfolio as an integrative, social pedagogy, and build from there. Others begin with assessment before delving into ePortfolio pedagogy. Still others begin at the program level, focusing on pedagogy and assessment across a single program; that program then serves as a model for others to

Getting Started
Six Scaling Strategies
for an ePortfolio Initiative

1. **Develop an effective campus ePortfolio team:** Building a cross-institutional leadership team helps create broad acceptance and sustain engagement as an initiative scales.

2. **Connect to departments and programs:** ePortfolio's integrative and longitudinal qualities align with cohesive degree programs. Working directly with programs and departments helps scale and build institutional acceptance.

3. **More deeply engage students:** Students are at the center of any ePortfolio initiative. Engaging students as active voices of an ePortfolio project through showcase events and as peer mentors builds support from stakeholders campus-wide.

4. **Make use of evidence:** Collecting, analyzing, and sharing evidence of the impact of ePortfolio on student learning can garner campus support.

5. **Leverage resources:** ePortfolio leaders must seek external funding and work with campus administrators to leverage internal resources.

6. **Align with institutional planning:** Connecting to key institutional initiatives, governance structures, and strategic planning processes helps solidify ePortfolio as an essential component of the college's work, broadening support and advancing the scaling process.

follow. Successful ePortfolio projects, as depicted in Figure 7.1, have a scaling trajectory that increases the depth and breadth of their work over time. That trajectory may or may not be linear and may have starts and stops along the way. What the scaling stories of the most successful ePortfolio campuses have in common is that they are all moving toward the upper-right quadrant where ePortfolio practice is "done well" on a broad scale. Following are brief excerpts from scaling stories of successful C2L campuses.

When Three Rivers Community College (TRCC) began testing ePortfolio in 2004, the "focus was initially on technology" and ePortfolio's use for assessment in the nursing program.[5] In 2006 campus ePortfolio leaders realized they needed to shift their focus from technology and assessment to pedagogy; they began building reflective practice into the nursing program, course by course; "each semester through a planned progressive addition of the next nursing course, ePortfolio was integrated throughout the program."[6] In the years that followed, while continuing to use ePortfolio for programmatic assessment, the Three Rivers team began to share their scaffolded use of ePortfolio pedagogy with colleagues to improve student learning. In 2012 they presented their experience and evidence to the TRCC General Education committee, and in the 2013–2014 school year TRCC began moving toward cross-campus ePortfolio implementation. The TRCC team keeps student learning at the center and uses professional development to deepen ePortfolio pedagogy as the college enters this new phase of scaling up.[7]

Boston University's (BU's) College of General Studies (CGS) is a two-year liberal arts college that began using ePortfolio for assessment in 2009. Since that time, "each CGS student has maintained a single ePortfolio for all CGS courses" and the CGS program has successfully used these ePortfolios for assessment.[8] Taking part in C2L from 2011 to 2015, BU's ePortfolio leaders realized that student and faculty ePortfolio use was uneven and began to focus on pedagogy and professional development. In 2012 they formed a partnership with BU's Center for Excellence and Innovation in Teaching to offer professional development on integrative ePortfolio pedagogy. BU's team noted its plans to extend "efforts to meet with faculty and staff across campus to encourage them to have their students use ePortfolios."[9] CGS's use of ePortfolio for assessment has gained institutional attention at BU, which may lead to broader implementation on other parts of the university.

A small group of faculty and instructional designers at San Francisco State University (SFSU) launched an ePortfolio initiative in 2005, initially using reflective pedagogy to deepen student learning. In their scaling story, they tell us about their growth, how they expanded from "one graduate program" to implementation in 22 programs.[10] SFSU leaders made a conscious decision to only work with programs, believing that in a programmatic context they could drill down and focus on effective practice. In 2009 they began working with SFSU's Metro Academies Program, a two-year, structured learning community that brings together a number of High-Impact Practices. As SFSU took part in C2L, every student in the Metro Health Academy and the Metro STEM (science, technology, engineering, mathematics) Academy programs was given an ePortfolio to use in course work. SFSU leaders have gathered evidence

Figure 7.1. A Developmental Trajectory of ePortfolio Practice.

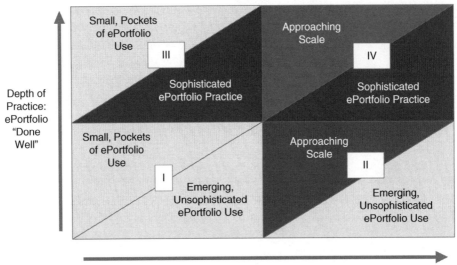

Breadth of Practice: Growing to Scale

Note. Although institutions may begin at different points and in different quadrants on this trajectory, the goal should be to develop an implementation plan and time line that will lead to the fourth quadrant, sophisticated, high-impact ePortfolio practice approaching or at scale.

demonstrating that the combination of ePortfolio and other High-Impact Practices in the Metro Academies has a powerful benefit for student success, building retention and graduation rates (see Chapter 8). SFSU leaders have used that evidence to mobilize support for further scaling. "The vision is to expand to 4 new departments in the next 5 years with 24% of the incoming freshmen (1,000 students) being tracked annually into a Metro program (STEM, child development, health, etc.)."[11] To accomplish that, the SFSU ePortfolio team identified four needs: funding, high-level administrative support, capacity building for Metro Academy teams, and space for labs and other student support structures.[12]

When Stella and Charles Guttman Community College (CUNY) welcomed its inaugural class in 2012, every Guttman student began using ePortfolio for learning and assessment. Guttman was the first college in the country to build ePortfolio into its structure, at scale, from its inception. Guttman's ePortfolio initiative has strong institutional support. Each year, 10 Assessment Days are built into the academic calendar, dedicated to faculty and staff assessment of ePortfolios. But even with high-level support, there are challenges. Although used widely, ePortfolio practice remains uneven. Guttman's ePortfolio leaders have developed a sustained focus on ePortfolio pedagogy, working to ensure that ePortfolio is used to create an integrative, reflective learning space and not just as a repository for student artifacts. As Guttman grows, ePortfolio leaders must bring in new faculty and staff each year, introducing them to ePortfolio as a technology, pedagogy, and its role in the assessment of student learning. In its scaling up story, the Guttman team wrote:

> There is much work still to be done developing and sustaining a pervasive culture of ePortfolio and assessment for learning at Guttman. We continue to work across the multiple layers of the institution (students, faculty, programs, institution) engaging our students and developing and deepening our use of ePortfolio as an integrative social pedagogy as well as for institutional assessment of authentic student work.[13]

IUPUI's ePortfolio initiative began in 2000, with a goal of using ePortfolio to assess student achievement of the institution's Principles of Undergraduate Learning. With few examples to follow, ePortfolio leaders forged ahead with the ambitious task of a campus-wide ePortfolio initiative. They didn't anticipate "the magnitude of the paradigm shift that ePortfolios represented, and, consequently, underestimat[ed] faculty development and support needs."[14] When their initial attempts faltered, they persevered; with ongoing institutional support they refocused and started at a more granular level. "Beginning in 2005–06, ePortfolio leaders offered incentives to departments and programs that themselves identified a need related to the ePortfolio."[15]

Working at this smaller scale, the IUPUI team moved forward by recognizing the importance of two sectors of the *Catalyst Framework*: Professional Development and Pedagogy. A pivotal event in the team's story is the development of a student personal development framework embedded in ePortfolio, the ePDP (described in Chapter 3). The success of the ePDP and institutional participation in several national projects (including C2L), helped propel broader use of ePortfolio across IUPUI. After a long history of working with the Sakai ePortfolio platform, which students and faculty found difficult to navigate, the school began a transition to the Canvas platform in 2014. "Today, the campus ePortfolio team supports a diverse array of ePortfolio projects in academic and co-curricular units across the campus, rather than a single ePortfolio initiative with a uniform approach and a shared set of purposes."[16]

LaGuardia's ePortfolio program dates from 2002. Since then, the college has grown and refined its use of ePortfolio, moving from 800 ePortfolios to a cumulative total of more than 130,000 (see Figure 7.2). The first effort was a faculty research team studying the possibility and making recommendations. Then came a pilot, focused on reflective pedagogy:

> Twenty-two faculty from across the disciplines helped to pilot LaGuardia's first ePortfolio platform, a homegrown FTP system, experimenting with ePortfolio pedagogy in the classroom and sharing their experiences. The seeding of ePortfolio continued via attachment to First-Year Academies, learning communities for basic skills students, whose faculty honed their approaches through participation in a year-long professional development seminar.[17]

Based in LaGuardia's robust Center for Teaching and Learning, the team developed professional development activities to involve faculty in integrative pedagogy and

Figure 7.2. LaGuardia Community College Student ePortfolio Use by Year.

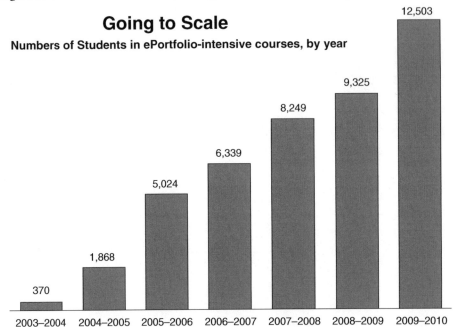

Going to Scale

Numbers of Students in ePortfolio-intensive courses, by year

						12,503
					9,325	
				8,249		
			6,339			
		5,024				
	1,868					
370						
2003–2004	2004–2005	2005–2006	2006–2007	2007–2008	2008–2009	2009–2010

Note. LaGuardia's ePortfolio initiative has grown steadily since 2003. With careful planning and implementation, it now has broad institutional use. From J. Elizabeth Clark, "Growth and Change at LaGuardia: Our Scaling Up Story," *Catalyst for Learning: ePortfolio Resources and Research,* January 25, 2014, http://lagcc.mcnrc.org/scaling-story

student learning. In 2009, as an institutional accreditation visit approached, ePortfolio leaders took on the task of authentic assessment; linking programs and general education, they built a nationally recognized assessment process. However new challenges emerged: faculty and students began to express frustration with the college's ePortfolio platform, which, as of this writing, has yet to fully support social pedagogy. And some faculty began to associate ePortfolio primarily with assessment, not integrative pedagogy.

In this context, the ePortfolio initiative at LaGuardia recently entered a period of renewal. The integration of ePortfolio practice into a newly redesigned, discipline-based, required first-year seminar (FYS) has attracted new faculty interest and revitalized the focus on pedagogy. Each year, 7,000 students are now introduced to ePortfolio as they begin their careers at LaGuardia. Building on the FYS and taking advantage of a new college emphasis on "alignment"—improved linkages between student affairs and academic affairs, a connection focused on better serving the "whole" student—campus ePortfolio leaders launched efforts to use ePortfolio in advisement and co-curricular learning (using ePortfolio-based digital badges). Meanwhile, LaGuardia ePortfolio leaders formalized a broad campus-wide ePortfolio leadership team designed to build engagement and deepen campus ePortfolio culture.

Scaling an ePortfolio initiative is different on every campus. And some scaling stories are not as positive as LaGuardia's. Across the country, many ePortfolio projects remain stuck at the pilot phase. Sometimes there are setbacks. A Manhattanville College proposal to mandate ePortfolio as a graduation requirement, advanced at a time of fiscal uncertainty and threatened cutbacks, met with faculty resistance; the campus ePortfolio team had to re-group. They are now moving forward with a more patient approach, tailored to the current campus context.

Even the successful scaling stories shared here are distinct and varied; each college had its own initial goals and followed different growth paths. But these stories have in common a couple of related themes: (a) The most successful campuses started with either a focus on assessment or on pedagogy, but eventually saw the importance of doing both in tandem; and (b) effective use of professional development plays a central role in most success stories.

Both themes reflect an underlying emphasis on the ability to learn and adapt evolving strategies to meet challenges as they arise. Moreover, these stories are ongoing. Scaling is a continual process, requiring ongoing effort. When attention is paid to all sectors of the *Catalyst Framework*, that ongoing process is more likely to generate a high-impact ePortfolio initiative.

Getting Started: Six Scaling Strategies for an ePortfolio Initiative

As we've seen, attention to the entire *Catalyst Framework* supports efforts to deepen and expand a campus ePortfolio initiative. Are there effective strategies native to the Scaling Up sector itself? In our work with C2L campuses, we observed an array of additional strategies that effective ePortfolio project leaders employ to expand their work. We've distilled our findings to a set of six Scaling Strategies. Some focus on ways to engage and work with specific stakeholder groups, and others highlight campus-wide connections that help foster learning-centered collaboration.

In reviewing these strategies, there are several considerations: (a) although any one of these strategies will help support an ePortfolio initiative, attention to all six will be more likely to help an institution develop a high-impact ePortfolio practice; and (b) while these strategies are particularly useful to consider in the early stages of an initiative, they can also benefit campuses at more advanced stages of implementation.

Scaling Strategy 1: Develop an Effective Campus ePortfolio Team

Leadership is key to the success of any ePortfolio implementation. And although many institutions have one designated point person, such as an ePortfolio director, that person needs to work with a strong team of faculty and staff from across the institution.

The members of an effective leadership team should have strong communication and collaboration skills, budgeting and resource management abilities, and the habits of adaptive learning. Team members should understand ePortfolio pedagogy. Faculty and staff should be active ePortfolio users, modeling good pedagogy and practice. It helps when multiple members are involved in the larger ePortfolio field, participating in ePortfolio conferences and staying abreast of current research.

Faculty play key roles on a leadership team. Based on their classroom experience with students, faculty leaders can model effective ePortfolio pedagogy. As professional development leaders, they can engage peers in designing effective ePortfolio practices. Faculty leaders are persuasive spokespeople for an ePortfolio initiative, building buy-in from faculty colleagues and campus leaders. Effective ePortfolio teams must gather a strong group of faculty leaders and involve them in key stages of the planning process.

An effective ePortfolio leadership team should also include members who can connect with key areas of the college, including the Center for Teaching and Learning, Student Affairs, information technology, assessment, and institutional research. Each area plays a vital role in scaling an ePortfolio initiative. If the leadership team does not include an upper-level administrator, the ePortfolio director must have regular access to key members of the campus administration. Keeping campus administration informed about ePortfolio activities, accomplishments, and challenges is essential to ongoing funding and resources.

In their scaling up story, IUPUI ePortfolio leaders discuss the importance of their ePortfolio leadership team:

> Developing an Effective Campus ePortfolio Team is an ongoing process, evolving along with our understanding of what it means to be "effective." From the outset, [our] ePortfolio team members have represented diverse segments of the institution, including academic administration, the faculty, the Center for Teaching and Learning (CTL), and Planning and Institutional Improvement (PAII), the division that coordinates assessment.
>
> The core ePortfolio leaders come from the campus-level divisions that contribute to the ePortfolio budget or provide other resources: Academic Affairs (including the CTL), PAII, and UITS. Each member of the coordinating group brings to bear a background in two or more areas important to the effectiveness of the ePortfolio Initiative: assessment, faculty and professional development, communications, curriculum and instructional design, and management of technology-related change. In addition, over the past decade, ePortfolio team members have become seasoned ePortfolio leaders who have experience with both success and failure of ePortfolio efforts. They are deeply familiar with the ePortfolio literature, have worked with academic programs in many disciplines, have participated in multiple national and international ePortfolio projects, have advised other campuses undertaking ePortfolio initiatives, and have used ePortfolios in their own teaching and learning practices.[18]

ePortfolio leadership teams incorporate and nurture their capacity to work with a range of campus stakeholders, showing how ePortfolio connects their efforts with the larger work of the institution.

Scaling Strategy 2: Connect to Departments and Programs

Because of its longitudinal and integrative nature, ePortfolio practice works best when it is incorporated across a program or major. When fully integrated into the curriculum and practice of a degree program, ePortfolio practice enables students to more easily make connections among courses in the program and between general education and the major. ePortfolio teams must find ways to connect with the needs, goals, and daily practices of departments and programs.

ePortfolio practice can benefit degree programs by providing a structured context for program leaders to consider alignment of program goals, course goals, course assignments, and student work. Effective ePortfolio teams work with chairs or program coordinators to integrate ePortfolio into program curriculum and support implementation. Making connections to other initiatives, such as outcomes assessment, also helps in this process. At LaGuardia, for example, working directly with program coordinators to connect ePortfolio with program assessment strengthened the ePortfolio and outcomes assessment work.

Many C2L campus teams began their pilot programs by working with key faculty in degree programs. Those initial pilots then served as models for other programs. For example, Tunxis Community College began with pilots in computer information systems and dental hygiene. ePortfolio campus leaders then used those programs as examples to encourage ePortfolio use by other programs, including business administration and early childhood education.

Establishing strong connections with departments and degree programs helps campus ePortfolio teams advance the scaling process. Strategically determining which faculty, departments, and programs to begin with and then cultivating ties accordingly will help root ePortfolio practice in fertile soil. Building strong relationships with some programs encourages other departments and programs to understand and adopt ePortfolio practice.

In addition to degree programs, our C2L research revealed that many ePortfolio teams connect with the High-Impact Practices used on their campus. Effective leadership teams build ties not only with individual HIP faculty but also with programs charged with guiding a HIP initiative, a first-year experience office, for example, or a community-based learning program.

The SFSU team, for example, connected with Metro Academies, the first-year experience program, in 2010. Building connections with these programs, often outside traditional departments, ePortfolio teams strengthen purposeful, interdisciplinary cooperation.

> ePortfolios in Metro are seen as an additional High-Impact Practice in a model program with national attention and the potential to grow. The faculty learning community model provided a rich opportunity within the C2L project to introduce and integrate portfolios & leverage assessment/rubric development with specific application to GE disciplines.[19]

SFSU ePortfolio leaders use that connection as they scale ePortfolio across their institution.

Perhaps because of their emphasis on innovation and experiential learning, high-impact practices provide a natural home for ePortfolio practice. Meanwhile, integrative ePortfolio practice can enhance the value of a specific High-Impact Practice and create opportunities to connect multiple high-impact learning experiences. We explore this connection in Chapter 9.

Scaling Strategy 3: More Deeply Engage Students

Students are key stakeholders in any successful ePortfolio project, and effective leadership teams partner with them to advance scaling. Although our main focus with students is on enhanced learning and success, students are also active players on campus. They can be dynamic voices in the scaling process, making ePortfolio learning visible in ways that engage their peers and attract faculty, staff, and administrative attention.

Student ePortfolio mentors support ePortfolio learning by assisting their peers in building their ePortfolios. On some campuses, mentors work in ePortfolio labs, providing drop-in assistance to any student working with ePortfolio. Student mentors can also support faculty by offering technical assistance as well as working directly with a particular class. Mentors also serve as spokespeople for ePortfolio, encouraging peers and faculty to use ePortfolio in a meaningful way. To learn more, please read the vignette, *Why Student Mentors?*

Why Student Mentors?
Here's What LaGuardia Students Say

In "The Power of Peers: New Ways for Students to Support Students," Arcario, Eynon, and Lucca discussed the importance of student technology mentors and ePortfolio consultants. In this excerpt from that article we hear ePortfolio students report that the peer consultants work to encourage and motivate them. "They understand what you're going through. All the things you'll go through in college. . . . And they help you try to achieve it."[20]

As a consultant put it, "I try to give them a lot of encouragement in general" and "I always show my ePortfolio and encourage them to create a good ePortfolio."[21] Consultants also tried to encourage students by being role models, conveying the idea that if a consultant can do it, then all the students can as well:

> One more thing is that I'm like a role model for students. I tell them, "I'm an international student, I started to work as an STM and then I graduated and started to work this job." And they're like, "Wow, I can do that, too." . . . Because sometimes half of my class comes from all different countries. So they think, "I can do it, too." So I just want to show them they can do all this stuff. So that's really it, for me. That's really it.[22]

Many ePortfolio teams regularly host ePortfolio showcase events. Having students present their ePortfolios to the campus honors exemplary students. It also makes ePortfolio practice visible to stakeholders. Showcases can generate student interest in ePortfolio learning, encourage faculty ePortfolio practice, and build administrative support. At Tunxis, students are recognized in an annual student showcase each spring in which they present their final portfolios at a faculty-wide meeting. Faculty hear students discuss their ePortfolios and reflect on what they learned.[23] Tunxis also holds annual showcases for programmatic advisory boards in computer information systems, business administration, and dental hygiene, involving external stakeholders and helping students link their academic learning to career planning.[24]

Engaging students as active players in the scaling process helps make ePortfolios visible and tangible in ways that faculty, staff, and other stakeholders cannot ignore. The student voice is a powerful one and can be a positive force in the scaling up process.

Scaling Strategy 4: Make Use of Evidence

Effective ePortfolio leaders collect and analyze evidence of ePortfolio's impact on student learning and share their findings with institutional stakeholders. Across higher education, there is growing emphasis on the importance of evaluating the impact of educational innovations. Funders, accreditation agencies, and academic administrators increasingly want to see evidence and use it in decision-making. In this context, ePortfolio leaders have found that evaluation evidence also strengthens their own insights and helps garner needed resources.

Gathering and analyzing meaningful evidence of impact can be challenging. Evaluation takes planning, persistence, and skill. Proof of impact in education is rare, and rigorous control group studies are expensive and difficult to set up and manage. ePortfolio leaders often lack the training and resources to take on meaningful evaluation along with everything else they're doing. And on underresourced campuses, the institutional research office is often too overloaded to help. All too often, ePortfolio teams fall back on anecdotal evidence.

In C2L, the most effective campus teams were able to overcome the obstacles and gather evidence, indicating that ePortfolio use correlates with improvements in student learning and success (see Chapter 8). We found that careful planning was key to the work of these teams. Following are the four main steps in planning and implementing a meaningful and manageable evaluation process:

1. Consider and articulate project goals
2. Identify multiple measures for each goal
3. Collect and analyze evidence, identifying improvements and next steps
4. Share evidence and analysis with institutional stakeholders.

1. Consider and articulate project goals. In C2L effective ePortfolio teams considered project goals in order to identify the appropriate outcomes or measures. These leaders weighed what was important for their campus in terms of issues, needs, and institutional outcomes. They considered what stakeholders valued, what funders required, and what their ePortfolio project might reasonably accomplish. In most cases, these goals included improvements in student engagement and student learning as well as other goals important to their campus.

2. Identify multiple measures for each goal. Having articulated project goals, teams selected appropriate quantitative or qualitative measures for each goal. Depending on goals, outcomes, and needs, measures used included surveys, outcomes data, and qualitative evidence of student learning from ePortfolios. Using student work as evidence helps complement retention and other quantitative data by bringing the authentic student work and student voice into the evaluation process (see Table 7.1).

When evaluating an ePortfolio initiative, challenges arise around the questions of comparison groups and isolating the impact of ePortfolio. Isolating variables and scientifically proving causality in education are difficult tasks. Because the value of

TABLE 7.1
Make Use of Evidence: Tunxis Community College's 2011 to 2012 Evaluation Plan

Goal	Measure
1A. Create a vibrant teaching and learning community using ePortfolio 1B. Design a comprehensive faculty development plan centered on ePortfolio	• Faculty Training Survey • Number of faculty using ePortfolio in courses • Number of faculty who participate in the *ePortfolio Seminar Series* • Number of faculty who participate in the *ePortfolio Continuing Conversations* series • Faculty reflection narratives
2A. Student engagement with ePortfolio 2B. Increased student understanding of ePortfolio 2C. Student awareness of integration of knowledge within a degree program	• ePortfolio student survey (2009–2010) • Capstone student survey (2009–2011) • Number of student ePortfolios created
3. Increased student success and retention	• Comparison of success (C- or better) rates in ePortfolio/non-ePortfolio sections in developmental English • Retention rate comparison in developmental English • College-wide retention rates based on number of ePortfolio courses • Examination of student work
4. Effective use of ePortfolio for assessment	• Percentage of students using ePortfolio to demonstrate program outcomes • Percentage of students using ePortfolio to demonstrate general education outcomes

Note. From the beginning of their ePortfolio initiative, ePortfolio leaders at Tunxis worked to identify, gather, and analyze evidence of impact that aligned with project goals. From Laura M. Gambino, "Tunxis Community College Evaluation Plan" (Evaluation Plan, 2011). Reprinted with permission of Laura M. Gambino.

ePortfolio practice emerges from its ability to connect multiple learning experiences, eliminating multiple variables (or a randomized controlled trial) is virtually impossible. Given these challenges, evaluation plans often include mixed or multiple measures, used to identify correlations between ePortfolio use and gains in student success.

3. Collect and analyze the evidence, identifying improvements and next steps. Once data sources and measures are identified, the next step is to gather and analyze the data. C2L teams considered what collection and analysis they could do on their own and when and how to collaborate with their campus Institutional Research (IR) Office. IR can assist with planning evaluations, and with data collection and analysis. Some teams develop sustained partnerships with these offices; others incorporate someone from IR on their ePortfolio team. Either way, teams benefit from working with someone who brings sophisticated training in interpreting a range of data sources.

After the data are analyzed, teams must consider what they show in terms of project goals. What impact has ePortfolio practice had on student learning and success? Do the data reveal bottlenecks? Emergent strategies? Are there ways to improve ePortfolio pedagogy and practice? Given the evidence, what next steps can be taken to advance project goals? It is important to consider these questions when sharing findings with institutional stakeholders.

4. Share evidence and analysis with institutional stakeholders. When sharing findings and recommendations, effective ePortfolio leaders consider what evidence will be most meaningful to each stakeholder group. Faculty, for example, may be most interested in qualitative evidence of improved student learning, such as case studies. Administrators may want to focus on outcomes data; retention, success, and graduation rates, for example. This evidence can be used to garner resources needed to scale an ePortfolio initiative.

Making effective use of evidence is important to long-term project sustainability. Effective ePortfolio leaders do this early in a thoughtful, sustained, and systematic process. Leaders must also recognize that positive impact rarely occurs overnight; it can take several semesters or longer. In the long run, attention to evidence is vitally important to help stakeholders see the value of scaling up ePortfolio practice.

Scaling Strategy 5: Leverage Resources

Like any campus innovation, an ePortfolio project needs resources to thrive. Effective ePortfolio leaders work with key administrators to obtain funds from their college's budget; they also pursue external funding to advance scaling.

Across C2L, ePortfolio teams worked with administrators to obtain the resources to support ePortfolio leaders, professional development, and effective technology. Some campuses used faculty reassigned time or stipends to support the work of the ePortfolio leaders. Others went further to fund ePortfolio positions. Support for ePortfolio-related professional development is also critical. Funds are required to purchase an ePortfolio platform and provide technical support, even if it involves peer mentors. Physical space to house peer mentors and ePortfolio lab space are important as well.

In times of cutbacks, attracting internal funds can be challenging, and external funding can help. Grant funding helped some C2L teams expand their projects. LaGuardia's grant-writing success helped build its ePortfolio initiative. LaGuardia's ePortfolio work was launched in 2001 with a five-year grant from the Title V program for Hispanic-serving institutions of the U.S. Department of Education. ePortfolio leaders at LaGuardia have connected ePortfolio to other sources, such as Carl D. Perkins funds from the U.S. Department of Education (enhancing the success and technical literacy of vocational education students) and CUNY sources (supporting general education and assessment). A subsequent Title V grant focused on strengthening capstone education and helped build ePortfolio use in that area.[25] Boston University sity obtained funding from the Davis Educational Foundation to begin its ePortfolio initiative in the College of General Studies; subsequent Davis funding has allowed it to deepen assessment and pedagogical work.[26]

When seeking internal or external funding, evidence of impact is invaluable. Being able to demonstrate the positive impact of ePortfolio practice on student learning and success greatly strengthens funding requests. Using evidence and connecting to stakeholders are key elements of a successful funding strategy.

Scaling Strategy 6: Align With Institutional Planning

High-impact ePortfolio practice requires engagement and support from a broad range of campus stakeholders, from faculty to student affairs staff to administrators. To facilitate this, effective leadership teams connect ePortfolio work to key institutional initiatives, such as general education, outcomes assessment, and improving student success. To work across these areas, effective ePortfolio leaders ensure that ePortfolio is part of broader institutional planning efforts. They build partnerships with college administration and work with governance structures and strategic planning processes.

In C2L many campus ePortfolio leaders connected with institutional leaders who served as allies in their ePortfolio work. In their scaling up stories, C2L teams repeatedly emphasize the importance of having a good working relationship with a key administrator. In some cases academic leaders support the project from its initiation. Even if administrative support is not initially strong, successful ePortfolio leaders continually work to build administrative connections.

Effective ePortfolio leaders also work with college governance structures. Getting governance approval solidifies the role of ePortfolio practice. At Salt Lake Community College, after a successful pilot ePortfolio project, leader David Hubert took on this task and noted the following:

> [We] worked with an interested group of faculty, staff and administrators to develop a proposal to make ePortfolios a course-level requirement in all General Education courses. The initial proposal passed the General Education committee, but was defeated in the Curriculum Committee. A revised proposal later passed the Curriculum Committee and the Faculty Senate, and was approved by the President's Cabinet in the Fall of 2009. Six years later, SLCC has a vibrant and robust ePortfolio project.[27]

Seeking to scale beyond the nursing program, the Three Rivers Community College team worked with the college's General Education Task Force as they developed an institutional assessment plan. According to Hubert, "Through an open dialogue with faculty, administrators, and students, we have reached a consensus: ePortfolios will now be used college-wide for general education and programmatic assessment of student learning."[28]

At Pace University, ePortfolio leaders saw an opportunity to introduce faculty to ePortfolio through the promotion and tenure process. They developed a plan to have faculty submit promotion and tenure applications using ePortfolios. These leaders spoke with the provost, and after gaining support, received approval from the faculty council and the college's promotion and tenure committee. As of this writing, every faculty member seeking promotion or tenure submits an ePortfolio.[29]

Effective C2L campus leaders also worked to incorporate ePortfolio into their institution's strategic planning process. Achieving this milestone serves as a visible sign of long-term institutional commitment. And having ePortfolio in the strategic plan helps project leaders obtain needed resources and support. When a strategic plan guides the work of a college, incorporating the ePortfolio project in that plan can prompt departments to consider ePortfolio practice. In some smaller colleges, such as Tunxis and Guttman, ePortfolio is included in the institution-wide strategic plan. In larger universities, ePortfolio is more often included in college or departmental strategic plans that connect to broader institutional planning goals. One way or another, effective ePortfolio teams pay attention to strategic goals and plans, and it helps them build stakeholder support and scale their projects.

Each of the six strategies we have discussed can help strengthen and scale an institution's ePortfolio initiative. Many of these strategies work best in tandem. For example, gathering evidence can strengthen a team's ability to secure resources. Developing a diverse leadership team can help build connections with departments and programs and align an ePortfolio project with institutional planning efforts. Used together, the six Scaling Strategies can help institutions scale high-impact ePortfolio practice and advance toward an institutional learning culture.

Connections to the *Catalyst Framework*

The Scaling Up sector relies on each of the other sectors of the *Catalyst Framework*. Scaling an ePortfolio initiative cannot take place without focusing on Pedagogy and Professional Development, connecting to Outcomes Assessment, and making sure there is an effective Technology platform to support an institution's needs.

Pedagogy

Employing integrative social pedagogy to guide ePortfolio practice in courses and advising can make ePortfolio practice more effective, improve student learning, and engage faculty and staff. Evidence that ePortfolio practice advances student success can build campus support for scaling.

Effective C2L leaders use insight into pedagogy to advance scaling. Highlighting pedagogy invites faculty to see ePortfolio in new ways. C2L teams help faculty and staff share ePortfolio pedagogy through faculty showcases, mini conferences, and publications. Faculty leaders are crucial to this dialogue. When faculty leaders share effective ePortfolio practices and their impact on student learning, it sparks the interest of other faculty and staff. Supported with professional development, this increased interest can broaden campus use.

Perhaps most important, connecting scaling efforts with pedagogical innovations can focus campus attention on teaching and learning. Used well, ePortfolio's capacity to make student learning visible and the data on ePortfolio-enhanced student learning can help deepen understanding of the connections between teaching and learning, between student-centered pedagogy and improved outcomes. Highlighting innovative pedagogies encourages faculty to consider new ways of learning for students and for themselves, and it spurs institutions to keep student learning at the center of campus-wide decision-making.

Professional Development

ePortfolio initiatives grow when supported by thoughtful professional development that enables faculty and staff to explore ePortfolio pedagogy and practice. From workshops to year-long seminars, professional development processes help educators root ePortfolio activities and reflection practices in their course goals. Done well, professional development increases faculty understanding of ePortfolio as an integrative social pedagogy. Effective professional development helps to not only broaden campus ePortfolio use but also deepen its campus-wide impact on student learning and success.

Outcomes Assessment

Campuses face wide pressure to improve outcomes assessment. ePortfolio practice can enable an ecosystemic view of assessment and function as a circulatory system, giving multiple stakeholders a richer and more continuous flow of evidence (student work, student reflection, and faculty and staff reflection) on how students achieve key competencies. C2L leaders who connect ePortfolio with outcomes assessment tend to be successful in expanding campus ePortfolio use. Yet such connections must be approached with care to avoid obscuring ePortfolio pedagogy and its value in building student learning.

Assessment can advance scaling of an ePortfolio project by helping to attract campus resources and support. External accreditation requirements may add leverage. Alternatively, if there is already a strong connection between assessment and ePortfolio, this connection can catalyze growth in other sectors of the *Catalyst Framework* such as Pedagogy. Demonstrating the effectiveness of ePortfolio-based outcomes assessment with programs can encourage adoption across academic programs.

Technology

An ePortfolio platform that effectively meets a broad range of campus needs is critical to scaling. When selecting an ePortfolio platform, it is important to ensure that it will support institutional needs, from effective pedagogy to authentic assessment.

Scaling ePortfolio practice requires appropriate levels of support for using the technology. As mentioned earlier, student mentors are one way campuses provide technical support to students, faculty, and staff. Tutorial materials, videos, and other multimedia resources can also support users. Having a dedicated student ePortfolio lab is another valuable component of technology support. In their planning processes, successful campuses provide the financial and infrastructure resources needed to support the effective use of their ePortfolio platform.

Scaling requires attention across the *Catalyst Framework* sectors. Increasing faculty and staff use of effective ePortfolio pedagogy relies on Professional Development. Meaningful Outcomes Assessment that "closes the loop" depends on Technology and Pedagogy. And when faculty and staff know that the appropriate Technology supports are in place for students, they are more likely to integrate ePortfolio into their teaching and learning practices. Positioned at the intersection of all five sectors, ePortfolio leaders can more effectively plan and act to scale their ePortfolio project, growing from pilot to a broader, more well-established institutional use.

Conclusion

Scaling innovation is challenging. Building a robust and successful ePortfolio initiative demands thoughtful, sustained effort. Careful attention must be paid to work in each sector of the *Catalyst Framework*. The most successful ePortfolio teams intentionally work across sectors, developing reflective social pedagogies, managing new technologies, and guiding professional development and outcomes assessment processes.

Effective ePortfolio leaders also attend to a range of other tasks, issues, and processes that build campus engagement and institutional support. The most successful C2L campuses deployed most or all of the six Scaling Strategies reviewed in this chapter, from engaging students as stakeholders to focusing attention on evidence of impact and aligning with campus strategic planning. Used in combination with attention to the Catalyst sectors, these strategies help leaders scale their ePortfolio initiative and build campus-wide integration.

Notes

1. Phil Hill, "Pilots: Too Many Ed Tech Innovations Stuck in Purgatory," e-Literate (blog), August 12, 2014, http://mfeldstein.com/pilots-many-ed-tech-innovations-stuck-purgatory/

2. Everett M. Rodgers, *Diffusion of Innovations* (New York, NY: Free Press, 2005).

3. Hill, "Pilots."

4. Campus Computing Project, "The 2015 Campus Computing Survey," accessed August 19, 2015, http://www.campuscomputing.net/item/2015-campus-computing-survey-0

5. Lillian Rafeldt, "Scaling Up Is a Process," *Catalyst for Learning: ePortfolio Resources and Research*, January 25, 2014, http://trcc.mcnrc.org/scaling-story/

6. Rafeldt, "Scaling Up Is a Process."

7. Rafeldt, "Scaling Up Is a Process."

8. Natalie McKnight, Gillian Pierce, Amod Lele, and John Regan, "Our Scaling Up Story," *Catalyst for Learning: ePortfolio Resources and Research*, January 25, 2014, http://bu.mcnrc.org/bu-scaling-story/

9. McKnight et al., "Our Scaling Up Story."

10. San Francisco State University, "Scaling Up While Drilling Down: How an Expanding ePortfolio Initiative Dives Into the First-Year Experience," *Catalyst for Learning: ePortfolio Resources and Research*, January 25, 2014, http://sfsu.mcnrc.org/scaling-story/

11. San Francisco State University, "Scaling Up."

12. Ibid.

13. Laura M. Gambino, Chet Jordan, and Nate Mickelson, "Doing Things Differently: Scaling Up at Guttman Community College," *Catalyst for Learning: ePortfolio Resources and Research*, January 25, 2014, http://gcc.mcnrc.org/scaling-story/

14. Susan Kahn and Susan Scott, "Scaling Up ePortfolios at a Complex Urban Research University: The IUPUI Story," *Catalyst for Learning: ePortfolio Resources and Research*, January 25, 2014, http://iupui.mcnrc.org/scaling-story/

15. Kahn and Scott, "Scaling Up ePortfolios."

16. Ibid.

17. J. Elizabeth Clark, "Growth and Change at LaGuardia: Our Scaling Up Story," *Catalyst for Learning: ePortfolio Resources and Research*, January 25, 2014, http://lagcc.mcnrc.org/scaling-story/

18. Kahn and Scott, "Scaling Up ePortfolios."

19. San Francisco State University, "Scaling Up."

20. Paul Arcario, Bret Eynon, and Louis Lucca, "The Power of Peers: New Ways for Students to Support Students," in *Making Teaching and Learning Matter Tranformative Spaces in Higher Education,* eds. Judith Summerfeld and Cheryl C. Smith (Dordrecht, Netherlands: Springer, 2011), 201.

21. Arcario et al., "The Power of Peers," 201.

22. Ibid.

23. Amy Feest, George Sebastian-Coleman, Jen Wittke, and Marguerite Yawin, "Scaling Up at Tunxis Community College," *Catalyst for Learning: ePortfolio Resources and Research*, January 25, 2014, http://tcc.mcnrc.org/scaling-story/

24. Feest et al., "Scaling Up at Tunxis Community College."

25. Clark, "Growth and Change at LaGuardia."

26. McKnight et al., "Our Scaling Up Story."

27. Salt Lake Community College, "Hiking Over the Hump: SLCC's Scaling Up Story," *Catalyst for Learning: ePortfolio Resources and Research*, January 25, 2014, http://slcc.mcnrc.org/scaling-story/

28. Lillian A. Rafeldt, Heather Jane Bader, Nancy Lesnick Czarzasty, Ellen Freeman, Edith Ouellet, and Judith M. Snayd, "Reflection Builds 21st Century Professionals: ePortfolio and Nursing Education at Three Rivers Community College," *Peer Review* 16, no. 1 (Winter 2014), 19–23.

29. Pace University, "Scaling Up Story: Picking Up the Pace With ePortfolios." *Catalyst for Learning: ePortfolio Resources and Research*, January 25, 2014, http://pu.mcnrc.org/scaling-story/

FROM SCALING TO TRANSFORMATION

ePortfolio and the Rebundling of Higher Education

Randy Bass

Scaling ePortfolio initiatives from early implementation toward institutionalization requires system-level strategies that connect individual practices (students and faculty) to larger structures, frameworks, cultural practices and policies that make up the institution. Connecting pedagogy to assessment (and assessment to institutional outcomes), the necessity of effective professional development, and the need to leverage cross-boundary programs such as advisement and first-year experiences: these all speak to the interrelationship between scaling strategies and the institutional and cultural dimensions of high-impact ePortfolio practice.

As they scale in institutions, ePortfolio initiatives increasingly serve as a network of connections among students and faculty and programs and majors. As they leverage institutional initiatives, such as general education, outcomes assessment, and other High-Impact Practices, they also serve to integrate often-marginalized centers of innovation. Through such connections, ePortfolio initiatives inform and deepen pedagogical practices campus-wide and introduce increasingly rich views of student learning into the everyday flows of teaching, learning, assessment, and curriculum design.

The very qualities of ePortfolio that both enable and demand such connections are evidence of the ways that they straddle established and emerging paradigms of learning for higher education; this is their unique power. This also poses a distinct design challenge when understanding the nature of scaling and the relationship between scaling and institutional transformation.

The two paradigms can be understood more or less in the same vein as Robert Barr and John Tagg's well-known framing in 1995 that higher education was shifting from an "instructional paradigm" to a "learning paradigm."[1] The long-established instructional paradigm focuses primarily on the formal curriculum, courses, programs and majors; it emphasizes knowledge transfer and cognition, delivered through curricular design that is generally atomistic, linear, and built on inputs. Now growing in strength and momentum, the emerging paradigm is an extension of what they meant by the "learning paradigm." It encompasses the importance of both curriculum and co-curriculum, focuses on student learning as an outcome, and understands learning to be fundamentally integrative and iterative.

The most powerful scaling practices will be informed by the ways ePortfolio bridges the established instructional and the emergent learning paradigms—and the way that such scaling can advance the emergence of a new vision for higher education. In this deepening effect, the ePortfolio scaling process itself pulls institutions toward the emergent, learning-centered paradigm. The third C2L value proposition, detailed and documented in Chapter 8, addresses the difference ePortfolio can make in catalyzing such institutional change:

> *Proposition 3: ePortfolio practice, done well, catalyzes learning-centered institutional change. Focusing attention on student learning and prompting connection and cooperation across departments and divisions, ePortfolio initiatives can catalyze campus cultural and structural change, helping colleges and universities develop as learning organizations.*

As catalysts for organizational change, ePortfolio initiatives can help institutions meet the challenges of developing a learning culture and navigating a turbulent higher education landscape. In this landscape there are two distinct expressions of the learning paradigm—what we might call the integrative and the disintegrative. The disintegrative forces of the emerging learning paradigm arise out of the explosion of interest in massive online learning, adaptive learning systems, learning analytics, and granular certification. These all reflect the paradigm shift that places value on access to learning and personalization of learning and education. However, these forces threaten to advance the paradigm in disintegrative ways, unbundling education into a series of disparate and disconnected experiences; in turn, this unbundling creates challenges for more integrative efforts to advance local institutional value, the impact of community on learning, and the holistic dimensions of education.

It is in the landscape characterized by the tension between the integrative and the disintegrative that strategies for scaling ePortfolio practice become particularly salient. The capacity to bridge to a more integrative version of the emergent learning paradigm significantly enhances the value of ePortfolio in catalyzing organizational and institutional change.

Thinking in Ecosystems

Innovative ePortfolio practices can help solve problems and meet challenges that institutions did not have 30 years ago. This is where the true power of ePortfolio may lie—in its capacity to push toward new practices and a new paradigm, while at the same time operating under the design constraints of current structures. ePortfolio leaders must see scaling strategies as opportunities to connect ePortfolio initiatives to the core priorities for building a culture of learning in their institutions, which might include:

- an increasingly robust vision of general education that goes beyond knowledge areas to skills and dispositions;
- a vision of the first-year experience that looks very broadly at student success;
- a new priority on transparency and alignment of learning goals among courses, programs, and the institution, also including (but not limited to) the complementary pressures on assessment and accountability; and
- a growing appreciation for integrative learning experiences, including such curricular and co-curricular opportunities as learning communities, service-learning, community-based learning, and capstone experiences.

For the most part, these are new priorities for higher education, emerging in recent decades as part of a broad shift to a paradigm that is learning-focused, outcomes-driven, and student-centered. Co-evolving with these expanding practices, ePortfolios provide a context for bringing together stakeholders from across boundaries, creating a network of connections that respond to the ecosystemic nature of institutions.

By their integrative nature, ePortfolio initiatives foster collaborations across silos, connecting faculty, academic staff, student affairs professionals, advising professionals, writing centers, technologists, librarians, employers, alumni, internship coordinators, community partners, and many more. According to the *Catalyst Framework*, successful initiatives also work in tandem with departments and programs, general education, outcomes assessment, and High-Impact Practices, especially first-year and capstone experiences, as well as service-learning, undergraduate research, and study abroad (see Chapter 9).

Each of these connections is critical to the scaling and development of a high-impact ePortfolio initiative. Moreover, the network quality, or interrelationship, of these connections illustrate the intrinsic qualities of ePortfolio and the strategic opportunities it offers. For example, there is a critical relationship between the capacity of ePortfolio to enable students to more easily make connections among the courses in a degree program (and between general education courses and program courses), on the one hand, and on the other, for faculty, through their connection to ePortfolio initiatives, to think about the coherence of their programmatic curriculum and its relationship to the broader curriculum.

Similarly, on some campuses, ePortfolio provides the apparatus that links first-year experiences, general education programs, and outcomes assessment, efforts that are all too often compartmentalized. ePortfolio initiatives can build connections among such efforts and, by providing data and authentic evidence of student learning, help obtain support from allies in administration, faculty governance, or the strategic planning process.

Co-evolving with the practices of the emerging learning paradigm, ePortfolio initiatives strengthen a network of essential, reinforcing connections. Integrating ePortfolio practice into institutional culture helps create and catalyze an institutional ethos of learning.

ePortfolio as a Catalyst for Strategic Change

Perhaps the most fundamental connections forged by ePortfolios, as a student-owned integrative learning space, are between institutionally defined experiences (i.e., courses, assignments and goals as understood by faculty, programs, majors, schools) and the lived experience of the student. That connection is the first premise of ePortfolio's capacity for being a catalyst for change because it provides a context for working incrementally and transformatively at the same time.

What does it mean to be a catalyst for change? What's the vision of change that is prefigured by ePortfolio? There are at least three layers to this vision that have been implied in the discussion so far.

1. Integrative learning culture: Shift to a student-organized view of learning, bridging curriculum and co-curriculum, where learners pull from knowledge resources and offerings to construct an increasingly customized educational experience that is professionally productive and personally meaningful
2. Integrative learning analytics: Development of an institutional conversation on student learning that can provide a framework for integrating data on student achievement and move the institution toward a learning-centered culture and structure
3. Strategic change: Context for institutions to involve faculty and other stakeholders in institutional change and to define and renew their local institutional value and character

These all bear on scaling strategies for ePortfolio initiatives. For example, in the sphere of professional development, ePortfolio practice invites faculty and staff to understand the student learning space differently while at the same time anchoring ePortfolio assignments and reflection practices in their course goals. By its integrative nature, ePortfolio practice provides faculty with a way to think beyond their courses, connect course goals to program goals, and potentially connect course content to broader student experiences.

ePortfolio practice also provides a structured and concrete context for program and department leaders to think about alignment of program goals, course goals, course assignments, and student work. Faculty and staff engaged in ePortfolio initiatives regularly address issues of alignment among course and program goals, assignments and student work, assessment criteria, learning analytics, and institutional outcomes. This is one of the ways ePortfolio practice nurtures learning cultures that grow organically from the ground up, from pilot to broader implementation.

Through engagement with institutional planning and strategic initiatives, ePortfolio practice can help institutions think about investments made in structures that promote integrative experiences. Reflective social ePortfolio practice makes visible dimensions of the educational experience that are often invisible or at best, marginal. This visibility makes possible what has been called *institutional learning*, and it is crucial to the process in which ePortfolio forms a bridge to the emergent learning paradigm.

Enabling a "Positive Restlessness" About Student Learning

George Kuh and colleagues identified the characteristics of schools that outperform expectations with higher than predicted graduation rates and higher than predicted National Survey of Student Engagement scores.[2] Features that foster student engagement and persistence include:

- a living mission and lived educational philosophy,
- an unshakeable focus on student learning,
- environments adapted for educational enrichment,
- clearly marked pathways for student success,
- an improvement-oriented ethos, and
- shared responsibility for educational quality and student success.

They found that these institutions share an

> ethic that permeates the campuses—a tapestry of values and beliefs that reflect the institutions' willingness to take on matters of substance consistent with their priorities. Indeed they exude a sense of "positive restlessness" in how they think about themselves and what they aspire to be.[3]

In practice, an ethos of positive restlessness is difficult to mount and to sustain. In most institutions, it is a challenge to weave cycles of systematic improvement, based on rich evidence of student learning, into the fabric of everyday practice. This is difficult enough to achieve in individual programs, let alone across boundaries of all the areas of the institution that influence student learning. Although this kind of focus is highly valued, it is often perceived as pressure to do assessment imposed from the top down, adding to faculty work and therefore difficult to sustain.

ePortfolio can serve as a catalyst for change precisely by providing a set of practices and connections that enable an institution to carry out an unshakeable focus on student learning and a shared responsibility for educational quality and student success in ways that connect to faculty, students, and programs. This is illustrated throughout C2L by campus efforts to closely tie ePortfolio to outcomes assessment in ways that fit with faculty culture and can be sustained beyond periodic scrambles for accreditation or pressures for accountability. Such efforts can serve to bridge, in Helen Barrett's distinction, "assessment of learning" with "assessment for learning," arriving at a new framing of what Darren Cambridge has called assessment for institutional learning.[4]

This is an especially valuable framework in the context of rising interest in learning analytics that can be harvested from virtual learning systems, such as LMS and adaptive learning environments. As useful as these analytics can be in tracking student activity and attainment in circumscribed contexts of instruction, they are insufficient by themselves for building a portrait of the whole learner and incorporating learning that takes place in more diverse settings. Offering a different type of evidence and a more holistic perspective, ePortfolios can serve as an integrative space for drawing together learning analytics from multiple sources from the perspective of the student (empowering learners to read and contextualize their own analytics) and of the institution (enabling faculty to see alignment of parts to whole).

For this kind of integrative campus learning culture to thrive, it must function coherently at multiple levels, from course improvement to program improvement to institutional learning. This ecosystemic view of assessment can be significantly enabled by ePortfolio, which can serve as a connector or circulatory system for giving multiple stakeholders a continuous, structured flow of evidence (including student work, student reflection, and faculty and staff reflection) on how students are achieving institutional goals.

From Scaling to Transformation

As we have seen across the C2L campuses, ePortfolio initiatives can help institutions meet the challenges of building a culture of learning. ePortfolio practice prefigures an important part of what a learning-centered institution would look like by offering an integrative view of the student learning experience where learning goals are mapped over time, across courses and diverse experiences, within and beyond the walls of the classroom. This can serve as a critical bridge to a more integrative version of the emerging learning paradigm.

An integrative ethos has long framed the most meaningful education in privileged residential environments. Armed with new tools, knowledge about effective learning and a stronger drive for equity, we now have the opportunity to offer an integrative education to all students seeking any kind of college education.

The integrative version of the emergent learning paradigm is distinguished in part by its emphasis on greater access and success, engaging the growing new majority of low-income, minority, and first-generation students with the most powerful forms of learning and intensive educational support. There are also more qualitative differences to this integrative version of the emergent learning paradigm. In this version, institutions function more like integrative networks, with stronger internal connections and more porous boundaries to connections beyond the institution; in this version, stakeholders within institutions start to restructure relationships among programs and divisions that have typically been disconnected (e.g., student affairs and academic affairs). In addition, in this version, educators create new programs and pathways that facilitate the iterative opportunities for students to connect theory, practice and reflection, including ways to better integrate curricular and co-curricular learning.

The evolution of higher education in the next decade will be driven in no small part by the tensions and divergent impulses visibly present in the changing ecology of higher education. Changes in ecosystem are being driven by an intensive focus on student success, completion, and employability; widespread emphasis on accountability, standardized testing, and easily obtained metrics of attainment; and an accelerating interest in modularizing education so that it is more portable, flexible, and affordable. The explosion of digital learning environments is exponentially expanding the options for online learning from non-traditional providers and driving traditional institutions toward more standardized, interchangeable curricula. The granular qualities of many digital innovations, as discussed previously, have reinforced a decidedly disintegrative trend.

These impulses are set against other forces in the current ecosystem, including a robust democratic vision of the values of a liberal education for all students and the importance of higher order skills and dispositions for long-term success and personal fulfillment. This more integrative vision also values outcomes assessment and analytics but takes account of the complexity of learning that involves cognitive, affective, and metacognitive dimensions through iterative experience. It also takes note of the growing evidence, found in the research literature on "guided pathways," that new majority students, in particular, are most likely to thrive in a context of curricular coherence and sustained support.

ePortfolio practices can help institutions negotiate among these tensions and catalyze change that is incremental and potentially transformative at the same time. ePortfolio initiatives can do this in at least three ways:

- ePortfolio initiatives have demonstrated impact on retention and graduation rates, serving the ends of completion and student success; yet ePortfolio also serves to deepen the impact of learning by providing an integrative space where students can reflect on the meaning of their learning and articulate a sense of identity and purpose.
- ePortfolio initiatives can serve institutional priorities on assessment and accountability, not by reduction of learning to simple metrics or testing, but by making the richness of student work visible and engaging multiple stakeholders in ongoing conversation about the evidence of student learning calibrated to institutional and programmatic learning goals.
- ePortfolio can serve as an effective tool for connecting curricular parts to wholes. Organized around the student experience, ePortfolios bring together multiple stakeholders across silos to interrogate how often discrete components of the educational experience reinforce each other.

In this regard, ePortfolio practice supports the emergence of a "third way," an alternative to the polarized tensions between "unbundling" on one hand and simply staying the same, on the other. As Bass and Eynon argue in *Open and Integrative: Designing Liberal Education for the Digital Learning Ecosystem,* the most promising path for higher education is neither unbundling nor stasis, but rather *rebundling*—combining the best traditions of higher education with the powers of granular digital tools to offer more effective and integrative learning environments to all students.[5]

The role of ePortfolio practice in this vision anticipates the ways that institutions will, increasingly and necessarily, need to become recentered around the kind of learning that is most distinctive to colleges and universities: the kind of learning associated with High-Impact Practices, mentored inquiry, and integrative learning that links theory with experience. In the swirl of competing forces and disruptive changes, ePortfolio incorporates a set of powerful enabling practices for ensuring that institutions can be recentered around a high-impact integrative curriculum. High-impact ePortfolio practices draw on, connect, and intensify the rest of the curriculum, the modular, foundational, and interchangeable building blocks of an education. And at the same time, ePortfolio practices can take into account and spotlight the ways that individual practices, programs and pathways can be combined or rebundled in new ways.

In this emerging context for higher education, ePortfolio practice has a central role to play in bridging to this new world and in helping to make the argument that a high-impact curricular core is possible in this new landscape. Connecting what is fragmented; empowering students, faculty, and other stakeholders to transform learning, teaching and institutional practice; creating opportunities for rebundling in new forms: high-impact ePortfolio practice can help institutions shape a more intentional and integrative strategy for navigating the on-going disruptions of the higher education landscape.

Notes

1. Robert B. Barr and John Tagg, "From Teaching to Learning: A New Paradigm for Undergraduate Education." *Change*, November/December, 1995, 13–25.

2. George D. Kuh, Jillian Kinzie, John H. Schuh, Elizabeth J. Whitt, and Associates, *Student Success in College: Creating Conditions That Matter* (San Francisco, CA: Wiley, 2005).

3. George D. Kuh, Jillian Kinzie, John H. Schuh, and Elizabeth J. Whitt, "Never Let It Rest: Lessons About Student Success From High-Performing Colleges and Universities," *Change* 37, no. 4 (2005): 46.

4. Helen Barrett, "Balancing 'ePortfolio as Test' with 'ePortfolio as Story'" (presentation, International Society for Technology in Education and University of Alaska Anchorage), accessed August 15, 2016, http://electronicportfolios.com/portfolios/njedgenet.pdf; Bret Eynon, "'The Future of ePortfolio' Roundtable," Academic Commons, accessed June 20, 2009, http://www.academiccommons.org/commons/essay/future-eportfolio-roundtable

5. Randy Bass and Bret Eynon, *Open and Integrative: Designing Liberal Education for the New Digital Ecosystem* (Washington, DC: American Association of Colleges and Universities, 2016).

PART THREE

THE DIFFERENCE
ePORTFOLIO MAKES

WHY ePORTFOLIO?

The Impact of ePortfolio Done Well

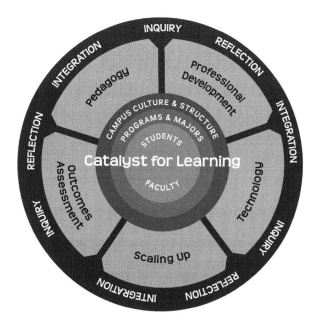

Does ePortfolio practice, done well, advance student learning? As we saw in Chapters 2 through 7, the *Catalyst Framework* offers strategies colleges can use to launch, develop, and sustain high-impact ePortfolio practice. With its interlocking sectors—Pedagogy, Professional Development, Outcomes Assessment, Technology, and Scaling Up—educators have a framework for effective ePortfolio implementation. In this chapter we address the questions that clearly come next: What difference does ePortfolio make? What is the impact of ePortfolio practice done well on student, faculty, and institutional learning? What evidence did the Connect to Learning (C2L) campuses generate? What does this evidence suggest?

This chapter is adapted from an article published in the *International Journal of ePortfolio* by Bret Eynon, Laura M. Gambino, and Judit Torok: "What Difference Can ePortfolio Make? A Field Report from the Connect to Learning Project." Vol 4, no. 1, Spring 2014, http://www.theijep.com/pdf/IJEP127.pdf

Educational practices are considered "high-impact" when they "appear to engage students at levels that elevate their performance across multiple engagement and desired outcomes measures such as persistence."[1] In this chapter, we share C2L data that suggest that when "done well," ePortfolio practice correlates with advances in student engagement, learning, and success. We also find that sophisticated ePortfolio projects can build connections and catalyze the development of colleges as adaptive learning organizations.

These findings address an important need. Facing dwindling resources and new pressures to improve student success, colleges must evaluate the value of ePortfolio practice or any other innovation before mainstreaming it. Faculty and administrators want to know why they should use ePortfolio: What difference can ePortfolio make? Can ePortfolio practice help advance student learning? Is ePortfolio worth an investment of institutional resources? What evidence demonstrates the value of an ePortfolio initiative?

Recognizing this issue, C2L teams paid sustained attention to evidence. C2L leaders encouraged campus leaders to develop evaluation plans and gather evidence of ePortfolio's impact. As data began to come in, we used the information to consider the impact of ePortfolio on student, faculty, and institutional learning. Based on this research, we developed the following interrelated value propositions:

- **Proposition 1:** ePortfolio practice done well advances student success;
- **Proposition 2:** Making student learning visible, ePortfolio practice done well supports reflection, integration, and deep learning; and
- **Proposition 3:** ePortfolio practice done well catalyzes learning-centered institutional change.

Sophisticated ePortfolio initiatives can help colleges and universities improve student outcomes and engagement, addressing what some call the Completion Agenda. When done well, ePortfolio practice also deepens student learning, which could be called a Quality Agenda. C2L evidence suggests that the power of ePortfolio practice emerges from its capacity to serve as a connector. High-impact ePortfolio practice can help students link and make meaning of diverse learning experiences across time and space; and an integrative campus ePortfolio initiative can spur collaboration across departments and divisions, catalyzing the growth of institutional learning cultures, which might be envisioned as a Change Agenda.

Proposition 1

ePortfolio practice done well advances student success. At a growing number of campuses with sustained ePortfolio initiatives, student ePortfolio usage correlates with higher levels of student success as measured by pass rates, GPA, and retention.

Colleges have long sought to improve student success. Now government and funders are pressing higher education to demonstrate improved retention and graduation rates. In this context, we examined the evidence of the relationship of ePortfolio practice to student success. As we did so, we found that a constellation of C2L campuses generated evidence showing that ePortfolio practices correlate with substantially higher levels of student success as measured by widely recognized indicators, including course pass rates, GPA, credit accumulation, retention across semesters, and graduation.

An important caveat: Definitive proof of causality related to student learning is always elusive. As discussed in Chapter 7, ePortfolio projects are rarely designed to permit randomized control group studies or to isolate the impact of ePortfolio. In the case of C2L, our network intentionally spanned diverse campus projects, marked by differences in focus, purpose, and student population. A rigorous, tightly controlled randomized controlled trial (RCT) study could not have easily accommodated this diversity. And FIPSE funds were in no way sufficient to support customized RCTs, individually administered on each campus. Consequently, campus data processes were shaped by local conditions, goals, and needs, as well as the quality of campus institutional research offices. The C2L data have limitations, yet they are nonetheless suggestive and intriguing.

A Growing Body of Success Data

In its initial years, the ePortfolio field produced relatively little evidence that focused on the relationship of ePortfolio and student success.[2] But there were some efforts to document this linkage. Two studies discussed data on ePortfolio's relationship to student success. Hakel and Smith noted that, at Bowling Green State University, students who built ePortfolios demonstrated higher GPAs, credit accumulation, and retention rates than control groups.[3] And LaGuardia Community College presented data showing that students in ePortfolio-intensive courses across the campus had a course pass rate of 74.9%; for students in non-ePortfolio sections of comparable courses, the pass rate was 69.1%. Comparison of next-semester retention at LaGuardia showed that students enrolled in at least one ePortfolio-intensive course had a return rate of 75.0%; for the comparison group, the rate was 70.0%.[4]

LaGuardia has continued to regularly document and report on data from a wide range of courses. An example is this summary from a recent report to the US Department of Education:

> Data provided by the Office of Institutional Research over a period of years suggests that students building ePortfolio are substantially more likely to return the following semester; and 2011–12 was no different. The composite one-semester retention or graduate rate for student in impacted courses [in 2011–12] was 80.4%, versus 61.7% for students in comparison courses. . . . Likewise, students enrolled in impacted courses had higher course completion (96.4%, +1.8 percentage points), course pass (79.7%, + 8.2 percentage points) and high pass–C and above (77.7%, +9.9 percentage points)—rates than students in comparison courses.[5]

Now other campuses have begun to examine the relationship of ePortfolio use to student success. On the *Catalyst for Learning: ePortfolio Resources and Research* site, a constellation of C2L campuses, including the following, present ePortfolio-related student success evidence:

- At Rutgers University, the Douglass Residential College began using ePortfolio in 2008–2009 in a required first semester mission course. As described in Chapter 3, it used an ePortfolio pedagogy designed to help students develop a clearer sense of themselves and their direction. Data showed that student performance substantially improved. The average grade point in the course for the two semesters before ePortfolio was introduced was a B (3.213); in nine semesters with the ePortfolio, students earned an average of a B plus (3.508). In addition to the improved success in the course itself, the impact extended to student success in other first-semester courses. Prior to integrating ePortfolio pedagogy into the curriculum, the average student cumulative GPA was 2.933; in the nine semesters since, students' average cumulative GPA has been 3.095.[6]

- Since San Francisco State University (SFSU) integrated ePortfolio into the Metro Health Academy, a learning community for high-risk students, the university has closely tracked several indicators of success, including persistence, credits taken and earned, GPA, completion of remediation, and graduation. Compared to all first-time freshmen at SFSU, Metro Health students need remediation at a higher percentage and are more likely to be low-income, first-generation, and/or underrepresented (see Figure 8.1). As reported in their C2L ePortfolio,

  Metro students are outperforming their more advantaged SFSU peers in terms of retention and graduation. Metro students' four-year graduation rate is almost 10 percentage points higher than their SFSU peers. Metro students persist at a 19 percentage point higher rate into their 7th semester (senior year) compared to all first-time freshmen at SF State, when we take an average of all cohorts.[7]

- IUPUI uses ePortfolio across the campus. In many sections of IUPUI's first-year seminar, students complete an ePortfolio-based ePDP "designed to promote students' understanding of their educational goals, strengths, aspirations, and career. The reflective prompts also aid students in setting self-concordant goals and feeling a greater sense of purpose in pursuing their degrees." Data from 2010, analyzed with a linear regression to account for high school GPAs, SAT scores, and other variables, show that students in first-year seminar sections that required an ePDP had significantly higher fall cumulative GPAs (2.82) compared to students in sections that did not require the ePDP (2.73). In 2013 the ePDP-enhanced sections of the first-year seminar for exploratory students, those who enter IUPUI with an undeclared major, had significantly higher fall GPAs and fall-to-spring retention rates compared to exploratory nonparticipants. As the IUPUI C2L team reports,

Figure 8.1. San Francisco State University: Impact of ePortfolio Use on Student Success

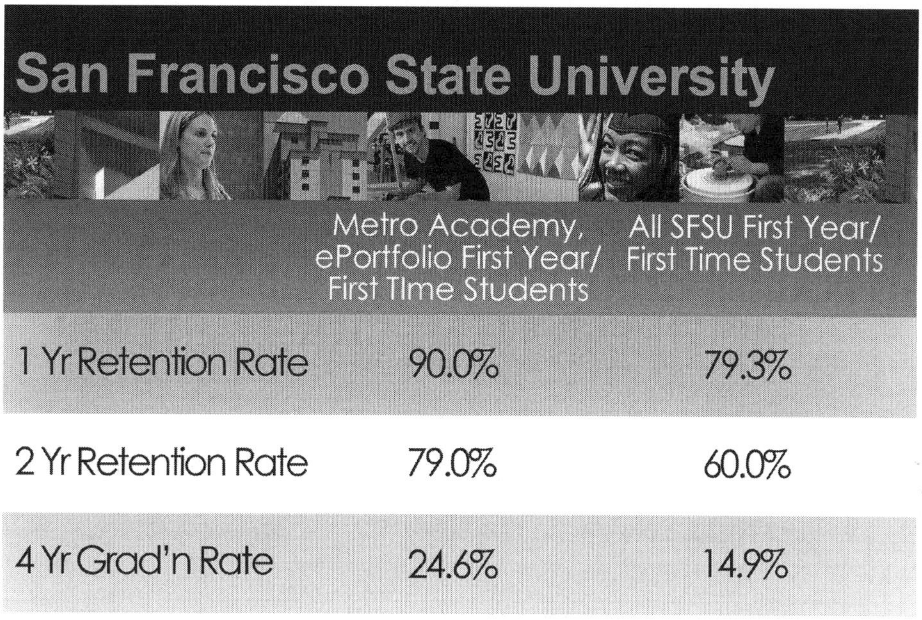

San Francisco State University		
	Metro Academy, ePortfolio First Year/ First TIme Students	All SFSU First Year/ First Time Students
1 Yr Retention Rate	90.0%	79.3%
2 Yr Retention Rate	79.0%	60.0%
4 Yr Grad'n Rate	24.6%	14.9%

Source. San Francisco State University, "Evidence," *Catalyst for Learning: ePortfolio Resources and Research,* January 25, 2014, http://sfsu.mcnrc.org/what-weve-learned/evidence/

"It appears that the ePDP process is particularly helpful for students who enter college as exploratory students."[8]

- At Queensborough Community College, all incoming students were enrolled in First-Year Academies, a set of thematic learning communities. One set of Academies sections used ePortfolio; the others did not. Overall, compared to college benchmarks, Academy courses showed improved course pass and next semester retention rates. The improvements in the ePortfolio sections of the Academy were larger still. The benchmark retention rate was 65%. First-Year Academies that did not use ePortfolio had an 88% retention rate. Those Academy sections that did use ePortfolio had a 97.8% retention rate (see Table 8.1).[9]

- At Connecticut's Tunxis Community College, a year-long comparison between ePortfolio and non-ePortfolio sections of developmental English courses showed that ePortfolio sections had 3.5 percentage points higher pass rates and an almost 6 percentage points higher retention rate. ePortfolio is also integrated into a number of programs at the college including computer information systems, dental hygiene, and business administration. Students use ePortfolio repeatedly in these programs. Data showed that students across the college who had taken multiple courses with ePortfolio, from first year to capstone, were more likely to be retained than students who had less or no ePortfolio exposure (see Figure 8.2).[10]

TABLE 8.1
Queensborough Community College

Retention	Percent	Intervention
Fall 2006–Spring 2007 Retention	65%	Benchmark
Fall 2009–Spring 2010 Retention	88%	Freshman Academy
Fall 2009–Spring 2010 Retention	97.8%	Freshman Academies With ePortfolio

- ePortfolio leaders at Pace University compared the 2011 and 2012 retention rates of ePortfolio and non-ePortfolio users across the university and "found some very positive trends of higher retention rates among ePortfolio users" across both years. For example, in the 2011 cohort, the overall university retention rate was 73.5%, for ePortfolio users the retention rate was 87.1%. Digging even deeper, they also identified a subgroup of ePortfolio users known as "super users," students who uploaded artifacts within their first academic year and had a total of 11 or more artifacts by May 2013. The retention rate of the 2011 ePortfolio super users group was 97.9%.[11]

Figure 8.2. Tunxis Community College: Impact of ePortfolio Use on Retention.

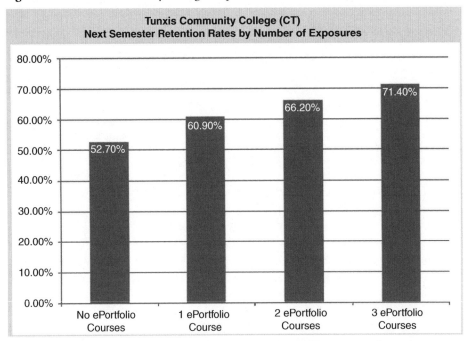

Source. Tunxis Community College, "Evidence," *Catalyst for Learning: ePortfolio Resources and Research,* January 25, 2014, http://tcc.mcnrc.org/what-weve-learned/evidence/

These and a range of other C2L campuses shared data correlating ePortfolio use with positive gains in student outcomes. Only one C2L campus out of the entire network shared data that failed to show gains. However, it should be noted that not all C2L campuses were able to collect comparative outcomes data. Some campus teams could not identify an appropriate comparison group. At Three Rivers, for example, all nursing students have used ePortfolios for almost a decade. Prior outcomes data were unavailable, and comparisons with non-nursing students were not meaningful. At Guttman, all students use ePortfolio, so no comparison is possible. Meanwhile, other C2L campuses were not able to effectively mobilize their campus institutional research offices to conduct comparison studies. Some teams, such as Salt Lake Community College, noted that they were moving toward gathering and analyzing evidence on ePortfolio's impact but were still in the early stages of that effort.

Given these limitations, we recognize that the C2L data are not conclusive. C2L was not a tightly focused research project, consistent in approach across campuses. Joined in a flexible community of practice focused on improvement and scaling, C2L partners represent the broad range of higher education sectors. They served very different student populations, with sharply divergent educational needs and trajectories, and their ePortfolio projects varied in breadth, depth, maturity, and scope. The controlled focus needed for rigorous, single variable research that spanned the entire network was far beyond the scope of the project. Consequently, campus teams chose measures appropriate for their needs. Data collection and analysis varied, given campus goals and institutional research capacities. Across the board, analysis was based on available comparison groups, not randomized control groups. Further research, funded and organized to address these issues, will be of clear value to the field.

That said, we believe that the constellation of outcomes data shared by C2L campuses represents an emergent pattern and compares well to the kinds of data widely used for decision-making by state agencies, funders, and higher education institutions. As such, we argue, it provides a suggestive body of evidence for the proposition that sophisticated ePortfolio practice correlates with improved student success, one of the performance indicators of a High-Impact Practice.

Specific aspects of these data are worth noting. One is that positive outcomes are seen across institutional type. As this evidence demonstrates, improved outcomes have been documented at community colleges, liberal arts colleges, urban public comprehensives, and Research I universities. Across these lines, high-impact ePortfolio practice correlates with elevated levels of student success and persistence, helping students make timely progress toward degree completion.

The impact on student success at the community college level is particularly notable. And the impact on high-need, first-generation students across institutional types is also striking, particularly considering that we know that other High-Impact Practices have been shown to have stronger benefits for high-risk students.[12]

It is notable that on many campuses, ePortfolio practice is linked to other High-Impact Practices, such as first-year experience programs, learning communities, and capstone courses.[13] When sharing their data, SFSU leaders noted:

> Our students are outperforming their more advantaged peers in terms of retention and graduation. It is, however, difficult to tease out the effect of each specific intervention or service we provide. Our program offers several wrap-around services including tutoring, academic advising, financial aid advising, and assistance with the registration process. We also enroll students in a cohorted learning community for two years while their instructors participate in a faculty learning community and receive regular trainings in pedagogy.[14]

It is impossible to isolate the impact of ePortfolio on positive student outcomes at SFSU, LaGuardia, Boston University, and other campuses. Because ePortfolio's value is rooted in connecting diverse learning experiences, examining it in isolation is difficult and perhaps meaningless. The case of Guttman Community College is revealing. At Guttman, ePortfolios are used with all students to intentionally link an array of High-Impact Practices, also implemented at scale, including learning communities, first-year seminars, service-learning, writing-intensive courses, collaborative projects, and common intellectual experiences. Early indicators of the success of Guttman's educational model are strong, including 49% and 45% three-year graduation rates for the first two entering classes. Given the way Guttman uses ePortfolio practice, there is no way to isolate the impact of that practice on a student's learning experience; Guttman leaders, however, argue that ePortfolio practice plays a vital role. Through recursive use of ePortfolio across curricular and co-curricular experiences, students connect their learning experiences into a cohesive whole, communicating their learning to themselves and the larger Guttman community.

Guttman's transformative approach adds to its power as a model of ePortfolio "done well;" however, it also eliminates the possibility of randomized, single variable research. While illustrating the ways that ePortfolio's value is rooted in its role as a connector, this example also highlights the broader tensions inherent to applying traditional education research models to integrative ePortfolio practice.

Some C2L teams were able to at least reduce the number of variables in play. Queensborough Community College compared data from first-year learning communities that used ePortfolio with those that did not and found that students in the ePortfolio-enhanced learning communities did much better (Table 8.1). Rutgers examined pre- and post-ePortfolio implementation data for comparison, and IUPUI used a linear regression to compare ePortfolio and non-ePortfolio users exposed to otherwise comparable learning experiences and saw statistically significant gains. These examples underscore an interesting point. The fact that data were gathered from multiple campuses with a variety of approaches may limit direct comparability, but it also created a breadth and diversity of data that evaluation focused on one campus rarely displays.

From another angle, it is interesting that much of the C2L data comes from contexts where ePortfolio use was linked with first-year seminars, capstone courses, and experiential learning. We suggest this supports an emergent proposition that the ePortfolio practice can connect and enhance the impact of other High-Impact Practices.[15] We discuss this connection between ePortfolio and other High-Impact Practices in Chapter 9.

Although these data are intriguing, it is worth noting what they do not show. If the data suggest that ePortfolio practice can support improved student success, it does not explain why or how it does so. How does ePortfolio use shape the student learning experience? Does ePortfolio practice advance students' sense of belonging to the campus community? Their sense of educational self-efficacy? Their ownership of their education? What kinds of ePortfolio pedagogies are effective? Success data alone cannot answer these questions. Other kinds of data can, however, help us better understand the ways ePortfolio practice affects the quality of the student learning experience.

Proposition 2

Making student learning visible, ePortfolio practice done well supports reflection, integration, and deep learning. Helping students reflect on and connect their learning across academic and co-curricular learning experiences, sophisticated ePortfolio practices transform the student learning experience. Advancing higher order thinking and integrative learning, the connective nature of ePortfolio helps students construct purposeful identities as learners.

Although student success data are vital, they provide limited insight into the ePortfolio learning experience. It might be tempting to leap from C2L data to a conclusion that ePortfolio practice automatically leads to improved student outcomes. We found, however, that the value of the ePortfolio experience for students depends on how it is implemented; that is, the pedagogy and practices of faculty and staff as well as broader support structures.

With this in mind, C2L took two steps. First, C2L campuses documented the practices shown to be the most powerful in enhancing student learning. Shared on the *Catalyst for Learning: ePortfolio Resources and Research* site and discussed in Chapter 3, this documentation illuminates the integrative, social pedagogy used by ePortfolio faculty across campuses. Second, C2L campuses also surveyed students, seeking insight into the ways students understand their ePortfolio experience. As discussed next, campus practices and the survey data suggest that the value of the ePortfolio experience emerges from the ways it makes learning visible, facilitating connective reflection; sharing; and deeper, more integrative learning.

Making Learning Visible: Reflection

What does it mean to make learning visible? Most obviously, ePortfolios can make the learning process more visible to students themselves. Curating a body of their own learning artifacts, collected over time and in different settings, provides students with opportunities to examine and reflect on their learning. As experienced ePortfolio practitioners know, however, meaningful reflection does not just happen. Skillful and intentional pedagogy is required from faculty and staff.

As discussed in Chapter 3, Carol Rodgers' framework for reflective thinking serves as a way to consider the following different types of reflective practice:

- Reflection as connection
- Reflection as systematic and disciplined
- Reflection as social pedagogy
- Reflection as an attitude toward change[16]

C2L teams incorporated Rodgers' insights into reflective pedagogy. The practices in Chapter 3 show how faculty and staff took advantage of ePortfolio's ability to make student learning visible, prompting reflective processes and helping students integrate their learning. In so doing, they engaged students in one or more key behaviors that High-Impact Practices elicit, particularly periodic, structured opportunities to reflect and integrate learning. Reflective strategies used by C2L campuses include scaffolding designed to help students:

- Connect diverse course-based experiences and build reflective skills. ePortfolio-based reflections at Pace University's Media and Communication Arts graduate program begin as "lower level reflection" on specific artifacts, a reflective essay completed at semester's end elicits "higher level reflection," asking students to examine their own strengths and weaknesses.[17]
- Link course-based learning to co-curricular learning and advisement. At Rutgers University's Douglass College, advisors structure ePortfolios to help students connect academic pathways to co-curricular programs and service-learning, building leadership skills.[18]
- Connect learning to academic competencies and professional standards. Boston University's College of General Studies uses ePortfolio to help students understand, focus on, and document growth in key competencies.[19]

These strategies are not mutually exclusive, of course. At Virginia Tech's College of Natural Resources, students use their ePortfolios to deepen their understanding of the discipline, connect with peer advisors, and think about their personal commitment to sustainability and environmental protection.[20] At Three Rivers Community College, nursing students use ePortfolio in every course offered by the program. They not only document competency-focused achievements also reflect on their clinical experiences, examine their personal attitudes and biases toward different types of patients, and work to develop their identities as nursing professionals.[21]

As C2L campuses integrated reflective strategies into their ePortfolio practices, they gathered survey data on student experiences. C2L leaders developed the C2L

Core Survey, administering it over five semesters from 2011 to 2013. Based in part on questions previously used at LaGuardia and other partner campuses, this instrument was designed to capture the attitudes and perspectives of students taking ePortfolio courses. Several additional items from the NSSE were also included (with permission) and slightly modified to fit the purpose of the C2L project. Student response data (n = 10,170) have now been collected, aggregated, and analyzed from all 24 C2L campuses.

The C2L Core Survey has three main goals: First, capturing student perspectives on ePortfolio, the survey offers evidence that can deepen our understanding of how ePortfolio usage affects the student learning experience. Second, survey evidence contextualizes the individual student ePortfolios available on the *Catalyst for Learning* site. Third, the large data set offered by this multi-campus implementation creates analytical opportunities that go beyond smaller surveys done only at individual schools and programs. The full C2L Core Survey is available at c2l.mcnrc.org.

Administered on campuses where faculty designed strategies based on Rodgers' framework, some Core Survey data reveal the ways such ePortfolio practice shapes student learning experiences (see Table 8.2). For example, students used a four-part scale to indicate their level of agreement or disagreement with the statement "Building my ePortfolio helped me succeed as a student." Nearly two-thirds (62.5%) of respondents Agreed or Strongly Agreed with this statement. Similarly, 68.6% Agreed or Strongly Agreed that "Building my ePortfolio helped me to make connections between ideas," suggesting that ePortfolio practice advanced "reflection as connection." Addressing Rodgers' understanding of "reflection as an attitude towards change," 66.0% Agreed or Strongly Agreed that "Using ePortfolio has allowed me to be more aware of my growth and development as a learner." This suggests that the integrative ePortfolio experience helps students build a more holistic self-portrait, a way of understanding themselves as learners.

TABLE 8.2
Student's Integrative ePortfolio Experiences

C2L Core Survey Items	% Agree or Strongly Agree
Building my ePortfolio helped me think more deeply about the content of the course.	63.8
Building my ePortfolio helped me to make connections between ideas.	68.6
Building my ePortfolio helped me succeed as a student.	62.5
Someday, I'd like to use my ePortfolio to show others, such as potential employers or professors at another college, what I've learned and what I can do.	70.2
Using ePortfolio has allowed me to be more aware of my growth and development as a learner.	66.0

The C2L Core Survey includes open-ended questions about the ePortfolio experience, asking students how it shaped their learning. The replies create a rich body of qualitative evidence, extending patterns demonstrated in the quantitative data. Sample responses include the following:

- ePortfolio has supported my growth and learning because I was able to bring my ideas together. I learned that I have accomplished a lot throughout my college career.
- ePortfolio has introduced me to my hidden goals in my life. Jotting down my goals in a place helped me work on them.
- I got to show who I was. While creating my ePortfolio, I learned more about myself.
- The best part was to be able to apply my own work into it. . . . I love how it links to assignments that you have done because these assignments can help other students continue their education. I also enjoy that I grew as a learner, and I developed skills that I didn't know before. It helps me connect between new ideas and old ones.

In the C2L Core Survey, these ePortfolio-specific questions were flanked by questions drawn from the NSSE (see Table 8.3). In 2011 the C2L Project received permission from NSSE to adapt a set of NSSE questions for use as part of the survey. Asked how much their ePortfolio-enhanced course work "contributed to [their] knowledge, skills, and personal development in understanding [themselves]," 75.8% responded Quite a Bit or Very Much, reinforcing the idea that reflective ePortfolio experiences supported what Rodgers refers to as an "attitude towards change" as well as self-understanding, and what Marcia Baxter Magolda has called "self-authorship."[22] Student responses were also

TABLE 8.3
Adapted Deep Learning Questions Drawn From the
National Survey of Student Engagement

C2L Core Survey Items To what extent has your experience in this ePortfolio-enhanced course...	Students (%) Responding Quite a Bit or Very Much
Contributed to your knowledge, skills, and personal development in writing clearly and effectively?	75.6
Contributed to your knowledge, skills, and personal development in understanding yourself?	75.8
Emphasized applying theories or concepts to practical problems or in new situations?	75.4
Emphasized synthesizing and organizing ideas, information, or experiences in new ways?	79.9

strong on questions related to integrative and higher order thinking. Drawing on the work of Tagg and others, Laird, Shoup, and Kuh have linked these questions to what they refer to as deep learning—reflection on the relationship between different pieces of information; focusing on substance and underlying meaning—and personal commitment to understanding.[23] When asked, for example, about engagement in "synthesizing and organizing ideas, information, or experiences in new ways," 79.9% of C2L students responded Quite a Bit or Very Much, again supporting the impact of what Rodgers describes as "reflection as connection."[24]

Although not conclusive, campus practices and the Core Survey data suggest that ePortfolio practice helps students make meaning from specific learning experiences and draw connections to other experiences. Integrative ePortfolio strategies prompt students to connect learning in one course to learning in other courses, co-curricular activities, and life experiences. Ultimately, students connect their learning to consideration of goals and values, constructing an openness toward learning, an attitude toward change, and a more purposeful sense of self.

Campus-Based Analysis of NSSE Data

The C2L Core Survey results from the NSSE questions we adapted are intriguing, but they have some limitations. Comparisons to national norms for these questions are not possible, because of the mix of institutions surveyed—community college and four year—and the range of programs and types of courses where the survey was administered. However, direct comparison on a single campus is possible and relevant. Two C2L campuses, Pace University and LaGuardia Community College, did their own institutional comparisons, which yielded meaningful findings.

Pace University examined their 2013 NSSE results for first-year students, comparing the responses of students who took courses using ePortfolio with those who did not. The analysis revealed positive correlations to ePortfolio in a number of areas. ePortfolio users were substantially more likely than non-users to report that their coursework had emphasized "solving complex real-world problems." ePortfolio users were also substantially more likely to report that their courses had helped them develop skills in "writing clearly and effectively" and "thinking critically and analytically." And ePortfolio-users were also more likely than other students to agree that technology contributed to "learning, studying, or completing coursework with other students."[25]

LaGuardia took a slightly different approach, using the Community College Survey of Student Engagement (CCSSE). Some questions on the Core Survey are found on both the NSSE and the CCSSE. Since LaGuardia regularly administers the CCSSE, LaGuardia researchers

(Continues)

(Continued)

were able to use the two surveys to compare the responses of ePortfolio users (who did the Core Survey) with the responses of the broader LaGuardia population, as well as with national CCSSE means.

Community college students nationwide, at campuses using the CCSSE, answered the question "How much has your work in this course emphasized synthesizing and organizing new ideas, information or experiences in new ways:" 64% of national respondents responded Very Much or Quite a Bit. In its campus-wide CCSSE survey, 73.4% of LaGuardia students responded Very Much or Quite a Bit to this question. For LaGuardia's ePortfolio-using students in Fall 2015 who answered the question in the C2L Core Survey, the comparable figure was 88.2%.

This pattern was repeated on question after question. For the question, "How much has your work in this course emphasized applying theories or concepts to practical problems or in new situations," 59.9% of students nation-wide answered Very Much or Quite a Bit. At LaGuardia, the college-wide mean was 65.8%. For students using ePortfolio, asked the question through the Core Survey, the comparable figure was 84.0%.

These responses underscore the power of the ePortfolio experience to advance student engagement in deep and integrative learning processes. On the question, "How much has your experience in this course contributed to your knowledge, skills, and personal development in understanding yourself," 58% of the community college students nationwide answered Very Much or Quite a Bit. The LaGuardia collegewide figure was 66.9%. The figure for ePortfolio students at LaGuardia was 87.4%.[26]

Making Learning Visible: Social Pedagogy

While students' individual reflections on their own learning are valuable, making learning visible can also have more collective aspects. Used with social pedagogy as described in Chapter 3, ePortfolio practice can facilitate collaboration and exchange as well as learning-centered connection with faculty, students, and other viewers outside the campus. Bass and Elmendorf described social pedagogies as the following:

> design approaches for teaching and learning that engage students in authentic tasks that are communication-intensive, where the representation of knowledge for an authentic audience is absolutely central to the construction of knowledge in a course. . . . By extension, through the use of integrative strategies such as ePortfolios, social pedagogies are also design approaches that help students deepen their reflections, build links across courses and semesters, and bridge between formal curricular and co-curricular learning.[27]

C2L faculty developed activities that used ePortfolio with social pedagogy and shared them on the *Catalyst* site. Reviewing these practices, Bass found the following ways campuses were using social pedagogy with ePortfolio (see Chapter 3 for a more detailed discussion):

- Peer response and social interaction deepen individual work.
- Team-based work creates a collectively produced artifact.
- External audiences raise the stakes on production.
- Forming students into an expertlike knowledge community of practice engages students with their learning.

Based on his review, Bass argues in his earlier essay (see Chapter 3), that a social pedagogy for ePortfolio—asking students to use ePortfolio to articulate their insights into learning to authentic audiences—can help them engage more deeply with content and concepts, integrate their understandings, and develop a more purposeful approach to learning. Social pedagogies for ePortfolio can be seen to directly align with three of Kuh and O'Donnell's operational characteristics of High-Impact Practices: (a) interactions with faculty and peers about substantive matters; (b) frequent, timely, and constructive feedback; and (c) public demonstration of competence.[28]

Five semesters of C2L Core Survey data support the idea that social pedagogy enhances the ePortfolio experience. Survey data examined interaction with two audiences for ePortfolios: instructors and peers. The role of instructors in ePortfolio-based interaction was analyzed based on students' reports that instructors had reviewed, discussed, and given feedback on their ePortfolios. (For a description of the analysis process, see C2L Senior Scholar Helen L. Chen's vignette, "Digging Deeper Into the Core Survey Data: Faculty and Peer Interaction" in this chapter.)

Correlating instructor feedback with student engagement with ePortfolio, we found a striking pattern. Students who reported instructor feedback as an important component of their ePortfolio experience (high feedback) placed significantly higher learning value on their ePortfolio experiences compared to their peers in the low feedback group. Across five semesters, 90.0% of students with high levels of instructor feedback Agreed or Strongly Agreed with the statement "Using ePortfolio has allowed me to be more aware of my growth and development as a learner." For students with low levels of instructor feedback, the comparable figure was 51.3%. This pattern was repeated across multiple survey items.

Similarly, students who reported peer feedback as an important component of their ePortfolio development (high feedback) reported significantly higher value experiences compared to their peers in the low feedback group. The data reveal that 94.4% of students who reported high levels of student feedback Agreed or Strongly Agreed with the statement "Using ePortfolio has allowed me to be more aware of my growth and development as a learner." The figure for students who received low levels of student feedback was 32.0% (see Figure 8.3).

This pattern is found in other items, such as "Building my ePortfolio helped me think more deeply about the content of this course," "Building my ePortfolio helped me succeed as a student," and "Building my ePortfolio helped me make connections

Figure 8.3. The Impact of Social Pedagogy on Student Engagement

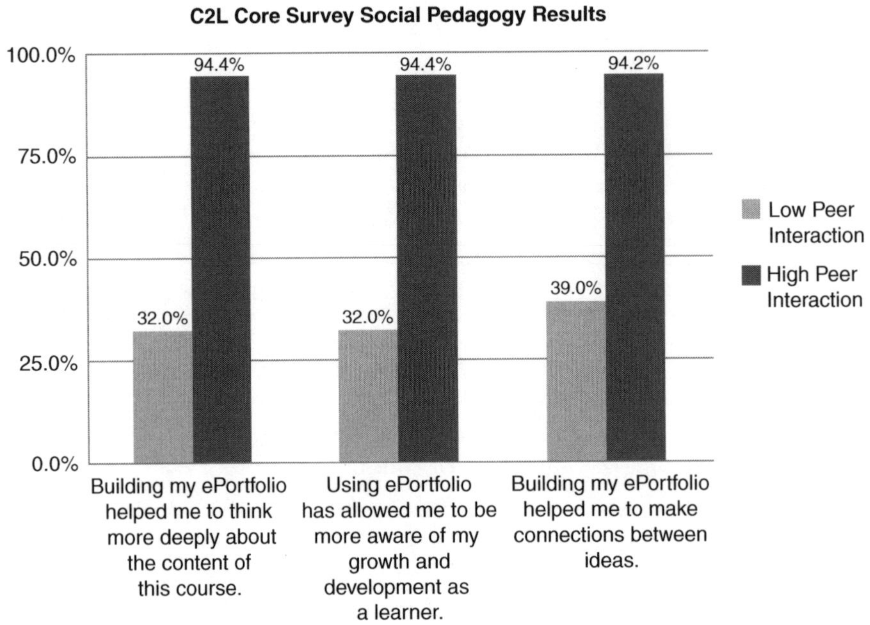

C2L Core Survey Social Pedagogy Results

between ideas." When students know someone, a faculty member or peer, is looking at their ePortfolio, its value as a vehicle for deepening contextualized learning is dramatically enhanced.

A similar pattern emerged with the questions drawn from the NSSE and associated with higher order and integrative thinking. Asked how much their course involved "applying theories or concepts to practical problems or in new situations," 92.9% of students with high levels of instructor interaction reported Quite a Bit or Very Much, for students with low levels of instructor interaction, the figure was 64.8%. On the same question, among students who reported high level of student interaction around the ePortfolio, 92.1% Agreed or Strongly Agreed. Among students who reported low levels of interaction, the figure was only 58.5%.

These data further suggest that a social pedagogy for ePortfolio practice enhances the integration of academic learning with the processes of identity construction. Asked how much their course "contributed to [their] knowledge, skills, and personal development in understanding [themselves]," 93.0% of students who reported a high degree of ePortfolio-based interaction with other students reported Quite a Bit or Very Much. Of students who reported a low degree of interaction, the comparable figure was 57.9%.

Qualitative data from the Core Survey illustrated the value of interaction to the portfolio experience. "ePortfolio has allowed me to receive feedback and criticism of my work from fellow classmates. I have learned where my weaknesses and strengths are as a designer," commented one student. "The best part was seeing other students' ePortfolios and getting to know them and their experiences," noted a second, and a third said, "The best part of working with ePortfolio is that I can share this with people and they can see what I have done in school."

Digging Deeper Into the Core Survey Data: Faculty and Peer Interaction
Helen L. Chen, C2L senior scholar

In considering Randy Bass' introduction of social pedagogies to the Connect to Learning network and the subsequent implementation of practices integrating the use of social pedagogy, we decided to see what impact, if any, the social pedagogy practices had on student engagement with ePortfolio. In our operationalization of these practices, we focused on the role of communication, interaction, and audience from two specific perspectives, instructors and peers. We created scales to explore how instructor and peer feedback on ePortfolio activities might influence student engagement outcomes across the six administrations of Core Survey data collected over five semesters from fall 2011 to spring 2014.

Instructor Feedback and Recognition

This scale, representing student recognition of the usefulness of instructors as an audience and as guides for ePortfolio creation and development, was created by taking the mean responses to the following instructor-related items:

- "My instructor provided useful feedback on my ePortfolio."
- "I know that my instructor looked at my ePortfolio."
- "My instructor(s) discussed the ways ePortfolio helps students to learn."

The scale values were represented on the same range as the response options for each individual item, from Strongly Disagree (1) to Strongly Agree (4). Cronbach's alpha, an estimated measure of internal consistency, was .85.

Peer Feedback and Recognition

Similarly, a peer-oriented scale was created by taking the mean of two peer-related items where respondents indicated agreement to the following statements on a four-point Likert scale ranging from Strongly Disagree (1) to Strongly Agree (4). The Cronbach's alpha for these items was .80.

- "My peers/classmates provided useful feedback on my ePortfolio."
- "I know my peers/classmates looked at my ePortfolio."

(Continues)

(Continued)

Discussion

Although the constructs of instructor and peer feedback and recognition and their corresponding scales require additional development and refinement, preliminary analyses identify their important contribution to providing a more nuanced understanding of feedback and guidance from instructors and peers. For example, in Figure 8.4, students who view instructors and peers as important sources of support in their ePortfolio development process (high and medium recognition) also reported stronger agreement (Agree/Strongly Agree) with the statement "Using ePortfolio has allowed me to be more aware of my growth and development as a learner" compared to students who did not recognize instructors and peers as important audiences (low recognition). These trends demonstrate how feedback from peers and instructors can potentially heighten student perceptions of ePortfolio on desired learning outcomes.

Figure 8.4. C2L Core Survey: Peer and Faculty Feedback Results.

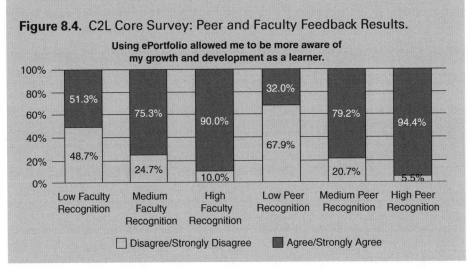

Making Learning Visible: Connection and Identity Formation

The Connect to Learning data suggest that high-impact ePortfolio practice, shaped by reflective and integrative social pedagogies, makes learning visible and helps students link different parts of their learning. A large majority of students reported that building an ePortfolio "helped . . . make connections between ideas" and "apply theories or concepts to practical problems or in new situations." This supports the argument that ePortfolio's value is rooted in its connective power, its ability to help students link a range of experiences. In 2009, in "It Helped Me See a New Me," Eynon did a close reading of multiple ePortfolios and examined LaGuardia survey data to argue that integrative ePortfolio practice engaged LaGuardia students in a process of identity construction, helping them understand themselves as learners and emerging professionals.[29] The C2L data support this claim and further indicate that interacting on ePortfolio helps students understand themselves as learners. This suggests that ePortfolio experiences shaped by integrative social pedagogies help students take ownership of their learning, building not only academic skills but also the more affective understandings of self regarded by Keeling, Baxter Magolda, and others as critical to student success and meaningful education.[30]

As researchers have redefined the dimensions of learning and development, the AAC&U has led a broad movement, encouraging practices that engage students as active learners, complex thinkers who connect learning in and beyond the classroom to address new challenges in education, careers, and personal and community lives. C2L findings suggest that ePortfolios "done well" can play a major role in helping colleges and universities address not only completion but also quality, advancing and supporting higher order thinking and integrative personal growth.

C2L evidence suggests that sophisticated ePortfolio pedagogies are more likely to engage students in higher order thinking, integrative learning, and other high-impact learning behaviors. These findings suggest that, by helping students integrate their learning, an effective ePortfolio initiative can help institutions deepen and transform multiple dimensions of the student learning experience.

Proposition 3

ePortfolio practice "done well" catalyzes learning-centered institutional change. Focusing attention on student learning and prompting connection and cooperation across departments and divisions, ePortfolio initiatives can catalyze campus cultural and structural change, helping colleges and universities develop as learning organizations.

As we have seen, C2L data show that ePortfolio practice, guided by a combination of reflective, integrative, and social pedagogies, supports improved student learning, engagement, and success, key indicators of High-Impact Practice. On campuses where ePortfolio is used effectively, however, the work of C2L teams extended beyond pedagogy. Working with faculty, staff, and programs, C2L teams addressed institutional structure and culture from multiple angles. C2L research suggests that effective ePortfolio initiatives build vibrant programs with work that links Pedagogy with the other sectors of the *Catalyst Framework*: Professional Development, Outcomes Assessment, Technology, and Scaling Up.

Actively addressing all five sectors of the *Catalyst Framework* is demanding, but it has a payoff. C2L teams that work effectively across the *Framework* build more robust and sustainable ePortfolio initiatives. And there is an additional bonus. Because an integrative ePortfolio initiative requires collaboration across multiple sectors of the campus, it has the potential to engage diverse campus groups that may otherwise rarely connect in a shared conversation about student learning. A cohesive ePortfolio project can build an integrated learning culture and help an institution develop as an adaptive learning organization.

As the higher education landscape becomes more complex, colleges must adapt to a fast-changing environment. With the emergence of massive open online courses (MOOCs) and other Web-based learning options, students can choose to learn everywhere. Facing calls to unbundle higher education, colleges must find ways to connect learning, create coherent purpose, and become adaptive learning organizations. Garvin describes a learning organization as one that is "skilled at creating, acquiring and transferring knowledge, and at modifying its behavior to reflect new knowledge and insights."[31] A learning college is, then, an institution able to use evidence of student learning, engagement, and success in processes of institutional learning and change.

If C2L's first and second propositions address what could be called the Completion and the Quality Agendas, the third addresses something equally important: the Change Agenda. How can colleges build capacity to adapt to changing conditions? How can administrators thoughtfully use faculty and staff expertise to advance campus-wide innovation? How can they build learning cultures and become more integrated and adaptive learning organizations? C2L's findings suggest that ePortfolio initiatives can help colleges address these increasingly pressing needs.

This third proposition is qualitatively different from the first two because it is more sweeping and more difficult to assess. The evidence for this proposition is complex, deriving primarily from the stories and practices shared by C2L teams. These self-reported data do not support hard and fast conclusions. But they are fascinating and, we believe, deserving of thoughtful consideration.

We use the *Catalyst Framework* to review our findings about the difference ePortfolio practice can make in this regard. Having discussed the impact of Pedagogy earlier in this chapter, here we focus on the *Framework's* other four sectors. We seek here to highlight the ways that ePortfolio practice in each sector prompts and supports the development of a more cohesive and agile learning organization.

Professional Development

When campus ePortfolio leaders organize meaningful professional development, it shapes a curricular and cultural context for student, faculty, and staff learning. The stories of C2L teams indicate that the most vibrant ePortfolio campuses pay sustained attention to professional development. Faculty development is key to ensuring the quality of ePortfolio practice, helping faculty test and adapt integrative, social pedagogy for ePortfolio. Professional development can extend beyond faculty, engaging advisors and other key staff members in integrating ePortfolio practice in advising and co-curricular learning experiences.

> Placing ePortfolios at the center of sustained professional development can encourage sophisticated pedagogy, build student achievement, and change campus conversations about teaching and learning.

Although critical to high-impact ePortfolio pedagogy, effective professional development can also advance faculty and institutional learning. As discussed in Chapter 4, professional development guided by the Catalyst design principles (Inquiry, Reflection, and Integration), can link faculty and staff to an engaging discovery process. Incorporating student ePortfolios in this dynamic can transform the impact of professional development. In examining students' ePortfolios, faculty can not only view student work but also student reflections on their learning and their lives. They can contextualize student learning, comparing work done in current courses to work done earlier or in different disciplines. They can consider the learning that takes place in co-curricular experiences. Highlighting student learning across boundaries, professional development can catalyze a powerful conversation that goes beyond courses and credits to focus on students and the holistic student learning experience.

The C2L team at Manhattanville College, for example, brought together faculty from traditional departments (such as English, psychology, and fine arts) with leaders of the Center for Career Development, the athletics department and others. The "open and integrated nature" of the process, team members said, deepened its impact:

> In all of our professional development programs, we actively recruit faculty and staff from across the disciplinary and programmatic spectrum. We work hard to disrupt "one size fits all" conceptions of ePortfolio by asking these diverse groups to collaboratively investigate the ways in which ePortfolios can meet their individual and collective goals for teaching, learning, programming and professionalism. In this way, ePortfolio professional development has become a catalyst for bringing faculty and staff who perform vastly different functions across our campus together to build an understanding of ePortfolio as a . . . way of thinking that can serve a complex web of interconnected goals and objectives.[32]

Through professional development, colleges build collaboration and identify strengths and areas for improvement. Effective professional development supports faculty and staff as they plan and integrate curricular and co-curricular improvements, helping institutions adapt, learn, and grow.

Placing ePortfolios at the center of sustained professional development can not only build ePortfolio initiatives and advance high-impact pedagogy but can also link different institutional stakeholders to conversations about curricular and co-curricular learning experiences. ePortfolio-related professional development can deepen campus conversations about teaching and ways to improve the student learning experience, contributing to institutional change.

Outcomes Assessment

Connecting ePortfolio to outcomes assessment can spur the growth of learning colleges. As discussed in Chapter 5, effective outcomes assessment begins with inquiry into authentic student work connected to real classroom activity. Examining and reflecting together on ePortfolios and student work, faculty and staff from across the college can more easily identify realistic recommendations and then close the loop, integrating appropriate improvement to pedagogy and practice across the institution. An

> ePortfolio initiatives can move outcomes assessment beyond accountability by spotlighting student work, engaging faculty and staff, and supporting student, faculty, and institutional learning.

ePortfolio-based outcomes assessment process that uses inquiry, reflection, and integration promotes institutional learning and change.

At Guttman, for example, Assessment Days are built into the academic calendar at the middle and end point of each semester. Faculty and staff attend these days and engage in a collective conversation about student learning based on authentic work from student ePortfolios. As Guttman's C2L team explained:

> We use these days to engage faculty in an inquiry and reflection process related to student learning and then connect, or integrate, the results of that process into our individual or collective practice. The use of ePortfolio during these activities allows us to keep the focus of our work connected to and centered on students and student learning.[33]

ePortfolio-based outcomes assessment processes such as these can spur a larger conversation about student learning. Building assessment processes so they engage faculty and staff in sustained and structured inquiry can help an entire institution become more of a learning college, a place where the college itself is a learner, continuously discovering ways to deepen and advance student learning in every aspect of its practice.

Technology

As discussed in Chapter 6, effective ePortfolio technology supports integrative student learning and links it to professional development and outcomes assessment. Making student learning visible and facilitating a campus-wide focus on pedagogy and student success, ePortfolio technology also has the potential to support broader institutional learning and change.

If sophisticated ePortfolio pedagogy asks students to document, reflect on, and integrate their learning, the most effective ePortfolio technology supports this process, helping students to (a) connect different elements of their learning, bringing together curricular, co-curricular, and experiential learning; and (b) share their contextualized learning with students, faculty, and other authentic audiences. Moreover, effective ePortfolio platforms also help faculty, staff, and other stakeholders connect to and focus on student learning. Facilitating the integration of artifacts into professional development and outcomes assessment processes, quality ePortfolio platforms help deepen faculty, staff, and institutional learning.

Linked to professional development and assessment, effective ePortfolio technology helps faculty and staff examine student work in a more holistic context, supporting learning about students and the improvement of pedagogy. As C2L's Northeastern

University team tells us, "When positioned properly within a conversation about pedagogy, 'ePortfolio as tool' can expand the dialogue about teaching and learning. . . . The conversation shifts from 'learning within courses' to 'learning across courses.'"[34]

> Effective ePortfolio technology can help catalyze change by making student learning visible, facilitating a campus-wide focus on pedagogy and student development.

Effective ePortfolio technology can help deepen faculty, staff, and institutional learning by facilitating professional development and outcomes assessment processes on a campus. Moreover, an ePortfolio platform has the potential to support the scaling of ePortfolio initiatives; enhancing a campus' ability to make student learning visible across an entire institution, catalyzing institutional learning and change.

Scaling Up

To build a successful initiative, ePortfolio leaders attend to a range of processes that build campus engagement and institutional support. Instrumentally important for building effective ePortfolio practice, these tasks inherently bring together diverse campus constituencies for collaboration focused on student learning, creating opportunities for deeper systemic change.

Reviewing campus practices, C2L identified six Scaling Strategies teams use to scale their initiatives. These demanding, recursive tasks, described in Chapter 7, include engaging students as stakeholders; gathering, analyzing, and using evaluation evidence; and building alliances with departments and programs. Northeastern's C2L team described the strategic value of building alliances with key programs. They established strong relationships with the undergraduate writing program, the honors program, and the Graduate School of Education. The team's scaling up story explains their approach:

> When a school elects to institute ePortfolios program-wide, the initiative is more likely to succeed during times of change and wavering support. Once one program has an ePortfolio requirement, and the system of support is put into place, it becomes easier for other programs to adapt the innovator's materials and systems for their own purposes. Diffusion of Innovations Theory predicts that successful programs in one area of an institution will breed similar programs within other areas of the institution.[35]

The Northeastern story highlights qualities that advance the scaling process: vibrancy, stamina, and interpersonal relationship building. They stress the need for bottom-up and top-down support. "Scale," they write, "springs forth from growth within the hearts and minds of many people within an organization, from intrinsic motivation and consensus that change will be beneficial. Scale is a manifestation of organizational learning."[36]

Scaling up refers to the strategies for expanding ePortfolio initiatives that align with programmatic and institutional priorities and share a continuous focus on student success and learning.

Scaling Up and work on Pedagogy, Technology, Professional Development, and Outcomes Assessment together demand sustained and intentional work. These efforts prompted C2L teams to build partnerships and facilitate collaboration, bringing together faculty from diverse disciplines, advisors and co-curricular staff, IT staff and professional development facilitators, and executives from multiple divisions. ePortfolio leaders at Pace University addressed the need to bring these groups together with an advisory board that included "members from each of our academic areas and also the library; Information Technology Services; Center for Teaching, Learning, and Technology; Office of Students Success; and Assessment Office."[37] For the Pace team, this was part of a broader change effort:

> One of our major goals has been to have ePortfolios permeate our Pace culture. . . . Integrating learning and making connections have been our mantras. . . . We have built partnerships with faculty, staff, and administrators from all schools, many disciplines, as well as Student Life, Office of Assessment, and Career Services. . . . ePortfolios are now being used by Student Life on one campus as part of a new Leadership Certificate Program; students in the program—first year and second year students, and their upper class mentors, are using the ePortfolio to document and reflect on their activities, workshops, and leadership development. . . . We are also using ePortfolios for Tenure and Promotion review, which has been helpful in getting faculty experienced with the platform.[38]

Successful ePortfolio leaders facilitate cross-campus collaboration, encouraging systemic conversations about student learning. Such sustained efforts to build an ePortfolio culture are critical to the ability to broaden and deepen ePortfolio initiatives. But such effort also yields dividends. The conversations required for ePortfolio success illuminate the holistic nature of the student learning experience, sparking structural change and building campus-wide commitment to learning-centered processes.

Growing commitment to a learning culture and related changes in institutional structure and culture were evident on many C2L campuses. As described earlier, ePortfolio-based assessment in Northeastern's education school has sparked deep curriculum change focused on integrative learning.[39] At Manhattanville, the ePortfolio team initiated sustained professional development, "the first on our campus after a long period of no professional development."[40] The ePortfolio-based process fed faculty interest in new opportunities for inquiry into teaching and learning, and this in turn led to administrative support. In 2013 the college created a new campus-wide Center for Teaching and Learning, responsible for ePortfolio and broader pedagogical support.

At San Francisco State University, the success of the integrative Metro Health Academies and the work of the ePortfolio team encouraged SFSU to rethink the way it supports entering students. In fall 2013 an ePortfolio-based learning community approach was expanded to serve 40% of the incoming student population.[41] The provost of Boston University recently called the ePortfolio initiative of the College of General Studies an assessment model for other BU Colleges.[42] Similarly, the successful effort to build ePortfolio culture in Three Rivers Community College's nursing program led to broad campus changes. As Three Rivers Community College ePortfolio leaders note, the successful integration of ePortfolio pedagogy and practice in nursing

> has catalyzed broader institution-wide change, helping us progress as a learning-centered college . . . through an open dialogue with faculty, administrators, and students, we have reached a consensus: ePortfolios will now be used college-wide for general education and programmatic assessment of student learning.[43]

At LaGuardia, the ePortfolio effort has long advanced the importance of integrative learning, addressing the whole student. In 2012 the college announced "a sweeping institutional change effort" reflecting a similar perspective, "aligning student affairs and academic affairs, rethinking advisement and rebuilding our First Year Experience."[44] The capacity of ePortfolio practice to support educational planning and identity development and link curricular to co-curricular experiences can help support bridges between academic and student affairs. These two areas worked in tandem to collaborate with academic departments and in spring 2014 launched a new discipline-based, credit-bearing first-year seminar, incorporating ePortfolio as a required and central element. That program has been very successful and is quickly scaling; in the 2015 to 2016 school year, LaGuardia offered nearly 300 sections enrolling 6,500 students. Early data show impressive gains in student learning and retention.[45]

Observing campus developments across C2L, particularly those related to scaling up processes, we see that the growth of an ePortfolio initiative requires and spurs broader changes in institutional culture and structure. In Chapter 7, Bass argues that ePortfolio initiatives grow and deepen most successfully when they are aligned with efforts to build a campus-wide culture of learning. He suggests that integrative ePortfolio initiatives can serve as a catalyst for positive change and identifies the following layers or dimensions of such a change:

1. Shift to a student-organized view of learning, bridging curriculum and cocurriculum, where learners pull from knowledge resources and offerings to construct an increasingly customized educational experience that is professionally productive and personally meaningful.
2. Development of an institutional conversation on student learning, moving toward a learning-centered culture and structure.
3. Shift in decision-making, investment, and allocation of resources and energy that optimizes the institution to be responsive to high-impact learning.

C2L evidence suggests that ePortfolio practice promotes learning-centered connection, making student learning visible to faculty and staff across institutional boundaries. Requiring and facilitating campus-wide collaboration, ePortfolio initiatives help break down traditional institutional silos. Supporting a richer, more holistic view of learning, encouraging a learning-centered institutional conversation, and catalyzing broad institutional change in structure and culture, ePortfolios can help colleges become more adaptive learning organizations.

Conclusion

Our work with C2L campuses allowed us to gather an array of evidence that supports three Catalyst value propositions: Integrative ePortfolio initiatives can build student success, deepen student learning, and catalyze institutional change. These findings add to our collective understanding of the power of integrative ePortfolio practice. They underscore the value of thoughtful investment in the development of sustained and sophisticated ePortfolio initiatives in collaborative communities of practice and exchange. Moreover, they suggest a host of promising avenues for further research, analysis, and theory building. We believe these three value propositions and their supporting evidence show that ePortfolio practice, done well, can and should play a vital role in the evolution of higher education.

Notes

1. George Kuh, *High Impact Practices: What They Are, Who Has Access to Them, and Why They Matter* (Washington, DC: American Association of Colleges and Universities, 2008), p. 14.

2. Lauren H. Bryant and Jessica R. Chittum, "ePortfolio Effectiveness: A(n Ill-Fated) Search for Empirical Support," *International Journal of ePortfolio* 3, no. 2 (2013): 189–198, http://www.theijep.com/pdf/IJEP108.pdf

3. Milton D. Hakel and Erin N. Smith, "Documenting the Outcomes of Learning," in *Electronic Portfolios 2.0: Emergent Research on Implementation and Impact,* eds. Darren Cambridge, Barbara Cambridge, and Kathleen Blake Yancey (Sterling, VA: Stylus, 2009), 133–136.

4. Bret Eynon, "Making Connections," in *Electronic Portfolios 2.0: Emergent Research on Implementation and Impact,* eds. Darren Cambridge, Barbara Cambridge, and Kathleen Blake Yancey (Sterling, VA: Stylus, 2009).

5. LaGuardia Community College, *Title V. Annual Report* (unpublished report, 2012).

6. Rebecca Reynolds, "Connect to Learning" (annual report, Rutgers University, 2014).

7. San Francisco State University, "Evidence," *Catalyst for Learning: ePortfolio Resources and Research,* January 25, 2014, http://sfsu.mcnrc.org/what-weve-learned/evidence/

8. Indiana University–Purdue University Indianapolis, *Program Review and Assessment Committee Annual Report 2013–2014,* accessed August 20, 2015, http://irds.iupui.edu/Portals/SDAE/Files/Documents/2013-14%20UCOL%20PRAC%20Final.pdf

9. Queensborough Community College, "What We've Learned," *Catalyst for Learning: ePortfolio Resources and Research*, January 25, 2014, http://qbcc.mcnrc.org/what-weve-learned/

10. Tunxis Community College, "Evidence," *Catalyst for Learning: ePortfolio Resources and Research*, January 25, 2014, http://tcc.mcnrc.org/what-weve-learned/evidence/

11. Pace University, "Evidence," *Catalyst for Learning: ePortfolio Resources and Research*, January 25, 2014, http://pu.mcnrc.org/what-weve-learned/evidence/

12. Kuh, *High Impact Practices*, 19.

13. Ibid.

14. San Francisco State University, "Evidence," *Catalyst for Learning: ePortfolio Resources and Research*, January 25, 2014, http://sfsu.mcnrc.org/what-weve-learned/evidence/

15. Susan Kahn and Susan Scott, "Scaling Up ePortfolios at a Complex, Urban Research University: The IUPUI Story," *Catalyst for Learning: ePortfolio Resources and Research*, January 25, 2014, http://iupui.mcnrc.org/scaling-story/

16. Carol Rodgers, "Defining Reflection: Another Look at John Dewey and Reflective Thinking," *Teachers College Record* 1, no. 4 (2002): 842–866.

17. Linda Anstendig, "Reflective Thinking and Writing as Systematic Practice at Pace University," *Catalyst for Learning: ePortfolio Resources and Research*, January 25, 2014, http://pu.mcnrc.org/ref-practice/

18. Rebecca Reynolds, "Rutgers University—I Got It Covered: Reflection as Integrative, Social Pedagogy," *Catalyst for Learning: ePortfolio Resources and Research*, January 25, 2014, http://c2l.mcnrc.org/ru-ref-practice/

19. Gillian Pierce, Natalie McKnight, John Regan, and Amod Lele, "Reflection as Integrative, Social Pedagogy: The College of General Studies' Freshman End-of-Year Reflection," *Catalyst for Learning: ePortfolio Resources and Research*, January 25, 2014, http://bu.mcnrc.org/bu-ref-practice/

20. Marc Zaldivar, "Connect to Learning Annual Report: Virginia Tech" (annual report, 2014).

21. Three Rivers Community College. "Campus ePortfolio," *Catalyst for Learning: ePortfolio Resources and Research*, January 25, 2014, http://trcc.mcnrc.org

22. Rodgers, "Defining Reflection"; David C. Hodge, Marcia Baxter Magolda, and Carolyn A. Haynes, *Engaged Learning: Enabling Self-Authorship and Effective Practice,* 2009, http://www.clarku.edu/aboutclark/pdfs/Hodge%20et%20al.pdf

23. Thomas F. Nelson Laird, Rick Shoup, and George D. Kuh, "Measuring Deep Approaches to Learning Using the National Survey of Student Engagement" (paper, Annual Meeting of the Association for Institutional Research, San Diego, May 14–18, 2005).

24. Rodgers, "Defining Reflection."

25. Pace University, "Correlations Between ePortfolio Use and NSSE Results 2011 Through 2013," *Catalyst for Learning: ePortfolio Resources and Research,* January 25, 2014, http://pu.mcnrc.org/what-weve-learned/evidence/

26. "Fall 2015 Survey Analysis" (Institutional Research Report, LaGuardia Community College, 2016).

27. Randy Bass and Heidi Elmendorf, "Designing for Difficulty: Social Pedagogies as a Framework for Course Design," https://blogs.commons.georgetown.edu/bassr/social-pedagogies/

28. Kuh, *High Impact Practices*.

29. Bret Eynon, "'It Helped Me See a New Me': ePortfolio, Learning and Change at LaGuardia Community College," 2009, accessed August 20, 2015, https://blogs.commons .georgetown.edu/vkp/files/2009/03/eynon-revised.pdf

30. Richard P. Keeling, MD, ed., *Learning Reconsidered 2: Implementing a Campus-Wide Focus on the Student Experience,* 2006, accessed August 21, 2015, https://www.nirsa.org/docs/ Discover/Publications/LearningReconsidered2.pdf; Hodge et al., *Engaged Learning*; John D. Bransford, Ann L. Brown, and Rodney R. Cocking, *How People Learn: Brain, Mind, Experience, and School* (Washington, DC: National Academies Press, 2000); Kuh, *High Impact Practices.*

31. David A. Garvin, "Building a Learning Organization," *Harvard Business Review,* accessed August 21, 2015, https://hbr.org/1993/07/building-a-learning-organization

32. Sherie McClam, "Faculty Development Offered With a lot of 'TLC'," *Catalyst for Learning: ePortfolio Resources and Research,* January 25, 2014, http://mville.mcnrc.org/pd-story/

33. Laura M. Gambino, Chet Jordan, and Nate Mickelson, "Outcomes Assessment: Making Student Learning Visible," *Catalyst for Learning: ePortfolio Resources and Research,* January 25, 2014, http://gcc.mcnrc.org/oa-story/

34. Gail Matthews-DeNatale, "The Ecology of Support," *Catalyst for Learning: ePortfolio Resources and Research,* January 25, 2014, http://neu.mcnrc.org/tech-story/

35. Laurie Poklop and Gail Matthews-DeNatale, "Ingredients for Scale," *Catalyst for Learning: ePortfolio Resources and Research,* January 25, 2014, http://neu.mcnrc.org/scaling-story/

36. Poklop and Matthews-DeNatale, "Ingredients for Scale."

37. Pace University, "Scaling Up Story: Picking Up the Pace With ePortfolios," *Catalyst for Learning: ePortfolio Resources and Research,* January 25, 2014, http://pu.mcnrc.org/scaling-story/

38. Pace University, "Scaling Up Story."

39. Gail Matthews-DeNatale, "Are We Who We Think We Are?" *Catalyst for Learning: ePortfolio Resources and Research,* January 25, 2014, http://neu.mcnrc.org/oa-story/

40. McClam, "Faculty Development."

41. San Francisco State University, "Scaling Up While Drilling Down: How an Expanding ePortfolio Initiative Dives Into the First-Year Experience," *Catalyst for Learning: ePortfolio Resources and Research,* January 25, 2014, http://sfsu.mcnrc.org/scaling-story/

42. Natalie McKnight, Gillian Pierce, Amod Lele, and John Regan, "Our Scaling Up Story, *Catalyst for Learning: ePortfolio Resources and Research,* January 25, 2014, http:// bu.mcnrc.org/bu-scaling-story/

43. Lillian A. Rafeldt, Heather Jane Bader, Nancy Lesnick Czarzasty, Ellen Freeman, Edith Ouellet, and Judith M. Snayd, "Reflection Builds Twenty-First Century Professionals," *Peer Review,* 16, no. 1 (2014), 19–23, http://www.aacu.org/peerreview/2014/winter/ reflection-builds-twenty-first-century-professionals

44. J. Elizabeth Clark, "Growth and Change at LaGuardia: Our Scaling Up Story," *Catalyst for Learning: ePortfolio Resources and Research,* January 25, 2014, http://lagcc.mcnrc.org/ category/scaling-up/

45. J. Elizabeth Clark, "Growth and Change at LaGuardia."

ePORTFOLIO AS
CONNECTOR AND CATALYST

9

JOINED AT THE HIP

In previous chapters we traced the link between ePortfolio practice and the HIP framework identified by Kuh, O'Donnell, AAC&U, and others.[1] We demonstrated that, done well, ePortfolio practice improves student learning and success, and it deepens the student learning experience, increasing engagement as well as higher order thinking skills. We outlined criteria for ePortfolio "done well", reviewing each sector of the *Catalyst Framework*: Pedagogy, Professional Development, Outcomes Assessment, Technology, and Scaling Up. We showed how ePortfolio practice "done well" elicits underlying behaviors common to HIPs, including public demonstration of competence, regular opportunities to reflect on and integrate learning experiences, and frequent peer and faculty feedback.

In this chapter, we examine the relationship of ePortfolio and HIPs from another angle. Shifting from the overarching HIP framework, here we spotlight dynamic linkages between ePortfolio and specific High-Impact Practices. Our Connect to Learning (C2L) research reveals that ePortfolio practices are well positioned to work in tandem with other HIPs, and to help integrate student learning across multiple high-impact learning experiences. We found that the connective capacities of ePortfolio practice supported key goals and outcomes of HIPs such as first-year experiences, internships, and capstone courses. In this chapter, we explore the ways ePortfolio practice supports these and other HIPs and examine the idea of ePortfolio as a meta High-Impact Practice.

Earlier chapters provided examples of the ways C2L campuses use ePortfolio in conjunction with HIPs. Across the C2L network, we saw example after example where ePortfolio practice was designed to work with one or more HIPs. Later in this chapter we delve into the details of such partnerships. Before we do, we want to ask: On a broad scale, what could explain this recurring linkage between ePortfolio and other HIPs? Why is this partnership so common? We see several possible reasons.

First, like ePortfolios, most HIPs inherently include a focus on the whole student as a human being, not just an academic unit. Attention is paid to identity development in many HIPs. First-year programs, capstones, service-learning, and study abroad all go beyond cognitive knowledge and skill acquisition. They also address affective learning, personal growth, and identity development. In this way, HIPs resonate with the deepest chords of ePortfolio pedagogy and practice, the ways ePortfolio can help students grow and change, become more aware of who they are, and draw on their curricular, co-curricular and lived experiences to purposefully shape new identities as learners.

Second, we consider that the reason may be more contextual than conceptual. Working with HIPs can be challenging; they require educators to think in new ways about teaching and learning. Consequently, HIPs tend to attract more adventurous faculty and staff. Those interested in teaching in such areas are almost by definition risk takers, willing to step outside the routine and try new approaches. Implementing a HIP is best suited for faculty or staff open to learning from disruption; ePortfolio practice can be similarly disruptive, spurring changes in the classroom and beyond. Faculty accustomed to the challenges of High-Impact Practices may be more open to the risks and challenges of ePortfolio practice and vice versa.

Third, many High-Impact Practices are intentionally integrative, and so is ePortfolio practice. Bass argued that most HIPs exist on the margin of traditional curricular disciplines and departments.[2] Faculty and staff who engage with HIPs must establish links to the institutional mainstream. For example, the faculty and staff of a high-impact service-learning program carefully help students see links between their field experience and the curricula of their disciplinary major. Similarly, in a capstone course, faculty help students draw on prior learning to complete a summative capstone project. Nurturing such relationships, HIP faculty and staff develop integrative strategies that resonate with high-impact ePortfolio practice.

If all HIPs are in some way integrative, high-impact ePortfolios are *essentially* integrative—integration stands at the core of ePortfolio practice. In the predigital context, a portfolio signified a curated and connected collection of artistic work, for example, or architectural drawings. The emphasis is on curated connection, the creation of unity from multiplicity. In today's higher education world, ePortfolios live in a unique institutional space, creating connections that extend vertically across semesters and horizontally across disciplines as well as co-curricular and life experiences. This enables ePortfolio practice to uniquely support or embody integrative learning. ePortfolio's essential connective quality allows it to support deeper and more far-reaching kinds of integration. In this sense, ePortfolio practice can link a range of high-impact learning experiences into a cohesive whole, becoming in the process a unique demonstration of signature learning.

Joined at the HIP

Across the C2L network, we often found ePortfolio practice linked with other HIPs, including first-year experiences, learning communities, capstone courses, service- and community-based learning opportunities, and undergraduate research. These connections have potential value; research has shown a cumulative positive effect of multiple HIPs on student learning and success. Students who participate in multiple HIPs demonstrate levels of engagement and deep learning higher than those of their peers who do not participate in a high-impact experience.[3] With this in mind, let's examine the ways C2L teams linked ePortfolio with specific High-Impact Practices, starting with the first-year experience (FYE).

First-year experience.   FYE programs introduce students to college and help them develop skills needed for success. In 1992 Barefoot and Fidler described six categories of first-year seminars: extended orientation seminars, academic seminars with uniform content across sections, academic seminars with variable content, pre-professional or discipline-linked seminars, basic study skills seminars, and hybrid models.[4] Across categories, FYE seminars tend to emphasize critical inquiry, writing, and collaborative learning activities that develop students' intellectual and practical competencies, building dispositions essential for student success.[5] FYE programs help students make the transition to college, develop an educational plan, and discover who they are as learners and scholars.

When first-year experience programs incorporate high-impact ePortfolio practice, it helps students achieve each of these goals. Integrated into the FYE, ePortfolio practice helps new students identify strengths and growth areas and develop an academic plan. High-impact ePortfolio work uses peer reviewing, a powerful activity for entering college students, engaging them in the practice of learning with and from peers. Most important, ePortfolio practice helps new students advance a process of identity development, using reflection to articulate who they are and who they want to be. Incorporating all these processes, high-impact ePortfolio practice can deepen the impact of an FYE program.

In C2L, we saw ePortfolio practice incorporated into FYE programs and seminars across institutional type, from community colleges such as Tunxis Community College to liberal arts colleges such as Manhattanville College and universities such as Virginia Tech and Rutgers. In each case, ePortfolio practice was used to deepen the first-year experience, helping build engagement and support the transition to college. At Manhattanville, for example, ePortfolio pedagogy is integrated into a first-year seminar titled "Sustainability: Creating a Future We Can Live With," in which students undertake two interrelated ePortfolio-based projects:

> In the first, entitled "Learning for a Sustainable Future," students use ePortfolios as spaces for reflecting on, integrating and representing their learning about sustainability and for engaging seminar peers in a collaborative process of learning from each other. In the second, titled "Social Media for Social Change/Action," teams of first-year students work together to use ePortfolio as a social media platform through which they seek to convince peers outside of their seminar to reflect and take action on an issue that is affecting the Manhattanville community's capacity for living sustainably and contributing to a sustainable future.[6]

In this example, ePortfolio practice supported students' collaborative research as they learned to work together to address a real-world issue. As a vehicle to present their learning to external audiences, ePortfolio helped students value their research and see connections between what they learned at college and the world beyond the campus walls.

At Guttman Community College, ePortfolio is integrated into every aspect of the FYE, including its first step. A mandatory Bridge Program focuses on introducing new students to Guttman and facilitating the transition from high school to college. At the conclusion of the Bridge Program, students use ePortfolio to reflect on this experience and their transition in the following exercise and to envision next steps in the process.

> Before you started Bridge, how did you imagine your college experience? In what ways did the Bridge program reinforce or change your ideas about college?
>
> What did you learn about yourself during Bridge? What did you learn about Guttman and the Guttman Community?
>
> Please describe a Bridge activity or other experience that you believe helped prepare you for the transition to college and explain how it helped. If you still feel a bit unprepared for college, describe the ways in which you feel unprepared and any steps you can take to support your transition.[7]

FYE programs often focus on educational planning and the development of an academic identity. As we saw in Chapter 3, ePortfolio practice and its capacity for making learning visible can help students examine their growth processes over time, grounding and extending the planning process, deepening the process of self-authorship. At IUPUI, for example, the use of the ePersonal Development Plan (ePDP) in the first-year seminar addresses the FYE goals of educational planning and identity development:

> As students complete the ePDP, reflective prompts assist them in bringing narrative to their lives and aspirations. The content of the ePDP is, in essence, the student's self and understanding of self. Sections of the ePDP are ordered so as to help students build their reflective narrative. The About Me section provides the foundation for Educational Goals and Plans, which in turn leads the student to development of Career Goals. The student is firmly at the center of this narrative, thereby embedding the learning around critical thinking, reflection, and integration of experiences within the student's sense of self and lived experience.[8]

At LaGuardia, after studying the ePDP, the ePortfolio team created a similar planning module called the LaGuardia Graduation Plan. In 2014, they embedded the plan in the ePortfolio—and integrated ePortfolio into the college's redesigned first-year-seminar (FYS). Since that time, thousands of LaGuardia students have completed the Graduation Plan and shared it with faculty and advisors. Data reveal that this developmental process is making a difference. Next-semester retention is rising dramatically. Survey data are also revealing. More than 2,500 FYS students were asked "how much did the FYS contribute to [your] knowledge, skills, and personal development in understanding [yourself]," and 89.3% responded Very Much or A Lot. Similarly, 88% of FYS students Agreed or Strongly Agreed that "building [my] ePortfolio helped . . . focus on planning [my] education."[9]

As these examples illustrate, effective ePortfolio practice can enhance the FYE's overarching goals: making the transition to college, developing an educational plan, and learning to collaborate with peers. FYE programs and ePortfolio form a high-impact partnership that advances students' identity development as they make the transition to college.

Learning communities.   We saw a similar partnership emerge on C2L campuses between ePortfolio practice and learning communities. According to the literature, learning communities "encourage integration of learning across courses. . . . Students take two or more linked courses as a group and work closely with one another and with their professors."[10] Implemented well, learning communities help students develop relationships with peers and consider issues from multiple perspectives. Juxtaposing disciplines, learning communities introduce the habits of mind of specific disciplines and the importance of diverse disciplinary perspectives, preparing students to more effectively consider choices of major. According to the National Resource Center for Learning Communities, "learning communities—done well—create a collaborative environment where students thrive, faculty and staff do their best work, and learning fosters the habits of mind and skills to tackle complex real-world issues."[11]

As part of a learning community, ePortfolio practice offers students a reflective space to examine and make explicit connections among the community's different courses and disciplines. Using ePortfolio as a collaborative space for the construction of knowledge helps students develop academic identities in a community of scholars, building engagement and shared purpose. ePortfolio has an added benefit for faculty, making learning in each course visible to all faculty in the community and offering a holistic picture of their students, extending beyond his or her individual course.

Several C2L campuses linked ePortfolio with learning communities. At Tunxis Community College (see Figure 9.1), learning communities joined FYE courses with either a developmental English course or an Introduction to Business course. Integrated across courses, ePortfolio practice helped students connect and apply learning from one course to another:

> In FYE, students complete Academic Skills Plans (ASP) in their ePortfolio where they read about and choose strategies for: reading, taking notes, organizing study materials, rehearsing and memorizing, and taking tests. Students then use and apply their plans in corresponding assignments in their English or business course and then reflect on what they learned from this process in their FYE course. All courses use ePortfolio extensively for assignments and peer and instructor feedback. In Introduction to Business, instructors are looking to have either advisory board members or students in the capstone business course read and comment on these student portfolios. In a fall-to-fall retention comparison, students in the learning community have repeatedly had a higher retention rate than students who did not participate in a learning community.[12]

Using their ePortfolios, Tunxis students apply the note-taking strategies learned in FYE to readings in their Introduction to Business course. Connecting the courses, students consider the value of different disciplinary perspectives. At Tunxis and

Figure 9.1. Tunxis Community College: Learning Communities and Retention.

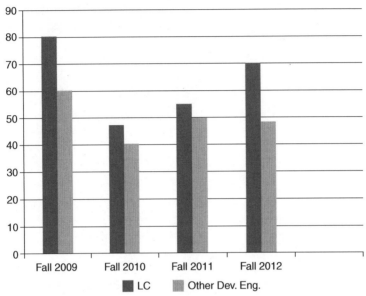

Learning Community: First Year Experience and Developmental English

Retention Rates: Fall to Fall
Learning Community Students Compared to Other Developmental English
Students were placed into the course based on their English placement scores.

Note. Students enrolled in the learning community, which used ePortfolio, had consistently had higher retention rates than a comparison group of developmental English students.
Source. Tunxis Community College, "Evidence," *Catalyst for Learning: ePortfolio Resources and Research,* January 25, 2014, http://tcc.mcnrc.org/what-weve-learned/evidence/

elsewhere, ePortfolio practice provides learning community students with opportunities to reflect and develop higher order thinking skills associated with deep learning. Using ePortfolios for communicating knowledge to peers supports the identity development process, as students develop a sense of academic purpose and an awareness of their place in a community of scholars.

Capstone courses.   Students often encounter learning communities and FYE programs early in their academic journeys. At the end of their journeys, capstone courses serve as a culminating High-Impact Practice. According to Cuseo, capstone courses have three key purposes:

> (1) to bring integration and closure to the undergraduate experience, (2) to provide students with an opportunity to reflect on the meaning of their college experience, and (3) to facilitate graduating students' transition to postcollege life.[13]

The integrative, reflective nature of capstone courses aligns well with ePortfolio pedagogy. Used in a capstone, ePortfolio practice can help each student integrate his or her learning journey and reflect on the ways it has changed him or her. Moreover, ePortfolio's ability to make learning visible enables students to showcase their accomplishments to broader audiences: peers, potential employers, and transfer institutions.

ePortfolio is used in the capstone course in art history at IUPUI. According to the C2L team, the course goals are

> developing metacognition focused specifically on the art history major and integrating learning from prior courses and experiences; developing complementary professional personas as "reviewed academic researcher" and "peer reviewer of academic writing;" and deepening learners' understanding of writing as a way of thinking.[14]

Guided by reflective social pedagogy, students in this capstone use ePortfolio to participate in a writing and peer review process. IUPUI faculty report that this recursive, interactive, ePortfolio-enhanced process strengthens "students' professional identities by helping them learn to be peer reviewers of others' writing about art. The other students in the course constitute an intermediate yet authentic audience for efforts aimed at professional- or graduate school-level writing."[15]

LaGuardia Community College has offered professional development seminars to help faculty redesign capstone courses, using ePortfolio to support integration, reflection, and transition. One Liberal Arts Capstone course taught by Max Rodriguez exemplifies a process of intentional redesign:

> I have worked very hard to reposition assignments in the course to help students make critical connections looking back at the work they have done during their careers at LaGuardia and forward towards the work they want to do after they graduate.
>
> My favorite addition to students' ePortfolios was an assignment asking them to create a digital story of their journey through LaGuardia as they reflected on what they have learned. I have also worked to help students understand the difference between an ePortfolio they created earlier in their careers and the capstone ePortfolio at the end of their career at LaGuardia.[16]

At LaGuardia and other C2L campuses, a capstone ePortfolio provides students with the opportunity to look back and reflect on their college experience, integrate their learning over time and across boundaries, and consider their upcoming transitions. Capstone portfolios help students move to the next stages of identity development as they envision themselves as lifelong learners and emerging professionals.

The connections between ePortfolio and learning communities, first-year experiences, and capstone experiences are particularly strong; many additional examples can be found on the C2L website. We now shift our attention to other linkages we saw, including global learning and study abroad, service-learning, undergraduate research, and internships.

Diversity and global learning.   Global learning experiences "help students explore cultures, life experiences, and worldviews different from their own."[17] Study abroad is one of the most common global learning experiences. Because ePortfolio is accessible from anywhere with Internet access, it can help students studying abroad to document, reflect on, and share the cultural and educational experiences offered by study abroad. When done well, students use the ePortfolio to connect their classroom learning with their study abroad activities, applying that learning to their expanded experiences.

Salt Lake Community College, Guttman, IUPUI, and Boston University all use ePortfolio in study abroad experiences. At Salt Lake Community College, for example, ePortfolio leader David Hubert has his students document and reflect on their experiences in London. Each student creates an ePortfolio for the trip, gathers multimedia artifacts from each of his or her cultural experiences, and responds in writing to a series of reflective prompts. These prompts help students apply classroom learning as they explore new places and cultures. For example, students are asked to

> describe the domestic impact of World War II and the immediate postwar years in Britain. In a reflective piece, tell the reader what it was like and put yourself in the place of the typical Londoner during those times. Rely on your readings and what you learn from venues such as the Museum of London and the Imperial War Museum.[18]

Returning home, students share their ePortfolios and analyze their study abroad experiences in a showcase for faculty, staff, family, and friends.

Undergraduate research.   We also observed ePortfolio use in conjunction with undergraduate research. At Pace University, LaGuardia, Virginia Tech, IUPUI, and the University of Delaware, ePortfolio offers students a space to document and reflect on the research process as well as a vehicle for sharing research findings with external audiences. At Delaware, for example, ePortfolio is used in the Undergraduate Research Summer Scholars Program. As part of this program,

> Students use an ePortfolio to share their research with their research team, which is comprised of undergraduates of unrelated disciplinary areas. By continually discussing their research with students both within and outside of their subject area over the course of ten weeks, students gain the ability to communicate their research to multiple and diverse audiences.[19]

Through scaffolded reflection, University of Delaware students also connect their learning from the program to general education or program competencies.

Service-learning and community-based learning.   Service-learning and community-based learning programs are increasingly common in higher education. As HIPs, "these programs model the idea that giving something back to the community is an important college outcome, and that working with community partners is good preparation for citizenship, work, and life."[20] These experiential activities can help students think in new ways about their course work, and apply problem-solving skills in real-world settings. Reflecting on their learning, ePortfolio helps students to make meaning of their experience as citizen scholars.

At Virginia Tech (VT), ePortfolio leaders became partners with VT's Students Engaging and Responding Through Volunteer Experiences (SERVE) Living Learning Community program. Students in SERVE use the ePortfolio to document a year-long journey and write a series of reflective essays. In one piece, students describe their "Personal Call to Service," and in another they identify personal strengths before and after their service-learning experience. Prior to their service, students complete a reflection titled, "What I Bring to the Table," where they consider their strengths and potential areas for growth. After they complete their service experience, students write a second essay, "What I Bring to the Table—Revisited," reflecting on their growth and reconsidering their strengths and weaknesses. The SERVE ePortfolio is a space for students to develop academic and civic identity and connect service-learning experiences to academic and career plans.[21]

Internships.   Similar in some ways to service-learning, internship experiences provide students with the opportunity to apply their learning in a professional setting for an extended period of time. The term *internship* can apply to a range of experiences: working in a business or other work environment, clinical practica in a health-care setting, or a student-teaching experience. When done well, ePortfolio helps students make meaning from their internship experiences, considering the ways they are growing and developing as professionals. The following are among the many examples of internship-related ePortfolio practices documented on the C2L site:

- Three Rivers Community College nursing students use ePortfolio throughout their coursework. In Family Health Nursing, one of the required clinical experience courses, students use their ePortfolio to compose a reflection that describes the clinical issue/problem related to care of their patient, include an assessment and analysis with viewpoints from two scholarly resources, analyze any assumptions presented by themselves or others, and include a nursing care plan to address the issue.[22]
- At IUPUI, "the Life-Health Sciences Internship [LHSI] Program is exploring how the ePDP can help deepen students' learning through their year-long mentored research internships. Through regular in-person and online discussions facilitated by peer mentors, LHSI aims to help interns—usually sophomores and juniors—develop professionalism, connect their research with other curricular and co-curricular learning, and prepare for future job and internship searches."[23]
- In St. John's University's Teacher Preparation Program in the School of Education, students use ePortfolio throughout the program. During their student teaching experience, "Students are asked to collect artifacts from lessons they've taught along with samples of student work which are captured in the ePortfolio. Students are then asked to reflect on the related tools to assess the quality of teaching and learning. They are guided through a series of questions that lead them to question if this lesson was stellar or [if there] were ways that it could have been improved."[24]

From the FYE to capstone, undergraduate research to internships, ePortfolio practice helps deepen the impact of High-Impact Practices. The integrative qualities of reflection, with the connective capacities of ePortfolio technology, can help faculty, staff, and students make HIPs more meaningful. While providing a valuable space for collaboration and making learning visible to external audiences, ePortfolio practice most importantly helps students make connections that deepen their learning. Whether connecting prior learning to a new experience, as in FYE programs and capstones; bridging disciplines; or connecting classroom learning to the real-world problems encountered in undergraduate research, internships, and service-learning, ePortfolio practice can facilitate the connective process so essential to the impact of High-Impact Practices on students' deep learning and success.

ePortfolio as a Meta High-Impact Practice

One of the unique characteristics of ePortfolio practice done well is its longitudinal quality, its ability to "exist" across an entire student learning experience, from course to co-curricular, spanning semesters and helping students connect what would otherwise be seemingly disparate experiences into a cohesive whole. This longitudinal quality of effective ePortfolio practice can facilitate the integration of multiple HIPs across a student's academic trajectory. In this way, ePortfolio practice can, to borrow a phrase from IUPUI's Susan Kahn and Susan Scott, serve as a "meta" HIP, creating a unique and transformative learning experience for students.[25]

As a meta High-Impact Practice, ePortfolio provides a space between and among other HIPs for students to see the linkages among practices and create their own role in those relations. HIPs' reflective ePortfolio pedagogy helps students draw lessons from the other HIPs, make connections between the disciplines represented in the HIPs, and make connections between HIPs and their own experiences outside higher education. Additionally, ePortfolios are ideal for showcasing the powerful work students do in High-Impact Practices to authentic audiences.

In a recent article in *Peer Review,* Hubert, Pickavance, and Hyberger suggested, somewhat tongue-in-cheek, that ePortfolio can be seen as Tolkien's ring of power, "the high-impact practice that unites and connects all the other HIPs."[26] They ask readers to imagine a student who takes part in a series of HIPs—Summer Bridge, FYE, a learning community, undergraduate research, and a capstone course in the student's major. In each, they suggest, students would use ePortfolio to document and reflect on their learning. "Over time," they write, "the e-portfolio would become signature work itself, as it documented the student's engaged learning arc, growing sophistication and emergence as a reflective practitioner."[27] The ePortfolio is uniquely qualified for this task:

> Curated [ePortfolios] are ideal venues in which to showcase the work that results from student engagement with HIPs. They allow for text to be combined with multimedia representations to create shareable representations that transcend time and distance. As such, they allow student work to escape the confines of a discrete

educational event and formally intersect with the broader range of curricular, co-curricular and life experiences that define what it means to be liberally educated.[28]

This *Peer Review* piece spotlights the work done at Salt Lake Community College, a C2L campus that uses ePortfolio to connect a series of HIPs. Other C2L campuses are moving in similar directions. At Guttman Community College for example, where ePortfolio is used at scale, the curriculum was intentionally designed to provide every student with access to an array of HIPs, carefully scaffolded across the two-year learning sequence. All students participate in a required Bridge Program where they are introduced to their learning community cohort. They remain with their learning community throughout the entire first year of coursework. The First-Year Experience extends to a required two-semester curriculum, including an advisor-led seminar, "Learning About Being a Successful Student," focusing on identity development and educational planning. At the midpoint of the fall and spring semesters, two Community Days provide students with the opportunity to participate in service- and community-based learning experiences connected to their first year of coursework. Intentionally designed group projects in the first year provide common intellectual experiences for students. In the second year of coursework, students have at least two required writing intensive courses in their program of study, and most programs have a capstone course (see Figure 9.2).

Figure 9.2. Guttman Community College's Guided Pathway.

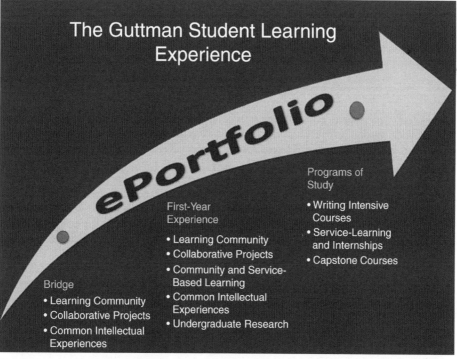

Note. At Guttman Community College, ePortfolio helps students connect and integrate multiple HIPs and serves as a signature student learning experience. Created by Laura M. Gambino.

ePortfolio practice is integrated across each of these High-Impact Practices, thereby creating a cohesive signature learning experience where students connect and deepen knowledge and understanding gained at each step of their learning journey. During the Bridge Program, students create a learning ePortfolio to be used across their academic trajectory. As students advance through their studies, scaffolded assignments leverage ePortfolio's reflective capacities to prompt them to examine their learning processes and their educational plans and goals. For example, students reflect on the ways they were able to apply classroom-based learning to their Community Days activities. Students recursively revise their educational goals and plans, helping them prepare for their major or program of study and consider post-Guttman plans. At multiple points, reflective prompts ask students to explicitly identify and make integrative meaning across diverse experiences and to connect their learning to Guttman's institutional student Learning Outcomes, or GLOs. For example, at the end of their first year, students are asked to reconsider their experience beginning in the Bridge Program and its impact on their learning:

> How have you changed as a student since you started at Guttman? In what ways did this first year of college at Guttman affect who you are as a student? Tell us where you began as a learner. What skills and aptitudes did you possess at the beginning of the semester? Where are you now? What skills did you acquire and hone? Is there a particular posting or page in your ePortfolio that highlights these changes?[29]

Similarly, at the conclusion of their program of study, all students complete a capstone reflection describing in their own words the role these High-Impact Practices played in their success as a Guttman student as well as the ways their learning demonstrates each of the Guttman Learning Outcomes.

Guttman Community College Capstone Reflection Prompt
Before you begin writing this reflection, please review your ePortfolio, including the reflections you wrote at the end of the Bridge program and your First Year Experience. Think about what you've accomplished and the ways in which you have grown and evolved as a learner and scholar.

How Do You GLO?
Broad, Integrative Knowledge: General Education: Your first year experience focused on general education. Describe the ways you built on that learning through your programs of study courses. Please provide a specific example (or two) that highlights this.

   Applied Learning: In what ways did the knowledge you gained in your First-Year Experience courses help you in your major-specific courses? What connections can you make between what you learned in your courses and your life outside the classroom?

(Continues)

(Continued)

Looking Back/Looking Forward
What did you initially anticipate about your experience as a Guttman student? In what ways did your experience align with your expectations? In what ways did it surprise you?

What have you learned about yourself as a learner and scholar? How have you grown academically? Socially?

What are your future goals? Who do you want to be in two to three years? In what ways has Guttman helped prepare you to achieve these goals and become the person you want to be?[30]

Although there is much analysis to be done on Guttman's ePortfolio–enhanced educational model, early evidence points to a positive impact on student learning and success. The two-year graduation rates for the first three cohorts of students were 28%, 29%, and 31%, respectively, and the three-year graduation rate for the first two cohorts was 49% and 45%, far above the national three-year community college graduation rate, which is typically around 20%.[31]

Other campuses in the C2L network are also using ePortfolio as a meta HIP. At LaGuardia, some majors scaffold ePortfolio practice into the first-year seminar, advising, internships, and capstone courses. Majors such as biology and environmental science, integrate ePortfolio practice into undergraduate research as well. At SFSU, the Metro Health Academies build a number of HIPs into the student learning experience: learning communities, first-year experience, and writing intensive courses.[32] At Boston University, ePortfolio connects a first-year seminar, writing-intensive courses, and study abroad.[33] At all three, ePortfolio practice is designed to help students link these experiences and understand them as a cohesive whole.

ePortfolio practice has a unique capacity to serve as a cohesive, signature learning experience for students. Its longitudinal and integrative capacities provide students with a powerful opportunity to link what would otherwise be disparate course, co-curricular, and lived experiences, melding them into a cohesive whole. And, at the same time, it provides a means for campus faculty and administrators to see and consider the student learning experience in new ways. ePortfolio practice can do this with any set of diverse learning experiences. But the potential value is higher when the experiences being linked are those generated by High-Impact Practices. Building on, connecting, and ultimately multiplying the impact of those experiences, the high-impact ePortfolio can, by design, become the signature work for a truly transformative college experience.

Conclusion

ePortfolio works well with many, if not all, of the other High-Impact Practices. Its longitudinal capacity and its ability to exist outside traditional course boundaries uniquely position it to transform the student learning experience and to transform institutional learning as well. We know HIPS are, according to Kuh, "developmentally powerful."[34] But we also know that we have yet to realize the full potential of ePortfolio as a High-Impact or meta High-Impact Practice. We must not only broaden student access to ePortfolio practices but also ensure they are implemented effectively as described in the *Catalyst Framework* because it is "only when they are implemented well and continually evaluated to be sure they are accessible to and reaching all students will we realize their considerable potential."[35]

Notes

1. George Kuh, *High-Impact Educational Practices: What They Are, Who Has Access to Them, and Why They Matter* (Washington, DC: Association of American Colleges & Universities, 2008); George Kuh and Ken O'Donnell, *Ensuring Quality & Taking High Impact Practices to Scale* (Washington, DC: Association of American Colleges & Universities, 2013); Jayne E. Brownell and Lynn E. Swaner, *Five High-Impact Practices: Research on Learning Outcomes, Completion, and Quality* (Washington, DC: Association of American Colleges & Universities, 2010); Ashley Finley and Tia McNair, *Assessing Underserved Students' Engagement in High-Impact Practices* (Washington, DC: Association of American Colleges & Universities: 2013).

2. Randall Bass, "Disrupting Ourselves: The Problem of Learning in Higher Education," *Educause Review* 47, no. 2, (2012): 23–32.

3. Finley and McNair, *Assessing Underserved Students' Engagement in High-Impact Practices*.

4. Betsy O. Barefoot and Paul P. Fidler, *National Survey of Freshman Seminar Programming, 1991. Helping First Year College Students Climb the Academic Ladder* (Columbia, SC: National Resource Center for the Freshman Year Experience, 1992): 2.

5. Kuh, *High-Impact Educational Practices*.

6. Sherie McClam, "Learning for a Sustainable Future and Using Social Media for Social Change," *Catalyst for Learning: ePortfolio Resources and Reseearch,* January 25, 2014, http://mville.mcnrc.org/soc-practice/

7. Guttman Community College, *Milestone Reflection Prompts* (internal document, 2016).

8. Catherine A. Buyarski, "Reflection in the First Year: A Foundation for Identity and Meaning Making," *Catalyst for Learning: ePortfolio Resources and Research*, January 25, 2014, http://iupui.mcnrc.org/ref-practice/

9. LaGuardia Community College, "First in the World Evaluation Report," (unpublished document, 2016).

10. Kuh, *High-Impact Educational Practices*.

11. National Resource Center for Learning Communities, "Learning Communities at Evergreen," accessed August 24, 2015, http://www.evergreen.edu/washingtoncenter/

12. Jen Wittke, Marguerite Yawin, and Amy Feest, "Social Pedagogy Practice for Learning Communities: Developmental English-FYE & Introduction to Business-FYE," *Catalyst for Learning: ePortfolio Resources and Research*, January 25, 2014, http://tcc.mcnrc.org/soc-practice/

13. Joseph Cuseo, "Objectives and Benefits of Senior Year Programs," in *The Senior Year Experience: Facilitating Reflection, Integration, Closure and Transition*, ed. John N. Gardner, Gretchen Van der Veer, and Associates (San Francisco, CA: Jossey-Bass, 1998), 22.

14. R. Patrick Kinsman, Susan Kahn, and Susan Scott, "Social Pedagogy: Working Together to Develop Metacognition and Professional Identity," *Catalyst for Learning: ePortfolio Resources and Research*, January 25, 2014, http://iupui.mcnrc.org/soc-practice-2/

15. Kinsman et al., "Social Pedagogy."

16. J. Elizabeth Clark, "Faculty Development Practices at LaGuardia: Capstone Courses, ePortfolios, and Integrative Learning," *Catalyst for Learning: ePortfolio Resources and Research*, January 25, 2014, http://lagcc.mcnrc.org/faculty-development-practices-laguardia-rethinking -the-capstone-experience-seminar/

17. Kuh, *High-Impact Educational Practices*.

18. David Hubert, "Mixed Media Reflection: ePortfolios in an SLCC Study Abroad Program," *Catalyst for Learning: ePortfolio Resources and Research*, January 25, 2014, http:// slcc.mcnrc.org/ref-practice-1/

19. Lynnette Overby and Meg Meiman, "Assessing Student Learning in Undergraduate Research," *Catalyst for Learning: ePortfolio Resources and Research*, January 25, 2014, http:// ud.mcnrc.org/ref-practice/

20. Kuh, *High-Impact Educational Practices*.

21. Virginia Tech, "ePortfolio Initiatives at Virginia Tech: SERVE: Students Engaging and Responding Through Volunteer Experiences," accessed August 24, 2015, https://eportfolio .vt.edu/gallery/DeptsProgs/serve.html

22. Three Rivers Community College ePortfolio Team, "Connecting Theory to Practice in Gerontology-Reflective Practice," *Catalyst for Learning: ePortfolio Resources and Research*, January 25, 2014, http://trcc.mcnrc.org/ref-practice-4/

23. Indiana University–Purdue University Indianapolis, "Our Project," *Catalyst for Learning: ePortfolio Resources and Research*, January 25, 2014, http://iupui.mcnrc.org/who-we-are/our-project/

24. St. John's University, "St. John's University—Reflective Pedagogy Practice—Reflective Practices in Student Teaching With ePortfolios," *Catalyst for Learning: ePortfolio Resources and Research*, January 25, 2014, http://c2l.mcnrc.org/sju-ref-practice/

25. Susan Kahn and Susan Scott, "Scaling Up ePortfolios at a Complex Urban Research University: The IUPUI Story," *Catalyst for Learning: ePortfolio Resources and Research,* January 25, 2014, http://iupui.mcnrc.org/scaling-story/

26. David Hubert, Jason Pickavance, and Amanda Hyberger, "Reflective E-Portfolios: One HIP to Rule Them All," *Peer Review* 17, no. 4 (2015), accessed February 20, 2016, https://www.aacu.org/peerreview/2015/fall/hubert

27. Hubert et al., "Reflective E-Portfolios."

28. Ibid.

29. Guttman Community College, *Milestone Reflection Prompts* (internal document, 2016).

30. Guttman Community College, *Milestone Reflection Prompts*.

31. Elisa Hertz, *Data Snapshot* (unpublished report, 2015).

32. San Francisco State University, "Scaling Up While Drilling Down: How an Expanding ePortfolio Initiative Dives Into the First-Year Experience," *Catalyst for Learning: ePortfolio Resources and Research,* January 25, 2014, http://sfsu.mcnrc.org/scaling-story/

33. Natalie McKnight, Gillian Pierce, Amod Lele, and John Regan, "Our Scaling Up Story," *Catalyst for Learning: ePortfolio Resources and Research,* January 25, 2014, http:// bu.mcnrc.org/bu-scaling-story/

34. Kuh, *High-Impact Educational Practices*.

35. Ibid.

NEXT-GENERATION
ePORTFOLIO PRACTICE

Higher education is in the midst of rapid and tumultuous change, prompted in part by the emergence of a new digital learning ecosystem. High-impact ePortfolio practice can help students, faculty, and institutions successfully adapt to and take advantage of these changes. To accomplish this, thoughtful educators must engage in sustained examination of the emerging ecosystem and work together to develop next-generation ePortfolio practices and platforms. This chapter introduces some key questions, concepts, and examples that can help educators in this process.

The media frenzy around massive open online courses (MOOCs) has passed, but more substantial developments in digital learning continue to advance. The boundaries of traditional classroom learning are yielding to environments that are more porous and connected. According to a recent report from the Alliance for Excellent Education:

> In the twenty-first century, learning takes place almost everywhere, at all times, on all kinds of paths and at all kinds of paces. With a click of a mouse or the touch of a screen, young people and adults can access a wealth of information, analyze it, and produce new knowledge at any time.[1]

The result, the report concludes, has broad implications for all educational institutions. "These learning opportunities break wide open the traditional confines of school walls and school days."[2]

In a 2016 essay, *Open and Integrative: Designing Liberal Education for the New Digital Ecosystem,* Bass and Eynon argue that two key features define the new digital world in and beyond education: the multiplying capacities of networked information systems and the proliferation of highly sophisticated, algorithmically driven systems that track, analyze, and respond to user actions. Driven by these forces, a new educational landscape is taking shape, characterized by digital badges, learning analytics, Internet-based learning resources such as Khan Academy, and adaptive learning systems, such as those developed by the Open Learning Initiative.[3] As a result, students are learning in new ways, and universities no longer have the exclusive franchise on advanced learning.

Other factors also contribute to the turbulence of this moment in higher education history. For-profit colleges run aggressive recruitment campaigns, distracting attention from their often dismal track records. Widespread cutbacks in state funding for public higher education have forced many traditional colleges to place an unsustainable tuition burden on students, generating student debt and public dissatisfaction. This adds to growing pressure on colleges and universities to more explicitly document their outcomes and demonstrate the value of a college education.

The student body itself is also in flux, marked by the emergence of a new majority of previously underrepresented groups, including growing numbers of Black and Hispanic students. More college students than ever before are first generation, coming from low-income families and communities. These "new majority" students bring invaluable energy, perspective, intellectual capacity and cultural capital to higher education. Our society needs these students as the leaders of the future, equipped with the skills and knowledge required to deal with looming environmental, economic, political, and cultural challenges. But students who come from communities and education systems scarred by poverty and discrimination often bring uneven educational preparation and require new levels of remediation and support. Meanwhile, across all demographics, the new generation of college students is shaped in complex ways by the increasing prevalence of advanced technology and social media in everyday life.

These and other factors all combine and interact, contributing to the complexity of the challenges facing higher education. Many factors are important, but the digital revolution is a salient touchstone, the starting place for many of those who say that higher education must be radically changed if not eliminated.

The rapid development of adaptive digital tools and networked systems contributes to a powerful narrative, focused on the need to "unbundle" higher education. Online courses, badging, nano degrees, and other developments, according to this narrative, create opportunities for the market to provide advanced training and education in structures more flexible and efficient than traditional colleges. An argument that has become familiar is expressed in a 2015 *Newsweek* article:

> Technology tends to unbundle stuff. Look how it's unbundling television, or how it unbundled the music album. The college degree is a bundle that doesn't work for everybody and creates unnatural market conditions. . . . The next generation will be able to pull apart the college bundle the way people today are pulling the plug on cable.[4]

More serious observers have struck similar notes. *Chronicle of Higher Education* editor Jeff Selingo advocates for unbundling, arguing that "the real unbundling opportunities surround the content and delivery functions of a university . . . quickly remaking the idea that a college education must be delivered at one physical location by professors who create and curate their own courses."[5] Others go further, calling for an à la carte system where students pay for each service they need, ranging from digital advisement to online tutorials and office hours.

> At a time when a range of forces are driving a fragmentation of the educational experience, next-generation ePortfolio practice can create opportunities for maintaining and even strengthening connection and meaningful integration.

"There will always be a market for the elite bundled college experience," predicts Jose Ferreira, chief executive officer of EdX. But Ferreira suggests that for less elite students, the traditional college experience will increasingly be replaced by more discrete or disconnected pay-as-you-go structures. "New unbundled or partially bundled alternatives will emerge, and eventually they will dominate the industry," he said.[6]

Ironically, this discourse has emerged at the same time as an increased awareness of the importance of integrative learning. Surveys show that employers are highly interested in students' abilities to transfer skills and knowledge from one setting and apply it to another, a key facet of integrative learning.[7] As discussed earlier, a growing body of research, including much of the research on High-Impact Practices, emphasizes the critical processes of human connection, intellectual synthesis, and holistic education that address students' developmental and affective needs as well as their cognitive growth. New majority students, in particular, have been shown to benefit from educational approaches that bundle academic courses with advisement and other support services, creating a more cohesive learning environment. The growing literature on guided learning pathways further underscores the importance of thoughtful and cohesive integrative learning design across the entire student learning experience.[8]

This moment is thus marked by tension between themes of integration and disintegration. Although new technologies and market pressures push toward "unbundling," the needs of students suggest a need for "rebundling" in new forms. As detailed in *Open and Integrative*, the point is not to choose between digital technology and integration but rather to look for opportunities for synthesis, for using the capacities of the latest digital technologies to help address what we know about the real needs of students for integrative learning and support.[9]

In this context, we suggest that ePortfolio practice can play a uniquely valuable role. To the extent that unbundling moves forward, that learning increasingly takes place in and beyond the walls of the traditional college classroom, ePortfolio practice can help students connect learning experiences across diverse settings, supporting more integrative processes of reflection and assessment. Connecting the granular capacities of emerging digital environments to support more dynamic learning processes, ePortfolios can provide a cohesive foundation that links digital badges, learning analytics, and online learning to broader structures for student, faculty, and institutional learning. New forms of ePortfolios can provide a location for connecting students with advisors, faculty, and peer mentors, and for integrating academic learning with developmental support. At a time when a range of forces are driving a fragmentation of the educational experience, next-generation ePortfolio practice can create opportunities for maintaining and even strengthening meaningful integration.

To be effective in the new learning ecosystem, the next-generation ePortfolio practice must begin to integrate the functions of the newest digital learning spaces. It must become more interactive and expressive, promoting feedback and fluency. It must build in the strengths of new analytics and the flexibility of digital badging. But it must do so with a clear sense of purpose. Thinking about ePortfolios in the context of High-Impact Practices can be helpful in this regard.

The sections that follow briefly sketch some of the ways we believe ePortfolio practice must evolve in the years to come. Running across these distinct areas of innovation are threads of common purpose, suggested by the High-Impact Practice framework. Next-generation ePortfolio practice needs to mobilize new technical possibilities in ways that promote not only improved student outcomes but also the underlying behaviors that characterize all HIPs, including: interactions with faculty and peers about substantive matters; opportunities to discover relevance of learning through real-world application; frequent, timely, and constructive feedback; and periodic and structured opportunities to reflect on and integrate learning. Next-generation ePortfolio practice must also intentionally strengthen its capacity to link with and deepen the impact of other HIPs, such as learning communities and service-learning opportunities. Next-generation ePortfolio practice must deepen the power of ePortfolio as a meta HIP, as discussed in Chapter 9, broadening and deepening the integrative aspects of learning for students, faculty, and institutions. Keeping these priorities in mind will be important as the field considers opportunities and challenges offered by the new digital learning ecosystem.

Digital Badging

Digital badges are an interesting and potentially meaningful vehicle for adapting to the "learning everywhere" aspect of the new ecosystem, and they could become more effective when integrated into next-generation ePortfolio practice.

Based on analysis of digital gaming and learning theory that emphasizes recognition of incremental accomplishment, digital badges spotlight discrete learning experiences. In *7 Things You Should Know About Badges*, EDUCAUSE defines *badges* as

> digital tokens that appear as icons or logos on a web page or other online venue. Awarded by institutions, organizations, groups, or individuals, badges signify accomplishments such as completion of a project, mastery of a skill, or marks of experience.[10]

An influential report suggests that the badging process involves three groups: badge issuers, badge earners, and badge consumers.

- *Badge issuers* are "individuals, schools, employers, institutions, communities, or groups that create credentials to demonstrate mastery of skills and achievements that are of particular value to the issuer." Of particular importance, the badge issuer must identify the criteria for the badge, and what evidence

Digital Badging and ePortfolio: A Promising Opportunity
G. Alex Ambrose, University of Notre Dame

Digital badges are visual representations of accomplishments that make claims of what an individual knows or can do particularly in informal learning experiences. They are validated by embedded metadata such as issuer, criteria, and evidence.

The University of Notre Dame started a badging pilot project in the summer of 2012 with the 21st Century DaVinci ePortfolio Award badge. Students who earned this badge developed a website showcasing their diverse talents, interests, and a passionate drive for knowledge. Winners were able to share this badge in their ePortfolio. The badge image was linked (via image caption) to the university's ePortfolio directory to provide verification and evidence. Three and half years later, Notre Dame has developed 17 different ePortfolio badges that have been certified and issued to 226 students on campus. What began as an experiment has evolved into an award-winning initiative. In 2015, Campus Technology honored our ePortfolio-badging work with an Innovator's Award.

Notre Dame's badges recognize informal learning that takes place in co-curricular spaces—undergraduate research, service-learning, and peer advising. ePortfolios house the badges and the required evidence: research proposals or posters, photographs, videos, and journal reflections.

Notre Dame formed a partnership with an ePortfolio vendor, Digication, and a digital badge platform, Credly, to support a back-end integration where badges in Credly can be linked to evidence in a student's Digication ePortfolio. These badges can also be imported and displayed easily in the ePortfolio with metadata and a link back to Credly for verification (see Figure 10.1).

This next-generation mashup between digital portfolios and badges has revealed three promising implications. First, it demonstrates why ePortfolios need digital badges: If we want to keep the ePortfolio pulse alive across classes and after a course concludes, and if we want to connect employers to ePortfolios that communicate specific competencies, digital badges provide the motivation and opportunity for the students to make their learning visible. Second, it demonstrates why digital badges also need ePortfolios: If digital badges are going to be evidence-based and transferable, then the ePortfolio platform is best optimized to deliver that evidence and provide a logical space to showcase the badge. Third, together digital portfolios and badges provide a way to incentivize, make visible, and recognize competencies gained from informal learning on a residential traditional campus.

(Continues)

(Continued)

Figure 10.1. Notre Dame's Badge Directory.

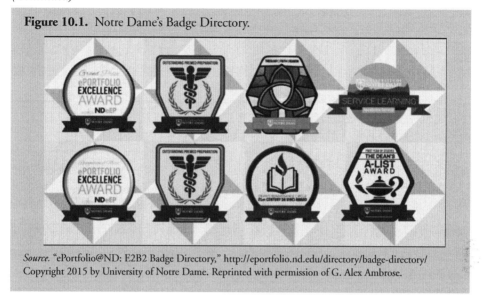

Source. "ePortfolio@ND: E2B2 Badge Directory," http://eportfolio.nd.edu/directory/badge-directory/
Copyright 2015 by University of Notre Dame. Reprinted with permission of G. Alex Ambrose.

of learning must be demonstrated. "A badge is hyperlinked to something that demonstrates the criteria for the badge and evidence such as an artifact, testimonial or document."[11]

- *Badge earners* are learners who want to demonstrate their skills and accomplishments to various audiences. "For example, individuals could demonstrate, to teachers, employers or others, knowledge and skills learned outside of school or skills that cannot necessarily be communicated by a standardized test, a resume, or a college application."[12]

- *Badge consumers* are a broad category, including "formal and informal education providers, individuals, employers, communities, or other groups that have a need for or interest in people with the skills and achievements symbolized by a badge."[13]

A range of institutions are experimenting with badges, from Notre Dame, Harvard, and the University of California, Davis to the National Aeronautics and Space Administration, the Smithsonian, and Khan Academy. A 2016 article in *Inside Higher Education* suggests that one in five colleges are now using badging in some form.[14] The badge system is "a way to structure the process of education itself,"[15] argues Kevin Carey:

> Students will be able to customize learning goals within the larger curricular framework, integrate continuing peer and faculty feedback about their progress towards achieving those goals, and tailor the way badges and the metadata within them are displayed to the outside world.[16]

Trent Batson, one of the founders of the ePortfolio movement and the director of the Association for Authentic, Experiential and Evidence-Based Learning (AAEEBL), has for several years argued that badges and ePortfolios have a natural affinity. Badges need a home base, according to Batson, a place where the learner can collect and display them. ePortfolios are an ideal home for badges, situating the specificity of the badge with the broader and more integrative capacities of the ePortfolio.[17]

Notre Dame uses badging to recognize co-curricular learning, including internships, study abroad, research assistantships, and service-learning activities, and links the badges to students' ePortfolios. In an interview with *Campus Technology*, Notre Dame's G. Alex Ambrose said, "I see the digital badge, displayed and supported in the ePortfolio, as a supplement to the transcript and the resume."[18] In a keynote speech to AAEEBL's international ePortfolio conference, Ambrose explained why badges benefit from being paired with ePortfolios. The ePortfolio provides not only a platform but also a context, the ability to connect specific achievement to a broader pattern of growth and change. "If digital badges are going to be evidence-based, stackable, and transferable, the ePortfolio platform is best optimized to deliver that evidence and provide a logical space to showcase the badge."[19]

If ePortfolio practice can enhance the value of badges, the reverse may also be true. Ambrose suggested that the specific and visual qualities of badges could invigorate the ePortfolio experience. Badges can help employers find the particular pieces of the ePortfolio they wish to examine, eliminating the need to search the entire portfolio, an obstacle to employer interest in portfolios. And for students, the ability to showcase specific achievements and the inherent motivation of winning badges can make the process of updating the ePortfolio more attractive. "If we want to . . . connect employers to ePortfolios that communicate specific competencies," Ambrose argued, "digital badges provide the motivation and the opportunity for students to make their learning visible."[20]

Integrating badging into next-generation ePortfolio practice can also strengthen the emergent work on developing a comprehensive student record, which expands the traditional student transcript to include recognition of co-curricular and competency-based learning and will be linked to evidence, such as a student ePortfolio. ePortfolio and badging can provide that evidence and link needed to create a comprehensive student record of learning.

Pairing badges and ePortfolios represents a key opportunity to use the strengths of high-impact ePortfolio practice to take better advantage of the new learning ecosystem. Accomplishing this requires ePortfolio vendors to develop the technical capacity to host and display badges and connect the accompanying evidence to the rest of the ePortfolio. More important, making this marriage a success will require educators to adapt their practice to more clearly address co-curricular learning and the off-campus educational opportunities that are rapidly emerging in the new learning ecosystem.

As educators work to integrate badging into ePortfolio practice, it will be helpful to keep in mind the strategies that make ePortfolio a High-Impact Practice. Clear criteria, designed to help students reach high expectations; public demonstration of competence, demonstrating achievements that matter to authentic audiences; frequent feedback connecting students with faculty and peers; and thoughtful pedagogy, incorporating Inquiry, Reflection, and Integration, will all be important. Taking advantage of the ways ePortfolio practice functions as a meta HIP, combining reflection and networked technology to connect one powerful learning experience to others, can make badges more meaningful (see Chapter 9 for a discussion of ePortfolio as a meta-HIP). Meanwhile, an integrative focus that spans the five sectors identified in the *Catalyst Framework* (Pedagogy, Professional Development, Assessment, Technology, and Scaling Up) will make a crucial difference in realizing the potential of a practice that joins badging with ePortfolio.

ePortfolio and Comprehensive Student Records
Helen L. Chen, C2L Senior Scholar

In a 2014 survey of 400 employers conducted by the AAC&U, just under half (45%) of the employers said they thought a college transcript would be useful in helping them determine prospective applicants' potential to succeed at their company. In contrast, a majority (80%) reported that an ePortfolio of student work would be a useful resource.

The limited usefulness of the traditional academic transcript has been acknowledged by employers, students, admissions committees, faculty, and staff as well as registrars themselves whose primary responsibility is to maintain the integrity of institutional student educational records. The contributions of extra- and co-curricular opportunities to learning, particularly those related to High-Impact Practices, are significant and often transformative to student growth and development.

The ideas behind the "enhanced" or "extended" transcript reflect how the traditional transcript is evolving in its purpose, audience, content, and in particular, the format and mode of delivery because of advances in technology standards for secure and trustworthy data transfer and acceptance of digital credentials. In fall 2015 the American Association of Collegiate Registrars and Admissions Officers and NASPA: Student Affairs Professionals in Higher Education, with support from the Lumina Foundation, selected 12 institutions, including LaGuardia, to develop models of "comprehensive student records" that document and validate student learning through more expansive means other than course titles, grades, and units. These prototypes range from the University of Maryland's competency-based transcripts for nontraditional students to LaGuardia's digital badging project and Stanford's certified electronic certificates mapped to learning outcomes and student work.

Diverse academic records (and not a singular transcript) can support students as they prepare to communicate what they have learned to external stakeholders. The pairing of formal academic transcripts with evidence, contextualized in a learner-created ePortfolio, highlights the potential benefits of an inclusive and meaningful record that has ongoing value, not only at the time of transfer or graduation but also, ideally, throughout students' postgraduate careers.

Social Pedagogy

As discussed earlier, C2L research indicates the value of using ePortfolios with a social pedagogy, involving interaction, collaboration, peer review, and feedback. Faculty interested in incorporating social pedagogy into their ePortfolio practice face a challenge, however. In this area, ePortfolio pedagogy has advanced more quickly than ePortfolio technology. Next-generation ePortfolio platforms must adapt to make social pedagogy easier and more effective for students and faculty.

Whether they use Twitter, Pinterest, Snapchat, or Instagram, today's students arrive on campus with extended experience using social media. Contemporary social media is increasingly sophisticated and fluid, allowing for a range of connections and interactions. Experiences in these environments create user expectations that shape the ways students perceive ePortfolios. High production values, fluidity, capacities for visual expression, and the capacity for personal customization all help signify to students that they are working on an exciting, up-to-date digital platform. Most important is the need for pervasive, nimble, and nuanced interaction. ePortfolio vendors ignore these issues at their peril.

At this writing, the most widely used ePortfolio platforms still appear to be functionally rooted in the idea of ePortfolios as primarily private spaces; most platforms support one-sided "showcasing," but not fluid interaction or collaboration. Despite sincere efforts on the part of developers, interaction and dialogue are difficult on most platforms. Commenting features are often stiff and clumsy. Conversation and exchange are often isolated, separate from and hard to link to the core processes of documentation, reflection, and integration. For ePortfolio to thrive in the new learning ecosystem, cutting-edge platforms must catch up to practice and facilitate fluid exchange, grounded in the portfolio itself. These features can enhance the behaviors that characterize HIPs, particularly regular feedback from faculty and peers, leading to increased engagement, more meaningful learning, and higher levels of educational success.

ePortfolios for Advisement

Advisement is widely recognized as a key to student success, particularly for first-generation and other new majority students. But less affluent colleges, particularly community colleges, struggle to provide advisement that meets students' needs. A range of digital systems hold promise for supporting advisement. Connecting ePortfolio with these systems can build on the work already under way, using ePortfolio to support meaningful advisement, as discussed in Chapter 3.

Across higher education, there is growing interest in digital advisement systems, sometimes called e-Advisement tools or Integrated Planning and Advisement for Student Success systems (iPASS). Austin Peay's Degree Compass and Penn State's eQuad are among the campus-developed platforms; meanwhile, vendors have developed Starfish, Simplicity, and Inside Track.[21] The details of iPASS systems vary from platform to platform, but functions often include some combination of the following: updateable and shareable degree planning and course scheduling; degree auditing and progress tracking; course recommendations; early alert systems and other tools for identifying at-risk students; and tools for communication among students, faculty, and advising staff, including e-mail, texting, and video chat. Often the purpose of iPASS is to enhance the ability of faculty and staff advisors to work together to help students develop and follow a guided pathway through the curriculum (see Figure 10.2). Automated communication tools that provide "nudges," "high fives," and other formatted "touch points" make it easier for advisors to not only follow student progress but also communicate quickly and easily to encourage students to stay on track.[22]

iPASS systems, according to the Community College Research Center (CCRC), "provide an array of student support-focused functions, including course management, degree planning and early alerts." Interestingly, CCRC researchers point out that, much like ePortfolios, iPASS implementation requires thinking well beyond the nature of the technology; and the impact of iPASS goes beyond the functions it provides:

> Ideally, it motivates a college to rethink its advising system and, in particular, the ways advisors do their jobs, thus encouraging and enabling large-scale and fundamental reform—reform that restructures college processes and that alters the attitudes and behaviors of college staff and students.[23]

Figure 10.2. The Next Generation Learning Challenge's Vision of an iPASS.

Source. Nancy Millichap, "Integrated Planning and Advising for Student Success: Focus on the Transformation of Advising," September 13, 2015, http://er.educause.edu/blogs/2015/9/integrated-planning-and-advising-for-student-success-focus-on-the-transformation-of-advising; Copyright 2015 EDUCAUSE, CC-BY 4.0. Reprinted with permission of EDUCAUSE.

We believe the next-generation ePortfolio practice must build on and link to iPASS systems. Some campuses have laid important groundwork for this effort. The ePersonal Development Plan (ePDP) developed at Indiana University–Purdue University Indianapolis (IUPUI) is particularly significant in demonstrating ways to use the ePortfolio to support advisement, connecting educational planning with reflection and feedback from advisors, faculty, and peers.[24]

As explained in Chapter 3, the ePDP is part of the IUPUI ePortfolio; embedded in the ePortfolio, ePDP prompts help students engage in structured processes of thoughtful self-assessment, goal development, and education and career planning. Initially built by IUPUI students as part of their first-year experience, the ePDP is then used longitudinally as an advisement tool. Faculty and staff advisors review the ePDP, and students update it throughout the student's career. The process builds intentionality for students and helps advisors see students' plans in the context of their entire educational experience, documented in the rest of the ePortfolio.

Incorporating planning with regular reflection and recurring feedback, the ePDP addresses the heart of the advisement process, helping students develop a stronger sense of themselves as learners and their relationship to the curriculum they are pursuing. ePortfolio practitioners and vendors can learn from the ePDP and high-impact ePortfolio practice and from the host of new iPASS systems now available. Guttman Community College is one year into their iPASS initiative, linking ePortfolio with Starfish by Hobsons, a student success software system, connecting the feedback and collaborative tools in Starfish with the reflective processes and integrative capacities of ePortfolio practice. Such a synthesis seems highly promising. Next-generation ePortfolio platforms can facilitate such efforts by finding ways to incorporate and link to e-advisement tools. Next-generation ePortfolio practice must increasingly partner faculty with advisors and peer mentors, helping them join forces to support students' progress and development.

Big Data and Formative Learning Analytics

Closely linked with e-advisement and iPASS systems is another major trend in digital learning. The tools to analyze so-called big data, also commonly known as analytics, are emerging as an important force in the new learning ecosystem. According to the International Conference on Learning Analytics and Knowledge, learning analytics is "the measurement, collection, analysis and reporting of data about learners and their contexts, for purposes of understanding and optimizing learning and the environments in which it occurs."[25] Next-generation ePortfolios could play an important role in making learning analytics more nuanced, more revealing, and more effective for students.

Analytics emerged in the business sector as Google, Amazon, and Netflix tracked and analyzed consumers' online behaviors to develop personalized marketing strategies. In recent years, colleges have recognized that they possess vast amounts of data on students, including application information, student profiles, course selection and completion information, and data generated by online course participation.

Analytics applications can mine at least some of this data, subject it to statistical analysis, and prepare reports or data visualizations to reveal patterns, trends, and exceptions. . . . Colleges and universities can harness the power of analytics to develop student recruitment policies, adjust course catalog offerings, determine hiring needs, or make financial decisions. In a teaching and learning context, data . . . can be used to build academic analytics programs that use algorithms to construct predictive models that can identify students at risk for not succeeding academically.[26]

The computing power of today's systems creates the possibility for analytics that are both fine-grained and sweeping. According to a 2015 New Media Classroom Horizon report:

The types of student data being analyzed vary, but include institutional information such as student profile information (age, address, and ethnicity), course selections, and pace of program completion; engagement data such as number of page views, contributions by students to discussion threads, percentage of students completing assignments, and number of logins; and learning analytics such as which concepts were mastered and which concepts were particularly difficult for a student. . . . The emerging science of learning analytics is providing the statistical and data mining tools to recognize challenges early, improve student outcomes, and personalize the learning experience.[27]

Next-generation ePortfolio practice can connect to the growing energy around analytics in at least two ways: as a potential source for additional data and as a site for students' own usage of analytics. On the first count, ePortfolios, particularly student reflections and their educational plans, could provide a rich source of unique data about students' actions and perceptions related to learning and change. Using sophisticated text scanning software, it is now possible to read the text that students post in their ePortfolios to look for key words and phrases related to progress, setbacks, attitudes, and plans. Simon Buckingham Shum, a leader in analytics design, has tested this process and uncovered possibilities for identifying students' development of the dispositions or habits of mind needed for college success.[28] Moving past simply tracking clicks to a richer data source can help analytics provide more powerful and perhaps more actionable insights into student experience of the learning process.

Analytics are widely understood to be particularly useful to advisors and faculty, as well as university administrators. One area that is only beginning to be explored is how analytics could be useful to students themselves, shifting the focus from *learning* analytics to *learner* analytics. The University of Michigan has pioneered the exploration of ways to help students use analytics to examine their own behaviors and compare them to models for success.[29] Now in the early stages of conceptualization and design, student-focused analytics dashboards could be embedded in ePortfolios, energizing the portfolio experience and creating a context for connecting the examination of analytics data to the reflective processes needed to move from inquiry to informed and sustained action. Building on high-impact ePortfolio practices, the

Catalyst Framework and ePortfolio's role as a student-centered, meta-HIP can deepen the power and value of analytics to students.

Analytics are still in their infancy, and the use of student data has its controversial side, generating concerns about privacy and profiling. Next-generation ePortfolio practitioners, with substantial experience grappling with issues of student visibility and protection, can play an important role in advancing the sophistication of analytics systems and the thoughtful use of analytics to support student success.

Making Twenty-First-Century Learning Visible

These four examples of next-generation ePortfolio practice are more suggestive than definitive. The new digital learning ecosystem is evolving rapidly, as is the broader higher education environment. Each day, new applications and trends emerge. Educators must be alert and agile to identify the kinds of possibilities that have the greatest promise.

It is already clear, however, that next-generation ePortfolio practice can play a vital role in the emerging educational environment. As the learning ecosystem evolves and the settings for learning multiply, reflective and connective ePortfolio practice can help students integrate learning experiences across boundaries. Connecting the discrete experiences offered by emerging digital environments, ePortfolios can provide a more cohesive foundation for new tools such as digital badges and learning analytics. Next-generation ePortfolios can help connect students with advisors, faculty, and peer mentors, integrating academic learning with developmental support. As the forces of technology and the market fragment the educational experience, next-generation ePortfolio practice can create opportunities for strengthening connection and meaningful integration.

Moreover, in this fast-changing context, it will be increasingly important for officials at colleges and universities to become more agile and adaptive, learning about their students and what helps them learn and succeed. In this regard, the demonstrated capacity of high-impact ePortfolio practice to support boundary-crossing professional development and assessment processes that effectively close the loop, guiding changes that improve student learning, can be crucial. Colleges must develop their capacities as learning organizations, and ePortfolio can play a critical role in this process.

From this perspective, the ongoing spread of the digital revolution not only adds functionalities and enhances the ePortfolio experience but also underscores the critical role that integrative ePortfolio practice can play in helping higher education to move beyond "unbundling," shifting to a more productive effort to shape a "rebundled" future. In high-impact ePortfolio practice, colleges and universities have an opportunity to better navigate the changing learning ecosystem and more intentionally design a transformed twenty-first-century university.

To be effective in the years to come, next-generation ePortfolio practice must take advantage of the exciting capacities of new digital learning spaces. ePortfolio platforms must build capacity for interaction and expression, feedback and fluency.

Platforms and practice must be redesigned to address the strengths of new analytics and the flexibility of digital badging. Vendors and practitioners must be well informed and guided by a clear vision. Understanding ePortfolio's potential as a High-Impact Practice must be part of this vision.

We have briefly sketched some specific examples of the paths ePortfolio practitioners must explore. Exploring these and other innovations, practitioners should bear in mind the themes suggested by the High-Impact Practice framework. Next-generation ePortfolio practice must incorporate new technical possibilities in ways that support the underlying behaviors that characterize all HIPs: frequent and constructive feedback, deepening classroom learning with real-world application, public demonstration of competence, and recursive opportunities to reflect on and integrate learning. Next-generation ePortfolio practice must link and support other HIPs, drawing on ePortfolio as a meta-HIP to deepen the integrative aspects of learning for students, faculty, and institutions.

As innovators work on next-generation ePortfolio practice, they will be well advised to draw on the *Catalyst Framework* as a guide. Simply coming up with new bells and whistles is not sufficient; innovations must embody well-crafted integrative social pedagogy and be supported with sustained and well-designed professional development for faculty and staff. Linkages with outcomes assessment informed by the Catalyst design principles—Inquiry, Reflection, and Integration—will strengthen the value of innovations such as badging and analytics. In addition, pursuing effective strategies for scaling innovations will continue to be of crucial importance.

The new ecosystem puts a priority on sustained, recursive, and integrative learning not only for students but also for practitioners and educational institutions. Increased focus on learning about students and learning about learning will help institutions become more agile and adaptive, two key survival skills in the decades to come. Guided by the design principles of Inquiry, Reflection, and Integration, high-impact ePortfolio practice can play a unique and invaluable role in helping students, faculty, and their colleges and universities survive and thrive in the twenty-first century.

Notes

1. The Alliance for Excellent Education, "Expanding Education and Workforce Opportunities Through Digital Badging," August 28, 2013, http://all4ed.org/wp-content/uploads/2013/09/DigitalBadges.pdf

2. The Alliance for Excellent Education, "Expanding Education and Workforce Opportunities Through Digital Badging."

3. Randy Bass and Bret Eynon, *Open and Integrative: Designing Liberal Education for the New Digital Ecosystem* (Washington, DC: American Association of Colleges and Universities, 2016).

4. Kevin Maney, "Cheaper and Smarter: Blowing Up College With Nanodegrees," *Newsweek*, October 16, 2015, http://www.newsweek.com/2015/10/16/college-nanodegrees-379542.html

5. Jeff Selingo, *College (Un)bound: The Future of Higher Education and What It Means for Students* (Boston, MA: Houghton Mifflin Harcourt, 2013).

6. Jose Ferreira, "The Unbundling of Higher Education," *Knewton Blog,* February 26, 2014, https://www.knewton.com/resources/blog/ceo-jose-ferreira/unbundling-higher-education/

7. Hart Research Associates, "Falling Short? College Learning and Career Success," accessed February 21, 2016, https://www.aacu.org/leap/public-opinion-research/2015-survey-results

8. Susan Scrivener, Michael J. Weiss, Alyssa Ratledge, Timothy Rudd, Colleen Sommo, and Hannah Fresques, "Doubling Graduation Rates: Three-Year Effects of CUNY's Accelerated Study in Associate Programs (ASAP) for Developmental Education Students" (New York, NY: MDRC, 2015), http://www.mdrc.org/sites/default/files/doubling_graduation_rates_fr.pdf; Thomas R. Bailey, Shanna Smith Jaggars, and Davis Jenkins, *Redesigning America's Community Colleges: A Clearer Path to Student Success* (Cambridge, MA: Harvard University Press, 2015).

9. Bass and Eynon, *Open and Integrative.*

10. "7 Things You Should Know About Badges," June 11, 2012, accessed February 22, 2016, https://library.educase.edu/resources/2012/6/7-things-you-should-know-about-badges

11. "Expanding Education and Workforce Opportunities Through Digital Badging," Alliance for Excellent Education, August 2013, accessed February 22, 2016, http://10mbetterfutures.org/wp-content/uploads/2013/11/Expanding-Workforce-and-Education-Opportunities-through-digital-badges.pdf

12. Ibid.

13. Ibid.

14. Paul Fain, "Digital, Verified, and Less Open," *Inside Higher Education,* August 9, 2016, accessed August 9, 2016, https://www.insidehighered.com/news/2016/08/09/digital-badging-spreads-more-colleges-use-vendors-create-alternative-credentials

15. Kevin Carey, "A Future Full of Badges," *Chronicle of Higher Education,* April 8, 2012, http://chronicle.com/article/A-Future-Full-of-Badges/131455/

16. Carey, "A Future Full of Badges."

17. Trent Batson, "12 Important Trends in the ePortfolio Industry for Education and for Learning," *Campus Technology,* September 19, 2012, https://campustechnology.com/articles/2012/09/19/12-important-trends-in-the-eportfolio-industry.aspx

18. Mary Grush, "Showcasing the Co-Curricular: ePortfolios and Digital Badges: A Q&A With Alex Ambrose," *Campus Technology,* January 27, 2015, https://campustechnology.com/articles/2015/01/27/showcasing-the-co-curricular-with-eportfolios-and-digital-badges.aspx

19. G. Alex Ambrose, "ePortfolios @ Scale and Beyond With Badges & Analytics" (closing keynote, Association of Authentic, Experiential Evidence-Based Learning Annual Conference, Boston, MA, July 30, 2015).

20. Ambrose, "ePortfolios @ Scale and Beyond."

21. "7 Things You Should Know about . . . IPAS," November 2014, accessed February 21, 2016, http://net.educause.edu/ir/library/pdf/ELI7114.pdf

22. Hoori S. Kalamkarian and Melinda Mechur Karp, *Student Attitudes Toward Technology-Mediated Advising Systems,* accessed February 21, 2016, http://ccrc.tc.columbia.edu/media/k2/attachments/student-attitudes-toward-technology-mediated-advising-systems.pdf

23. Jeffrey Fletcher and Melinda Mechur Karp, *Using Technology to Reform Advising*, accessed February 21, 2016, http://ccrc.tc.columbia.edu/media/k2/attachments/UsingTech-Insights-WEB.pdf

24. Catherine Buyarski, "Reflection in the First Year: A Foundation for Identity and Meaning Making," *Catalyst for Learning: ePortfolio Resources and Research*, January 25, 2014, http://iupui.mcnrc.org/ref-practice/

25. Phil Long and George Siemens, "Penetrating the Fog: Analytics in Learning and Education," accessed February 21, 2016, http://er.educause.edu/articles/2011/9/penetrating-the-fog-analytics-in-learning-and-education

26. "7 Things You Should Know," 1.

27. "NMC Horizon Report: 2015 K–12 Edition," accessed February 21, 2016, http://cdn.nmc.org/media/2015-nmc-horizon-report-k12-EN.pdf, 12

28. Simon Buckingham Shum, "Reflective Writing Analytics," YouTube video, 28.03. posted June 20, 2015, https://www.youtube.com/watch?v=Gom1wNZm1Bc

29. Steven Aguilar, Steven Lonn, and Stephanie D. Teasley, "Perceptions and Use of an Early Warning System During a Higher Education Transition Program," in *Proceedings of the Fourth International Conference on Learning Analytics and Knowledge* (New York, NY: Association for Computing Machinery, 2014): 113–117; "E2Coach: Tailoring Support for Students in Introductory STEM Courses," *Educause Review,* accessed February 22, 2016, http://er.educause.edu/articles/2013/12/e2coach-tailoring-support-for-students-in-introductory-stem-courses

ABOUT THE CONTRIBUTORS

Authors

Bret Eynon is a historian and associate provost at LaGuardia Community College (CUNY), where he guides collegewide educational change initiatives related to learning, teaching, curriculum, advisement, technology, and assessment. The founder of LaGuardia's Center for Teaching and Learning and its internationally-known ePortfolio project, Eynon's many articles and books include *Freedom's Unfinished Revolution: An Inquiry Into the Civil War and Reconstruction* (The New Press, 1996); and *1968: An International Student Generation in Revolt* (Pantheon, 1988); as well as *Who Built America?* an award-winning series of textbooks, films, and CD-ROMs. A senior national faculty member with the Association of American Colleges & Universities, Eynon's most recent book, with Randy Bass, is *Open and Integrative: Designing Liberal Education for the New Digital Ecosystem* (AAC&U, 2016). The national Community College Humanities Association has recognized him as a Distinguished Humanities Educator.

Laura M. Gambino is the associate dean for assessment and technology and professor of information technology at Guttman Community College (CUNY). In her role as associate dean, Gambino oversees the college's institution-wide ePortfolio program and the Integrated Planning and Advising for Student Success (iPASS) initiative. She serves as principal investigator for Guttman's EDUCAUSE/Achieving the Dream iPASS and GradNYC College Completion Innovation Fund grants. She also leads the assessment of Guttman's institutional student learning outcomes; her work in this area focuses on the intersection of assessment, pedagogy, and assignment design. Gambino, a leading ePortfolio and assessment practitioner and researcher, serves as a Degree Qualifications Profile (DQP)/Tuning Coach for the National Institute for Learning Outcomes Assessment (NILOA).

C2L Senior Scholars

Randy Bass is vice provost for education and professor of English at Georgetown University, where he leads the Designing the Future(s) initiative and the Red House incubator for curricular transformation. The author of numerous books, articles, and electronic projects, he has been honored with the EDUCAUSE Medal for Outstanding Achievement in Technology and Undergraduate Education. A consulting scholar at the Carnegie Foundation for the Advancement of Teaching, from 2003 to 2009, Bass is currently senior scholar at the Association of American Colleges & Universities.

Helen L. Chen is director of ePortfolio initiatives in the Office of the Registrar and a research scientist in the Designing Education Lab in the Department of Mechanical Engineering at Stanford University. She is a co-founder of Electronic Portfolio Action & Communication (EPAC), an ePortfolio community of practice, and serves as a board member for the Association for Authentic, Experiential and Evidence-Based Learning and as a co-executive editor for the *International Journal of ePortfolio*.

Foreword Author

George D. Kuh is adjunct research professor at the University of Illinois and Chancellor's Professor of Higher Education Emeritus at Indiana University. He is a senior scholar and founding director of the National Institute for Learning Outcomes Assessment (NILOA) as well as the founding director of Indiana University's Center for Postsecondary Research and the National Survey of Student Engagement (NSSE). Among his recent books are *Using Evidence of Student Learning to Improve Higher Education* (Jossey-Bass, 2015); *Ensuring Quality and Taking High-Impact Practices to Scale* (AAC&U, 2013); *High-Impact Educational Practices: What They Are, Who Has Access to Them, and Why They Matter* (AAC&U, 2008); and *Student Success in College: Creating Conditions That Matter* (Jossey-Bass, 2005, 2010).

Vignette Authors

G. Alex Ambrose, Associate Program Director of ePortfolio Assessment, University of Notre Dame

Susan Kahn, Director, Office of Institutional Effectiveness, Director, IUPUI ePortfolio Initiative, Indiana University–Purdue University Indianapolis

Kati Lewis, Assistant Professor, Salt Lake Community College

Gail Matthews-DeNatale, Associate Director, Center for Advancing Teaching & Learning Through Research, Northeastern University

Terrel Rhodes, Vice President, Office of Quality, Curriculum, and Assessment and Executive Director of VALUE, Association of American Colleges & Universities

Susan Scott, Coordinator, ePortfolio Initiative, Assistant Director, Office of Institutional Effectiveness, Indiana University–Purdue University Indianapolis

INDEX

This book—by presenting principles that teachers in higher education can put into practice in their own classrooms—explains how to lay the ground for this engagement and help students become self-regulated learners actively employing meta-cognitive and reflective strategies in their education.

Sty/us

22883 Quicksilver Drive
Sterling, VA 20166-2102

Subscribe to our e-mail alerts: www.Styluspub.com

Also available from Stylus Publishing

Leveraging the ePortfolio for Integrative Learning

A Faculty Guide to Classroom Practices for Transforming Student Learning

Candyce Reynolds and Judith Patton
Foreword by Terry Rhodes

"Candyce Reynolds and Judith Patton's *Leveraging the ePortfolio for Integrative Learning* is the most accessible book I have seen about using ePortfolios in higher education. They write this book as if it is their own ePortfolio, providing personal stories and many examples of faculty uses of ePortfolios. This book keeps you reading as if you are listening to the authors tell you all you want to hear [about ePortfolios]. . . from every aspect of defining your ePortfolio's campus purpose to choosing a platform to the structure of a showcase ePortfolio to tips and cautions. I was impressed with their thoroughness and lucidity. Thanks to Reynolds and Patton for this significant contribution to the field of ePortfolio studies."—*Trent Batson*, *President, The Association for Authentic, Experiential and Evidence-Based Learning*

"Integrative learning is often seen as the Holy Grail for various learning contexts, such as general education and lifelong learning. It's believed to exist, but it's often unclear how to foster such learning in meaningful ways. Destined to be a seminal text, what Reynolds and Patton provide here is a map to integrative learning through ePortfolios with practical advice leading to real outcomes. I will be providing this book as a manual for those who teach using ePortfolios."—*C. Edward Watson*, *Director, Center for Teaching and Learning, University of Georgia; and Executive Editor*, International Journal of ePortfolio

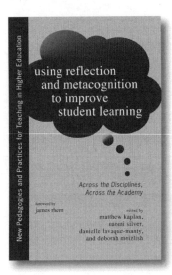

Using Reflection and Metacognition to Improve Student Learning

Across the Disciplines, Across the Academy

Edited by Matthew Kaplan, Naomi Silver, Danielle LaVaque-Manty, and Deborah Meizlish
Foreword by James Rhem

Research has identified the importance of helping students develop the ability to monitor their own comprehension, and to make their thinking processes explicit. Indeed, literature demonstrates that metacognitive teaching strategies greatly improve student engagement with course material.

(Continues on previous page)